STRIKE WHILE THE IRON IS HOT

by STEPHEN FRANCIS & RICO

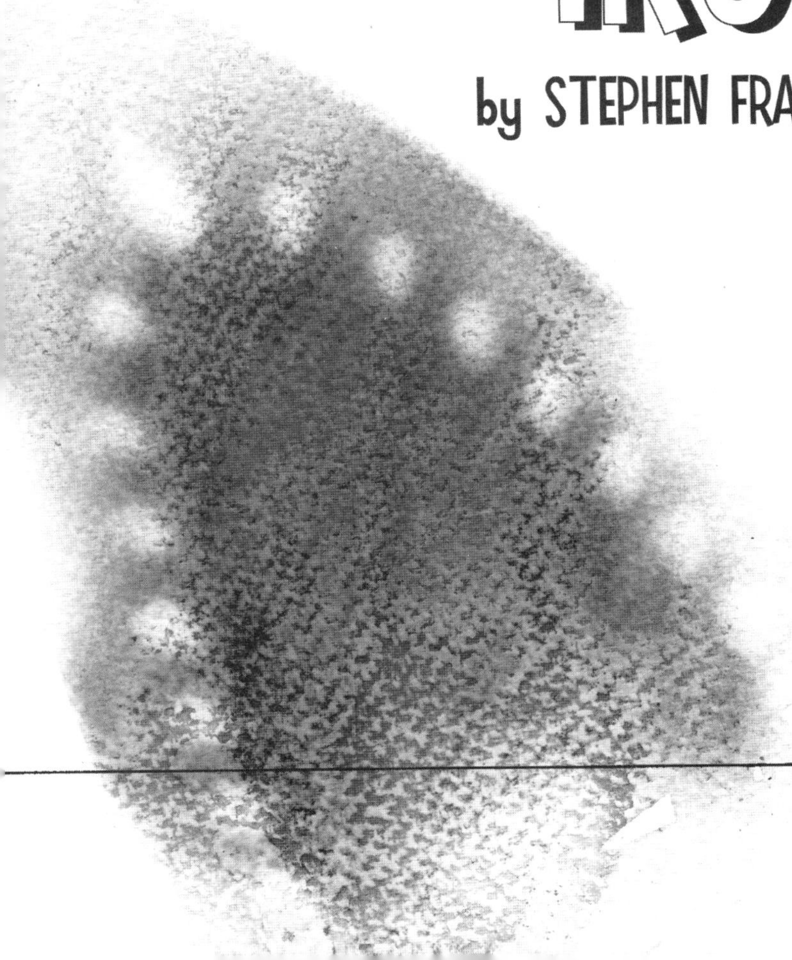

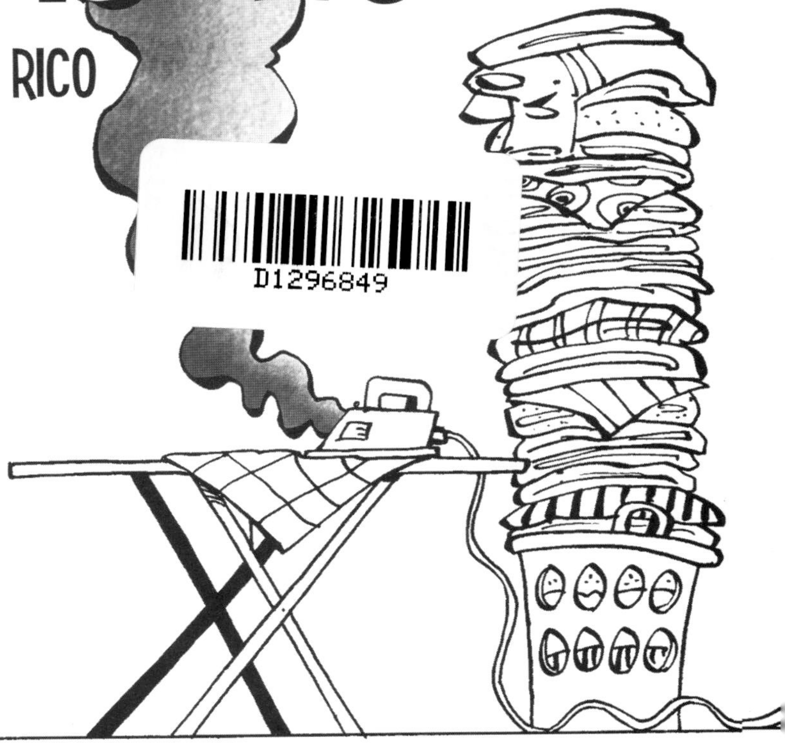

JACANA

Published in 2009 in South Africa by
Jacana Media
10 Orange Street, Auckland Park, 2092
PO Box 291784, Melville, 2109

JACANA

ISBN 978-1-77009-779-7

DTP by Dee Helling and Sandi Arrenbrecht

OTHER MADAM & EVE BOOKS

The Madam & Eve Collection	(1993, reprint 1999)
Free At Last	(Penguin Books, 1994)
All Aboard for the Gravy Train	(Penguin Books, 1995)
Somewhere over the Rainbow Nation	(Penguin Books, 1996)
Madam & Eve's Greatest Hits	(Penguin Books, 1997)
Madams are from Mars, Maids are from Venus	(Penguin Books, 1997)
It's a Jungle Out There	(David Philip, 1998)
International Maid of Mystery	(David Philip, 1999)
Has anyone seen my Vibrating Cellphone?	(interactive.Africa , 2000)
The Madams are Restless	(Rapid Phase, 2000)
Crouching Madam, Hidden Maid	(Rapid Phase, 2001)
Madam & Eve, 10 Wonderful Years	(Rapid Phase 2002)
The Maidtrix	(Rapid Phase, 2003)
Gin & Tonic for the Soul	(Rapid Phase, 2004)
Desperate Housemaids	(Rapid Phase, 2005)
Madams of the Caribbean	(Rapid Phase, 2006)
Bring me my (new) Wasing Machine	(Rapid Phase, 2007)
Madam & Eve Unplugged	(Rapid Phase, 2008)
Jamen sort kaffe er pa mode nu, Madam!	(Gyldendal, Denmark, 1995)
Jeg gyver Mandela Skylden for det her!	(Gyldendal, Denmark, 1995)
Alt under kontrol I Sydafrika!	(Bogfabrikken, Denmark, 1997)
Men alla dricker kaffet svart nufortiden, Madam!	(Bokfabrikken, Sweden, 1998)
Madame & Eve, Enfin Libres!	(Vents D'Ouest, France, 1997)
Votez madame & Eve	(Vents D'Ouest, France, 1997)
La coupe est pleine	(Vents D'Ouest, France, 1998)
Rennue-Ménage à deux	(Vents D'Ouest, France, 1999)
En voient de toutes les couleurs	(Vents D'Ouest, France, 2000)
Madame vient de Mars, Eve de Venus,	(Vents D'Ouest, France, 2000)
Madam & Eve	(LIKE, Finland, 2005)

MADAM & EVE APPEARS REGULARLY IN:
The Mail & Guardian, The Star, The Saturday Star, The Sunday Times, The Herald, The Mercury, The Witness, The Daily Dispatch, The Cape Times, The Pretoria News, The Diamond Fields Advertiser, Die Volksblad, EC Today, The Kokstad Advertiser, The Namibian, The SA Times (London).

TO CONTACT MADAM & EVE:
POST: PO Box 413667, Craighall 2024, Johannesburg, South Africa
E-MAIL: madamandeve@rapidphase.co.za
INTERNET: www.madamandeve.co.za

YOU KNOW WHAT THEY SAY, GWEN...
...YOU SHOULD ALWAYS "STRIKE WHILE THE IRON IS HOT!"
©RAPID PHASE - 2009
www.rapidphase.co.za
THANKS FOR THE ADVICE!
MORE PAY

I'LL TAKE THE SILVER MERCEDES -- FULLY EQUIPPED WITH CHROME EXTRAS AND COMPLETE ENTERTAINMENT CENTRE IN THE REAR.
CONGRATULATIONS! AN EXCELLENT CHOICE, MR MINISTER!
©RAPID PHASE - 2009
...AND MAY I ALSO COMMENT ON HOW CLEAN AND FRESH YOUR BREATH SMELLS!
WHY, THANK YOU.
Entitle Mints
Entitle Mints
...because you deserve them.

MADAM & Eve

BY STEPHEN FRANCIS & RICO

Panel: WHAT KIND OF **POKER** ARE WE PLAYING? "TEXAS HOLD'EM?"

Panel: ...OR "JOBURG LET 'EM ESCAPE?"

SHUT UP AND DEAL.

Panel: AM I ALLOWED TO PLAY THE **RACE CARD** IF THE OPPORTUNITY ARISES?

NO. EVERYONE'S EQUAL IN POKER. IT'S A CONSTITUTIONAL **RIGHT.**

Panel: LET'S SEE... I'LL BET... TWO CENTS.

...**YOUR** TWO CENTS... AND I'LL **RAISE** YOU TWO CENTS.

Panel: DID I HEAR SOMEONE SAY "RAISE?"

Panel: OKAY. HOW MANY CARDS DO YOU WANT?

I'LL TAKE **ONE** CARD.

Panel: ...AND DEALER TAKES SEVEN.

SEVEN?!! THIS IS FIVE-CARD DRAW!!

© RAPID PHASE · 2008

Panel: YOU CAN'T JUST **GIVE** YOURSELF AN **EXTRA** TWO CARDS WHENEVER YOU **FEEL** LIKE IT!!

Panel: I KNOW! I CALL IT **"THE B.E.E. DEAL."**

Panel: **SLAM!!** YOU ONLY **TAUGHT** ME POKER TWO MONTHS AGO! I'VE BEEN **PREVIOUSLY DISADVANTAGED!!**

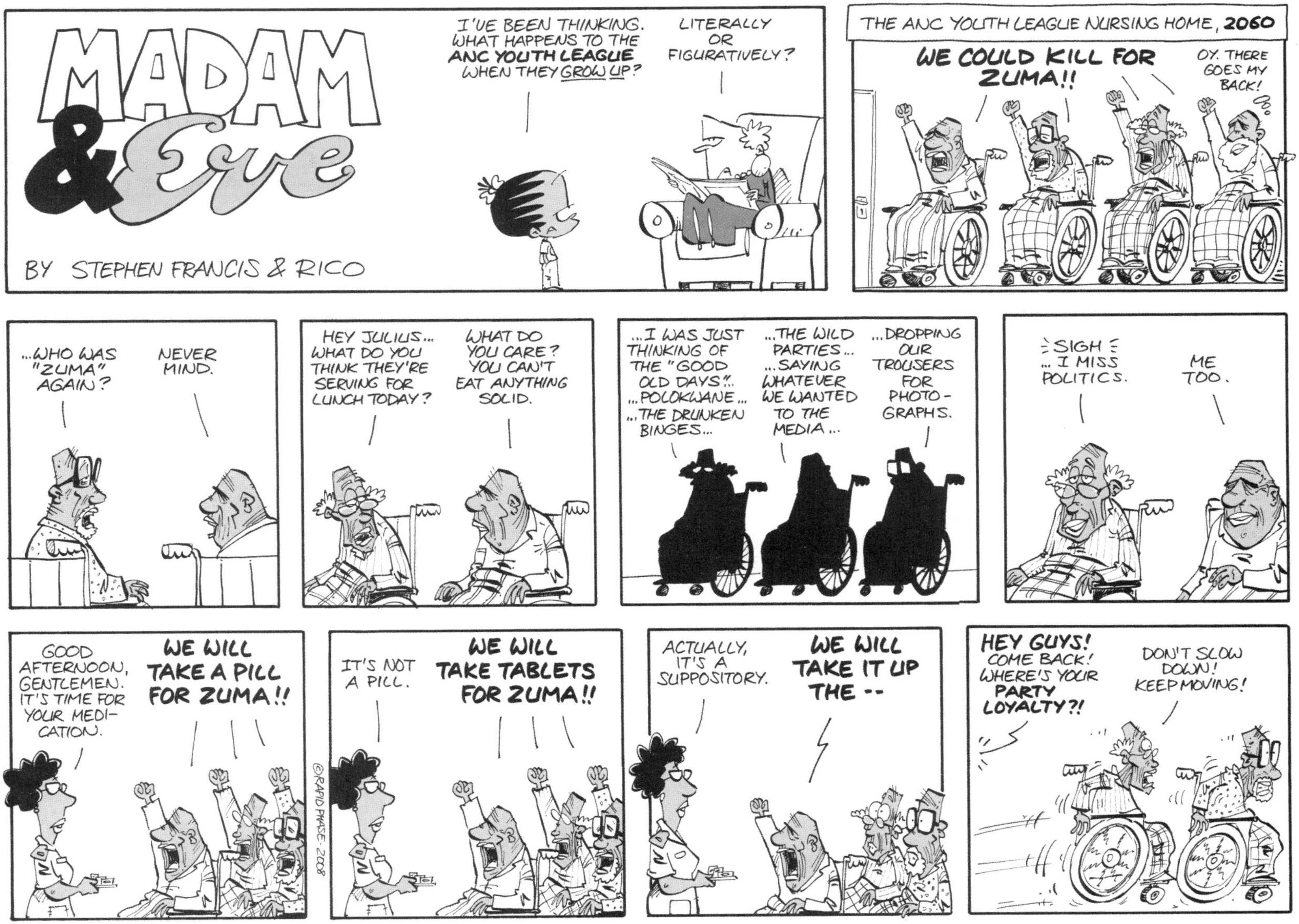
MADAM & Eve
BY STEPHEN FRANCIS & RICO
I'VE BEEN THINKING. WHAT HAPPENS TO THE ANC YOUTH LEAGUE WHEN THEY GROW UP?
LITERALLY OR FIGURATIVELY?
THE ANC YOUTH LEAGUE NURSING HOME, 2060
WE COULD KILL FOR ZUMA!!
OY. THERE GOES MY BACK!
...WHO WAS "ZUMA" AGAIN?
NEVER MIND.
HEY JULIUS... WHAT DO YOU THINK THEY'RE SERVING FOR LUNCH TODAY?
WHAT DO YOU CARE? YOU CAN'T EAT ANYTHING SOLID.
...I WAS JUST THINKING OF THE "GOOD OLD DAYS"... ...POLOKWANE... ...THE DRUNKEN BINGES...
...THE WILD PARTIES... ...SAYING WHATEVER WE WANTED TO THE MEDIA...
...DROPPING OUR TROUSERS FOR PHOTOGRAPHS.
SIGH ... I MISS POLITICS.
ME TOO.
GOOD AFTERNOON, GENTLEMEN. IT'S TIME FOR YOUR MEDICATION.
WE WILL TAKE A PILL FOR ZUMA!!
©RAPID PHASE · 2008
IT'S NOT A PILL.
WE WILL TAKE TABLETS FOR ZUMA!!
ACTUALLY, IT'S A SUPPOSITORY.
WE WILL TAKE IT UP THE --
HEY GUYS! COME BACK! WHERE'S YOUR PARTY LOYALTY?!
DON'T SLOW DOWN! KEEP MOVING!

HOLD IT! HOLD IT GUYS! EVERYONE STOP PLAYING!!
NOW WHAT?
THIS SONG NEEDS SOUND EFFECTS! BRING ME MY MACHINE GUN!
©RAPID PHASE · 2008
UH... JULIUS. DON'T WORRY ABOUT IT. I CAN PUT THEM IN DIGITALLY IN POST PRODUCTION.
OH.
LET'S TRY ANOTHER TAKE. BRING MY MY MICRO-PHONE.
WHY DID I EVER AGREE TO PRODUCE THE ANC YOUTH LEAGUE'S CD?

AND, IN OTHER NEWS...THE ANC YOUTH LEAGUE HAVE FORMED THEIR OWN BAND AND ARE RECORDING A CD FILLED WITH ELECTION AND STRUGGLE SONGS.
HOLD IT! STOP THE MUSIC! I SAID I WANTED THE DRUMS TO COME IN AFTER THE MACHINE GUN FIRE!
UH, JULIUS... BEFORE WE GO AGAIN... THESE RECORDING SESSIONS ARE EXPENSIVE. HOW DOES THE ANC INTEND PAYING FOR THEM?
©RAPID PHASE · 2008
WE WILL BILL FOR ZUMA.
WORKS FOR ME. READY WHEN YOU ARE.

JUST THINK: WE'RE MAKING HISTORY HERE, GUYS!
...ONE DAY, THESE ANC YOUTH LEAGUE SESSIONS COULD BE AS FAMOUS AS "THE BEATLES' WHITE ALBUM" ...OR EVEN "SNOOP DOGGY DOG!"
THE CLOCK'S TICKING, GUYS! WHAT'S THE NEXT TRACK WE'RE RECORDING?
I CALL IT "STAIRWAY TO HEAVEN WITH MY AK-47." ...IT'S A BALLAD.
HOW ABOUT A LITTLE MOOD LIGHTING?

HONK!!
POK! POK! POK! POK! POK! POK! POK!
www.madamandeve.co.za ©RAPID PHASE 2008
WHO SAYS THERE'S A "SKILLS SHORTAGE" IN SOUTH AFRICA?

www.madamandeve.co.za ©RAPID PHASE 2008
GWEN!!
IF YOU ASK ME, SHE'S TAKING THE PETROL PRICE DECREASE A LITTLE TOO FAR.
FILL IT UP!!

JACKPOT
YES!!
WAY TO GO, MOM!
CHING! CHING! CHING! CHING!
JACKPOT
©RAPID PHASE 2008
BOB'S PETROL CASINO
FILL IT UP.
JACKPOT
JACKPOT

COME ON, MON. DIS A DEMOCRACY! YOU GOT TO SHARE DE POWER!
NO, MON. I AIN'T BE SHARIN' NO POWER!
SHARE DE POWER WITH DE PEOPLE, MON.
WELL ... LET ME TINK ABOUT IT... WHILE I PUT ON SOME REGGAE MUSIC.
I SHOT DE SHERIFF...
©RAPID PHASE 2008
I SAID THE POWERSHARING TALKS IN ZIMBABWE WERE DEADLOCKED! -- DEADLOCKED!!
OH.

HOW DID THE ZIMBABWE POWER SHARING TALKS GO, PRESIDENT MBEKI?
TERRIBLE! THE ZANU PF WOULDN'T COMPROMISE ON ANYTHING!
SAND
©RAPID PHASE 2008
ALL WEEKEND, IT WAS THE SAME THING: "ROBERT WILL NEVER AGREE TO THIS!" OR-- "I GUARANTEE ROBERT WILL NEVER AGREE TO THAT!!"
SAND
SO... APPOINTING MUGABE'S WIFE AS HEAD MEDIATOR MAY HAVE BEEN A MISTAKE.
I'M STARTING TO SEE IT THAT WAY.

AND TODAY'S TOP STORY... THE POWER SHARING TALKS IN ZIMBABWE ARE ALMOST AT A CLOSE.
©RAPID PHASE 2008
YOU KNOW WHAT "POWER SHARING" IS, RIGHT?
DUH.
...SOMEONE CONNECTS AN EXTENSION CORD TO AN ESKOM LINE, THEN EVERYONE ON THE BLOCK PLUGS IN FOR FREE.
SLAM!!
MAYBE I SHOULD TAKE CURRENT EVENTS A LITTLE MORE SERIOUSLY.

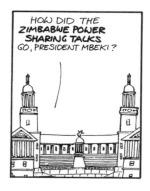

EVE! THE DISHES ARE STILL IN THE SINK!
...THAT'S BECAUSE I TOLD HER TO VACUUM!!
WELL, I WANT HER TO DO THE DISHES!
AND I WANT HER TO VACUUM!
DISHES!
VACUUM!
LET'S LET EVE SETTLE IT! EVE -- WHO SHOULD YOU LISTEN TO? ME... OR MY MOTHER?!
©RAPID PHASE · 2008
HI. I'M EVE. I'LL BE YOUR POWER-SHARING MEDIATOR FOR TODAY.

GREAT NEWS, PRESIDENT MBEKI! THE FIRST SAMPLES ARRIVED TODAY!
SAMPLES?
©RAPID PHASE · 2008
CHECK IT OUT! AND THIS TIME WE DIDN'T SKIMP ON QUALITY!!
WHAT THE HELL ARE YOU TALKING ABOUT?!
www.madamandeve.co.za
I THOUGHT YOU TOLD ME WE NEEDED TO UPGRADE THE COUNTRY'S NAVEL SITUATION.
NAVAL. --AS IN "NAVY!" THE COUNTRY'S NAVAL SITUATION!
HELLO? CALL FRANCE. TELL THEM TO CANCEL THE 37.5 MILLION BELLY-RING ORDER.
I HATE MONDAYS.

WHY IS **JACOB ZUMA** LIKE A CELLPHONE?
BOTH NEED **RECHARGING** ON A REGULAR BASIS.
©RAPID PHASE - 2008
SLAM!
I MADE THAT UP, IN CASE YOU'RE WONDERING.

WHY IS **THABO MBEKI** LIKE A **CELLPHONE?**
©RAPID PHASE - 2008
THEIR INTERNATIONAL ROAMING GETS REALLY EXPENSIVE.
"INTERNATIONAL **ROAMING!**" GET IT?! INTERNATIONAL **ROAMING!!**
HAHAHA!! HOHOHO!!
SLAM!!
I WONDER IF CHRIS ROCK STARTED LIKE THIS?

SLAM!!
FINE!! GO AHEAD AND THROW ME OUT! YOU KNOW WHAT THEY SAY! "ONE DOOR **CLOSES**... AND ANOTHER DOOR **OPENS!**"
©RAPID PHASE - 2008
...YOU FORGOT TO LOCK THE GARAGE.
...AND ANOTHER DOOR CLOSES AGAIN.

THIS WEEK'S TOP STORY... THE HIGH COURT HAS RULED THAT **JACOB ZUMA** WAS A VICTIM OF POLITICAL MANIPULATION.
YOU MEAN ZUMA WAS **RIGHT?!** IT **WAS** ALL A CONSPIRACY AFTER ALL!
FRANKLY, **NOTHING** SURPRISES ME ANY MORE.
www.madamandeve.co.za
©RAPID PHASE - 2008
AND IN OTHER NEWS, INTERNATIONAL SCIENTISTS HAVE DISCOVERED THAT TAKING A **SHOWER** AFTER SEX ACTUALLY **DOES** PREVENT HIV.
CRASH!
...MOM?

THIS WEEK'S TOP STORY... THE HIGH COURT HAS RULED THAT THE PRESIDENT **MAY** HAVE INTERFERED IN THE PROSECUTORIAL PROCESS AGAINST JACOB ZUMA.
YES! YES! I KNEW IT!!
BWAHAHAHA!!
www.madamandeve.co.za
©RAPID PHASE - 2008
AT LAST! A LIGHT AT THE END OF THE TUNNEL! I COULD BE **FREE!** ...**FREE!!**
COULD YOU HOLD IT DOWN, SHABIR? WE'RE TRYING TO WATCH **TV!**
GUARD! I WANT A PHONE CALL!

ELEVEN LITTLE MINISTERS, KNOWING IT'S THE END...
ONE CAME RUNNING QUICKLY BACK AND THEN THERE WERE **TEN.**
TEN LITTLE MINISTERS GOING OUT TO DINE.
ONE CUT A SWEETHEART DEAL. AND THEN THERE WERE **NINE.**
©RAPID PHASE - 2008
NINE LITTLE MINISTERS ...THE HOUR'S GETTING LATE.
ONE JOINED BIG BUSINESS. AND THEN THERE WERE **EIGHT**...
www.madamandeve.co.za
HEY!! THAT'S NOT HOW I REMEMBER IT!
IT'S THE UPDATED 2008 VERSION.

COMING UP... THE NEW REALITY SHOW "IT'S SO HARD TO GET GOOD HELP THESE DAYS."
FOLLOWED BY TODAY'S SHOE SALE BAROMETER AND A SPECIAL REPORT ON "THE TOP TEN SHOPPING MALLS."
BUT FIRST, STAY TUNED FOR OUR NEW DAYTIME DRAMA... "MAIDS OF OUR LIVES."
©RAPID PHASE · 2008 www.madamandeve.co.za
"THE MADAM CHANNEL?"
NOW THIS IS TELEVISION.

CRASH!
YOU IDIOT! WHY DON'T YOU WATCH WHERE YOU'RE DRIVING?!
WHY DON'T YOU WATCH WHERE YOU'RE DRIVING?!
www.madamandeve.co.za ©RAPID PHASE · 2008
DON'T YOU KNOW WHO I AM?! I'M ROBERT McBRIDE!!
DON'T YOU KNOW WHO I AM?! I'M JUDGE MOTATA
I SMELL ALCOHOL ON YOUR BREATH!!
WELL, I SMELL ALCOHOL ON YOUR BREATH!!
...YOU CALL THIS ONE IN.

NOW WATCH CLOSELY, LADIES AND GENTLEMEN... OR YOU MIGHT MISS THE MAGIC!!
www.madamandeve.co.za ©RAPID PHASE · 2008
ALAKAZAM!
ALA-KAZOO!!
POOF!
HEY! ALL MY MONEY'S GONE! MY BANK ACCOUNT... MY CREDIT CARD... MY LIFE SAVINGS!... MY INVESTMENTS!! GONE!!
CLAP! CLAP! CLAP! CLAP!
THOSE GUYS ARE GOOD.
THE FABULOUS LEHMAN BROTHERS

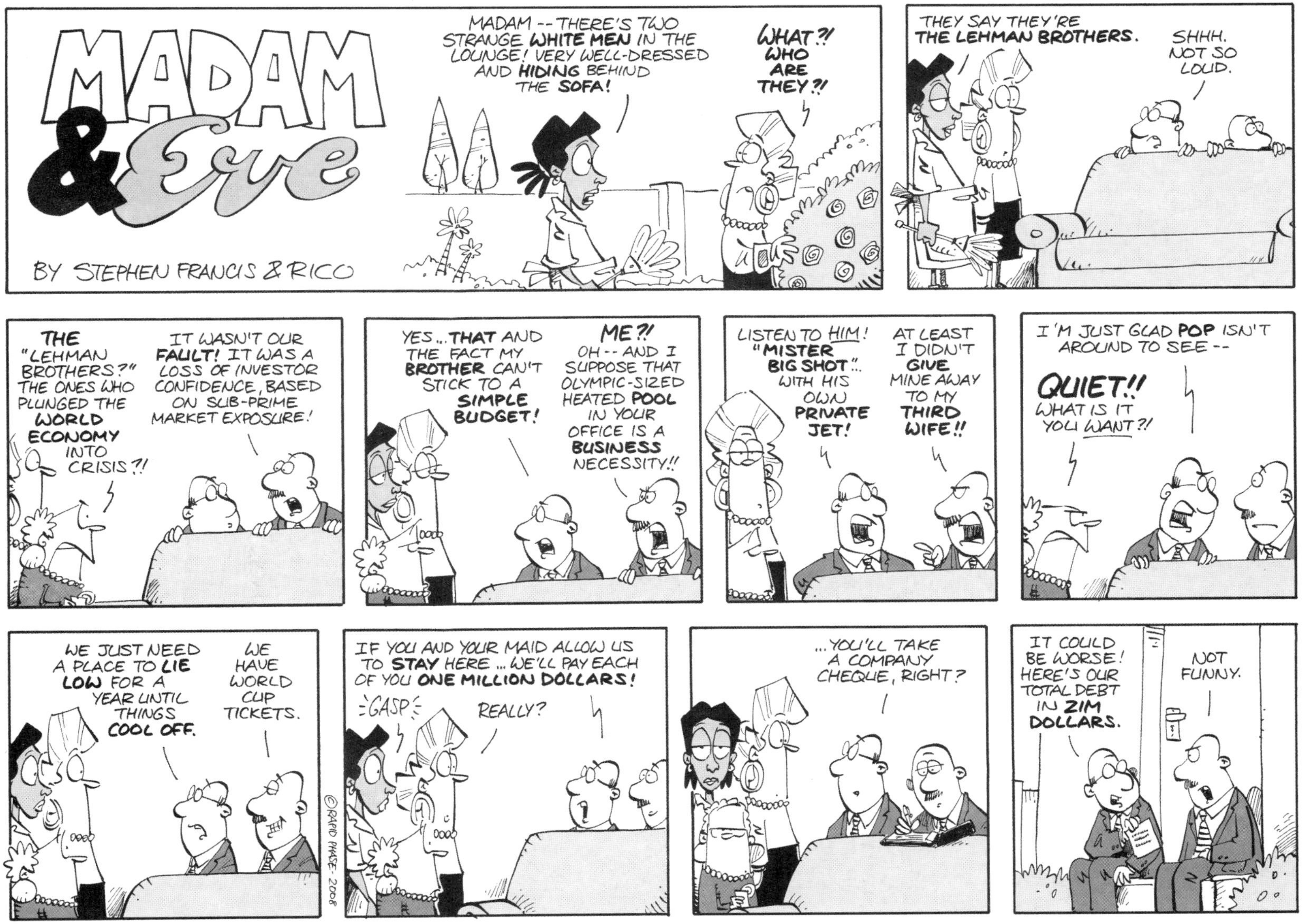

MADAM & Eve
BY STEPHEN FRANCIS & RICO
MADAM -- THERE'S TWO STRANGE WHITE MEN IN THE LOUNGE! VERY WELL-DRESSED AND HIDING BEHIND THE SOFA!
WHAT?! WHO ARE THEY?!
THEY SAY THEY'RE THE LEHMAN BROTHERS.
SHHH. NOT SO LOUD.
THE "LEHMAN BROTHERS?" THE ONES WHO PLUNGED THE WORLD ECONOMY INTO CRISIS?!
IT WASN'T OUR FAULT! IT WAS A LOSS OF INVESTOR CONFIDENCE, BASED ON SUB-PRIME MARKET EXPOSURE!
YES... THAT AND THE FACT MY BROTHER CAN'T STICK TO A SIMPLE BUDGET!
ME?! OH -- AND I SUPPOSE THAT OLYMPIC-SIZED HEATED POOL IN YOUR OFFICE IS A BUSINESS NECESSITY!!
LISTEN TO HIM! "MISTER BIG SHOT"... WITH HIS OWN PRIVATE JET!
AT LEAST I DIDN'T GIVE MINE AWAY TO MY THIRD WIFE!!
I'M JUST GLAD POP ISN'T AROUND TO SEE --
QUIET!! WHAT IS IT YOU WANT?!
WE JUST NEED A PLACE TO LIE LOW FOR A YEAR UNTIL THINGS COOL OFF.
WE HAVE WORLD CUP TICKETS.
IF YOU AND YOUR MAID ALLOW US TO STAY HERE... WE'LL PAY EACH OF YOU ONE MILLION DOLLARS!
GASP
REALLY?
©RAPID PHASE · 2008
...YOU'LL TAKE A COMPANY CHEQUE, RIGHT?
IT COULD BE WORSE! HERE'S OUR TOTAL DEBT IN ZIM DOLLARS.
NOT FUNNY.

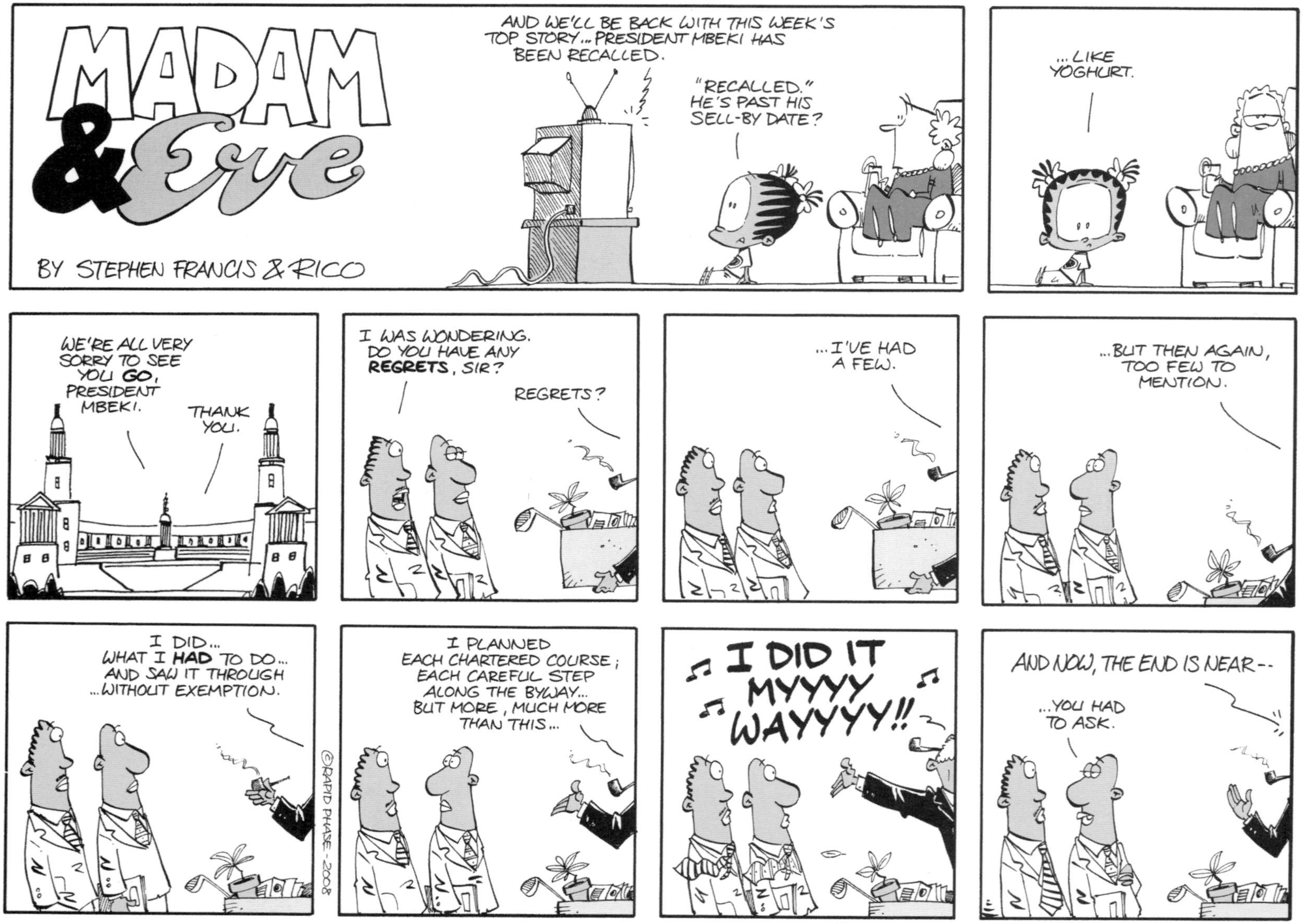
MADAM & Eve
BY STEPHEN FRANCIS & RICO
AND WE'LL BE BACK WITH THIS WEEK'S TOP STORY... PRESIDENT MBEKI HAS BEEN RECALLED.
"RECALLED." HE'S PAST HIS SELL-BY DATE?
...LIKE YOGHURT.
WE'RE ALL VERY SORRY TO SEE YOU GO, PRESIDENT MBEKI.
THANK YOU.
I WAS WONDERING. DO YOU HAVE ANY REGRETS, SIR?
REGRETS?
...I'VE HAD A FEW.
...BUT THEN AGAIN, TOO FEW TO MENTION.
I DID... WHAT I HAD TO DO... AND SAW IT THROUGH ...WITHOUT EXEMPTION.
©RAPID PHASE-2008
I PLANNED EACH CHARTERED COURSE; EACH CAREFUL STEP ALONG THE BYWAY... BUT MORE, MUCH MORE THAN THIS...
I DID IT MYYYY WAYYYY!!
AND NOW, THE END IS NEAR--
...YOU HAD TO ASK.

WELL, THAT'S IT. IT'S ALL DONE. PRESIDENT MBEKI HAS VOLUNTARILY AGREED TO STEP DOWN.
IT'S ABOUT TIME, TOO.
... SOME PEOPLE JUST CAN'T TELL WHEN THE PARTY'S OVER.
www.madamandeve.co.za © RAPID PHASE - 2008
... WILL THERE BE ANYTHING ELSE, PRESIDENT MUGABE?
I'LL LET YOU KNOW.

WE'RE ALL GOING TO MISS YOU, PRESIDENT MBEKI.
WHAT DO YOU THINK YOU'LL DO WITH YOURSELF AFTER YOU LEAVE OFFICE, SIR?
OH, I DON'T KNOW. PROBABLY SURF THE INTERNET FOR WACKY THEORIES, PLOT AGAINST MY ENEMIES, AND TRAVEL ALL OVER THE WORLD EVERY WEEK.
www.madamandeve.co.za © RAPID PHASE - 2008
... DON'T SAY IT.
HEY!! HAS ANYBODY SEEN MY GOLF CLUBS?!

REMEMBER -- WE'RE DOING THIS FOR THE GOOD OF THE COUNTRY... NOT AS SOME "VINDICTIVE PAYBACK!" FIRING MBEKI HAS TO BE DONE WITH SENSITIVITY.
"ALL THOSE WHO ARE STILL STATE PRESIDENT... TAKE ONE STEP FORWARD! -- NOT SO FAST, THABO!"
www.madamandeve.co.za
I'VE GOT IT! WE SEND A POEM! "ROSES ARE RED VIOLETS ARE BLUE WE'VE DECIDED TO PUT THE LAME DUCK IN THE STEW!"
© RAPID PHASE - 2008
WAIT! WE HOLD A NATIONAL LOTTERY! THE WINNER GETS TO FIRE MBEKI!
LET'S TAKE A BREAK.

LET ME GET THIS STRAIGHT: THE GUY FROM "THE BUCKET LIST" COST MBEKI HIS JOB?!
©RAPID PHASE · 2008
JUDGE NICHOLSON! NOT JACK NICHOLSON! JUDGE NICHOLSON!!
www.madamandeve.co.za
...YOU HAVE TO ADMIT... THINGS HAVE BEEN A LITTLE CONFUSING THESE LAST FEW WEEKS.

AND SO... SOUTH AFRICA'S NEW PRESIDENT BEGINS HIS FIRST WEEK IN OFFICE.
FINALLY.
NO MORE INSTABILITY.
NO MORE UNCERTAINTY.
www.madamandeve.co.za
...AND MAYBE NOW I CAN GET SOME PEACE AND QUIET.
©RAPID PHASE · 2008
WE WOULD KILL FOR MOTLANTHE!!

OKAY. LET'S TRY IT AGAIN.
... WE'VE BEEN TRYING FOR OVER AN HOUR! WE NEED A BREAK!
THIS IS THE ONE. I CAN FEEL IT. ...GO!
MO... MOLE...
www.madamandeve.co.za
MO - LANTHE! PRESIDENT MOLANTHE!!
©RAPID PHASE · 2008
I GUESS WE SHOULD BE PATIENT. "NKOSI SIKELELI" TOOK SIX MONTHS.
... EIGHT.
TEA BREAK!

HOW'S PRESIDENT **MOTLANTHE** DOING TODAY?
OH. YOU MEAN PRESIDENT **MOTLANTHE**?
YES. PRESIDENT **MOTLANTHE**.
BOLD AND DECISIVE, THAT'S PRESIDENT **MOTLANTHE**.
© RAPID PHASE - 2008
www.madamandeve.co.za
YOU KNOW... I **LIKE** PRESIDENT **MOTLANTHE**.
I LIKE PRESIDENT **MOTLANTHE** TOO.
WE SHOULD HAVE NEVER TAUGHT THEM HOW TO PRONOUNCE **MOTLANTHE**.
EXCUSE ME. ...DID SOMEONE MENTION **MOTLANTHE?**

NOOOOOO!!
ONE DAY WHEN YOU'RE **GONE**... HISTORY MIGHT **JUDGE** YOU AS A GROUCHY OLD **GOGO** WHO FORCED LITTLE BLACK KIDS TO GO PLAY OUTSIDE!!
© RAPID PHASE - 2008
...I CAN LIVE WITH THAT.
www.madamandeve.co.za
SLAM!
OBVIOUSLY SOME PEOPLE DON'T CARE ABOUT THEIR **LEGACY!**

WILL YOU BE NEEDING THIS, PRESIDENT **MOTLANTHE?**
WHAT IS IT?
SAND
PRESIDENT MBEKI'S **BUCKET OF SAND**. HE USED TO STICK HIS HEAD IN IT WHEN THINGS GOT ROUGH.
SERIOUSLY?! LET'S SEE!
SAND
...FEELING MORE **SECURE**, SIR?
UH... NOT REALLY.
SAND
www.madamandeve.co.za
© RAPID PHASE - 2008
I GUESS WE HAVE DIFFERENT STYLES OF GOVERNANCE.
I'LL PUT IT IN THE BASEMENT WITH THE GARLIC AND BEETROOT.
SAND

NATURALLY, I'M AWARE THAT INVESTOR CONFIDENCE HAS PLUMMETED, DUE TO THE CURRENT INTERNATIONAL FINANCIAL SITUATION.
HOWEVER, I SEEM TO HAVE INCURRED SOME UNEXPECTED YET UNAVOIDABLE EXPENSES WHICH CURRENTLY IMPEDE MY FISCAL STABILITY.
GET TO THE POINT.
www.madamandeve.co.za ©RAPID PHASE · 2008
I NEED AN IMMEDIATE BAILOUT.
NOT THAT KIND OF BAILOUT! A FIVE RAND BAILOUT!!

DON'T BOTHER MY MOTHER. SHE JUST STARTED HER NEW PART-TIME JOB AT HOME TODAY.
WHAT NEW PART-TIME JOB?
www.madamandeve.co.za ©RAPID PHASE · 2008
HELLO? FINANCIAL CRISIS HOTLINE! CAN I HELP YOU?
HOW SHOULD I KNOW?! THE NEW MOVIE COMES OUT IN NOVEMBER! UNTIL THEN, WATCH CASINO ROYALE!!
... SOME IDIOT WANTED TO KNOW WHAT I THOUGHT OF "THE BOND MARKET."
... CALLS CHARGED AT R 2.50 PER MINUTE.

POWER BLACKOUTS... PLUNGING FINANCIAL MARKETS... MYSTERY VIRUS PLAGUES...
WHAT HAPPENS NEXT?! RAINING FROGS?!
©RAPID PHASE · 2008 www.madamandeve.co.za
RIBBIT!!
AAAAAH!!
HAVE YOU SEEN MY PET FROG?

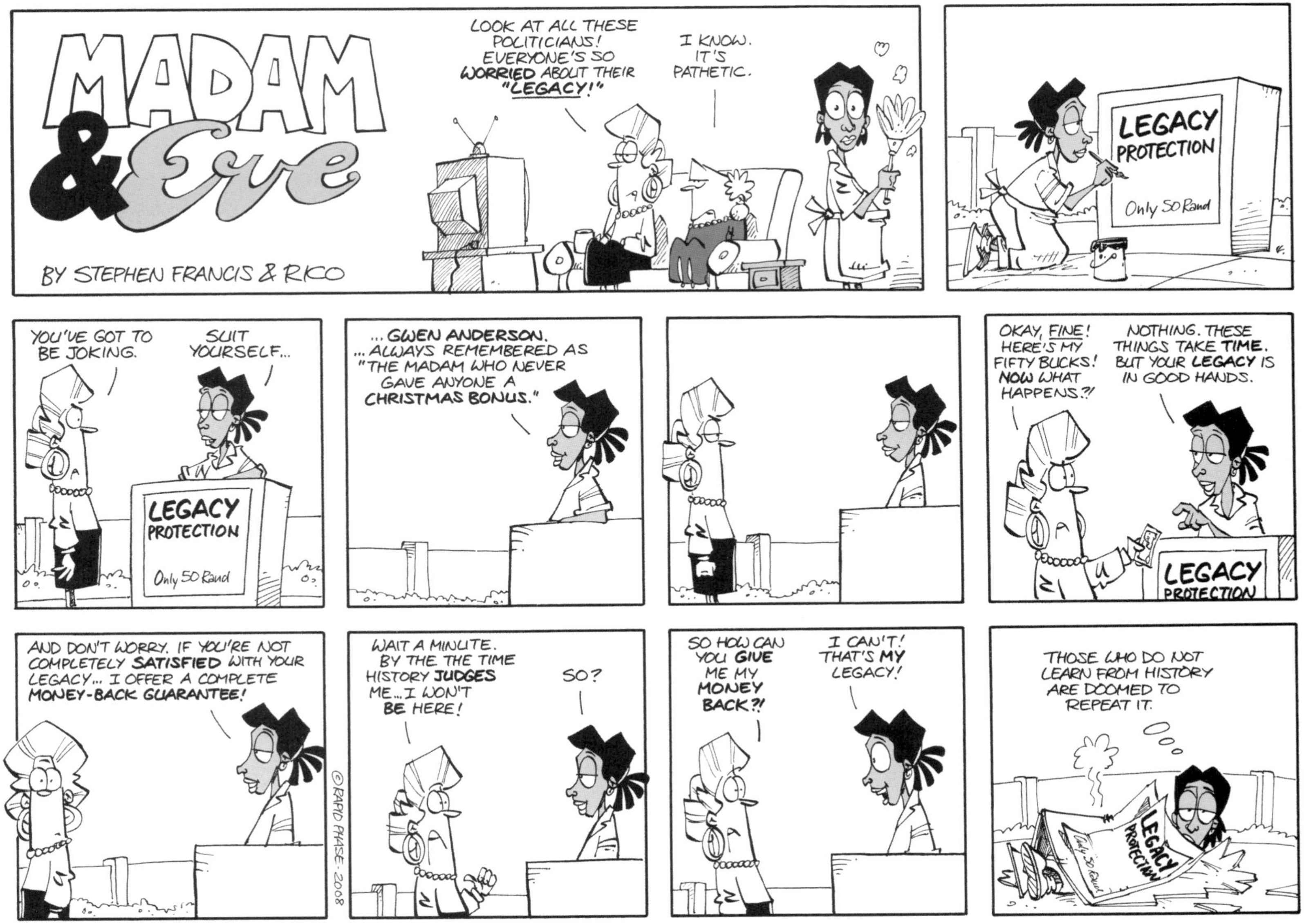
MADAM & Eve
BY STEPHEN FRANCIS & RICO
LOOK AT ALL THESE POLITICIANS! EVERYONE'S SO WORRIED ABOUT THEIR "LEGACY!"
I KNOW. IT'S PATHETIC.
LEGACY PROTECTION
Only 50 Rand
YOU'VE GOT TO BE JOKING.
SUIT YOURSELF...
LEGACY PROTECTION
Only 50 Rand
...GWEN ANDERSON. ...ALWAYS REMEMBERED AS "THE MADAM WHO NEVER GAVE ANYONE A CHRISTMAS BONUS."
OKAY, FINE! HERE'S MY FIFTY BUCKS! NOW WHAT HAPPENS?!
NOTHING. THESE THINGS TAKE TIME. BUT YOUR LEGACY IS IN GOOD HANDS.
LEGACY PROTECTION
AND DON'T WORRY. IF YOU'RE NOT COMPLETELY SATISFIED WITH YOUR LEGACY... I OFFER A COMPLETE MONEY-BACK GUARANTEE!
© RAPID PHASE · 2008
WAIT A MINUTE. BY THE THE TIME HISTORY JUDGES ME... I WON'T BE HERE!
SO?
SO HOW CAN YOU GIVE ME MY MONEY BACK?!
I CAN'T! THAT'S MY LEGACY!
THOSE WHO DO NOT LEARN FROM HISTORY ARE DOOMED TO REPEAT IT.
LEGACY PROTECTION
Only 50 Rand

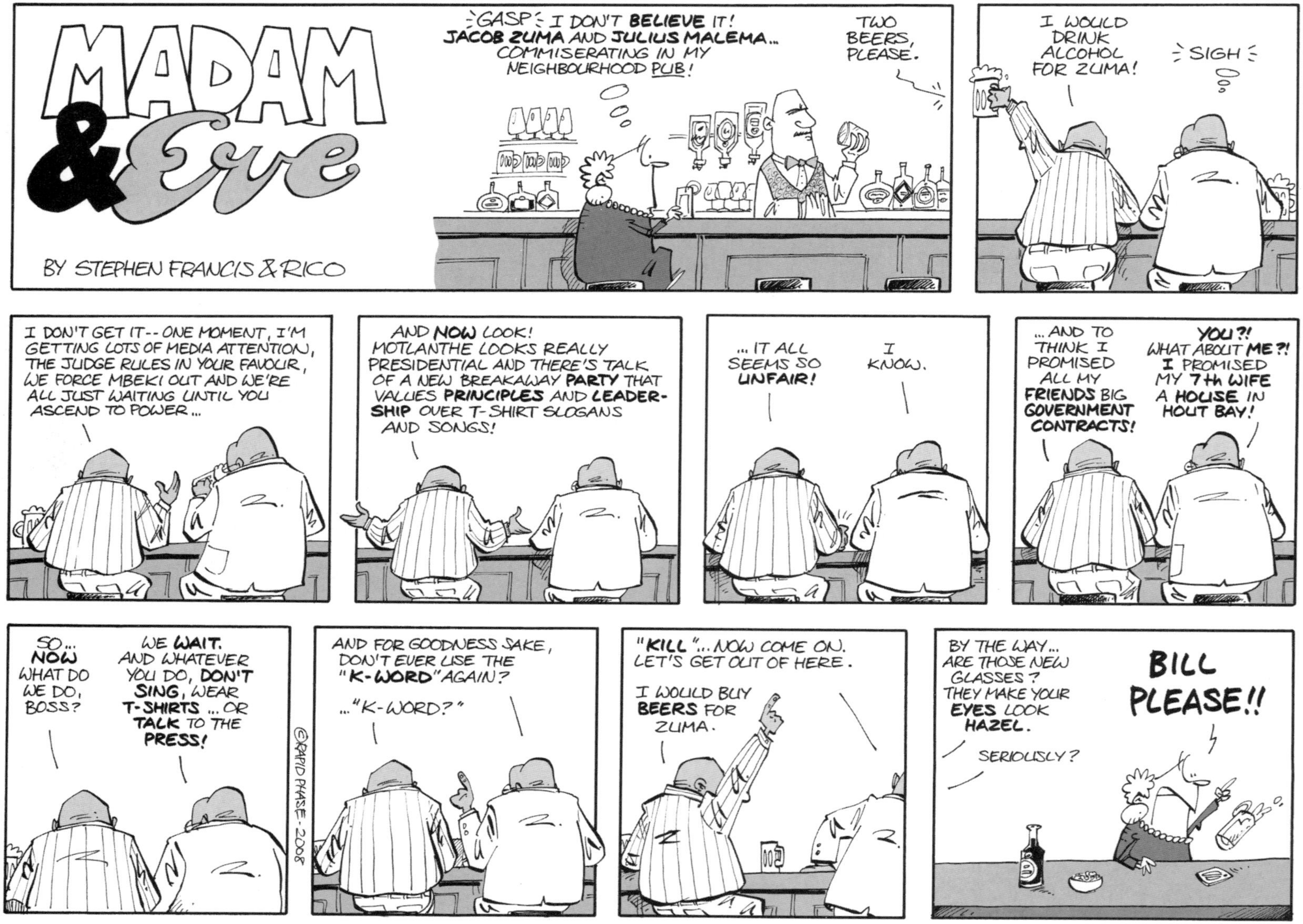

MADAM & Eve
BY STEPHEN FRANCIS & RICO
-GASP- I DON'T BELIEVE IT! JACOB ZUMA AND JULIUS MALEMA... COMMISERATING IN MY NEIGHBOURHOOD PUB!
TWO BEERS, PLEASE.
I WOULD DRINK ALCOHOL FOR ZUMA!
-SIGH-
I DON'T GET IT-- ONE MOMENT, I'M GETTING LOTS OF MEDIA ATTENTION, THE JUDGE RULES IN YOUR FAVOUR, WE FORCE MBEKI OUT AND WE'RE ALL JUST WAITING UNTIL YOU ASCEND TO POWER...
AND NOW LOOK! MOTLANTHE LOOKS REALLY PRESIDENTIAL AND THERE'S TALK OF A NEW BREAKAWAY PARTY THAT VALUES PRINCIPLES AND LEADERSHIP OVER T-SHIRT SLOGANS AND SONGS!
...IT ALL SEEMS SO UNFAIR!
I KNOW.
...AND TO THINK I PROMISED ALL MY FRIENDS BIG GOVERNMENT CONTRACTS!
YOU?! WHAT ABOUT ME?! I PROMISED MY 7th WIFE A HOUSE IN HOUT BAY!
SO... NOW WHAT DO WE DO, BOSS?
WE WAIT. AND WHATEVER YOU DO, DON'T SING, WEAR T-SHIRTS ...OR TALK TO THE PRESS!
©RAPID PHASE · 2008
AND FOR GOODNESS SAKE, DON'T EVER USE THE "K-WORD" AGAIN?
..."K-WORD?"
"KILL"... NOW COME ON. LET'S GET OUT OF HERE.
I WOULD BUY BEERS FOR ZUMA.
BY THE WAY... ARE THOSE NEW GLASSES? THEY MAKE YOUR EYES LOOK HAZEL.
SERIOUSLY?
BILL PLEASE!!

GASP I WON THE LOTTERY!!
www.madamandeve.co.za ©RAPID PHASE - 2008
I WON A LOTTERY THAT I DIDN'T EVEN ENTER!!
I WON A LOTTERY THAT I DIDN'T EVEN ENTER ... AND ALL THEY NEED ARE MY BANK DETAILS SO I CAN PAY A FEW SMALL ADMINISTRATION CHARGES!
I WON THE NIGERIAN LOTTERY! NO MORE BUDGET GIN!
YOU TELL HER ... OR SHOULD I ?

HELLO! FINANCIAL CRISIS HOTLINE! CAN I HELP YOU?
YES.
... I JUST WON 22 MILLION DOLLARS IN A LOTTERY... AND I DIDN'T EVEN ENTER IT. HOW'S THAT FOR LUCK?!
©RAPID PHASE - 2008
AFTER I GIVE THEM MY BANK DETAILS AND THEY SEND ME THE MONEY FROM NIGERIA ... HOW DO YOU THINK I SHOULD INVEST IT?
SIGH WHAT'S YOUR NAME?
www.madamandeve.co.za
JULIUS MALEMA. I WOULD WIN A LOTTERY FOR ZUMA.
MOM! I'M LISTENING TO THIS!

TRAITOR!
YOU'RE A TRAITOR!
OH, SHUT UP!
YOU SHUT UP!
www.madamandeve.co.za
WILL YOU TWO STOP ARGUING?! I'M TRYING TO RELAX!
...WE'RE NOT ARGUING, WE'RE PLAYING A GAME.
GAME?! WHAT GAME?!
"AFRICAN NATIONAL CONGRESS."
©RAPID PHASE - 2008
YOU SHUT UP!
NO, YOU SHUT UP!

HELLO. I'M LOOKING FOR TONIGHT'S ANC MEETING.
COULD YOU BE MORE SPECIFIC? THIS IS A BIG BUILDING. WHICH ANC MEETING?
©RAPID PHASE - 2008
... THE "PRO-ZUMA UBER-POPULIST SELF-ENRICHMENT T-SHIRT SLOGAN AND SONGS ABOVE REAL LEADERSHIP AND VALUES" ANC PARTY MEETING?
www.madamandeve.co.za
... OR THE "NEWLY-FORMED, YET UNTITLED, BREAKAWAY SILENT GRASSROOTS PARTY WITH A NAME AND MANIFESTO TO BE ANNOUNCED AT A LATER DATE" ANC MEETING?
... UH, ON SECOND THOUGHTS, WHERE'S TONIGHT'S DEMOCRATIC ALLIANCE MEETING?
... DOWN THE PASSAGE AND TURN LEFT.

MISTER LEKOTA?
WHAT IS IT?
©RAPID PHASE - 2008
THERE'S SOME PEOPLE HERE TO SEE YOU.
WHAT DO THEY WANT?
...THEY SAY THEY'RE LOOKING FOR THE REBEL CAMP.

IN A GALAXY NOT SO VERY FAR AWAY...

HMM... A DISTURBANCE IN THE STRUGGLE FORCE I FEEL.

FIND THE REBEL BASE AND DESTROY IT NOW!!

Y-YES LORD VADER.

...AND BRING ME MY LIGHT SABRE MACHINE GUN!!

ANC STAR WARS

Now playing everywhere at a theatre near you.

©RAPID PHASE - 2008

www.madamandeve.co.za

AND, IN OTHER NEWS... MBHAZIMA SHILOWA HAS BEEN CALLED A **BLACK SHEEP** FOR LEAVING THE ANC.

BLACK SHEEP?! THEY PLAYED THE **RACE** CARD!

... OR DID THEY PLAY THE "SHEEP" CARD?

©RAPID PHASE - 2008

SLAM!!

I'M JUST TRYING TO UNDERSTAND POLITICS AND YOU'RE NOT MAKING IT EASY!!

AND WE'LL BE RIGHT BACK ... WITH **MORE** ON PRESIDENT BUSH'S **NEW** WAR ON TERROR.

"WAR ON TERROR?!"

©RAPID PHASE - 2008

www.madamandeve.co.za

THE **AMERICANS** ARE GOING AFTER **LEKOTA** TOO?!

...ANYTHING'S POSSIBLE THESE DAYS.

23

AND IN OTHER NEWS, DOCTORS AT THE CENTRE FOR DISEASE CONTROL SAY THEY HAVE **CONTAINED** THE MYSTERY **VIRUS OUTBREAK** THAT IS PLAGUING GAUTENG.
-- HOWEVER, **FEAR** OF CONTRACTING THE ILLNESS IS STILL CAUSING WIDESPREAD **PANIC** AND MASS **HYSTERIA**.
©RAPID PHASE · 2008
www.madamandeve.co.za
...YOUR GIN & TONIC.
YOU **BOILED** IT FIRST?
... **AND** STERILISED THE LIME.

AND IN OTHER NEWS... **ROBBEN ISLAND** WILL BE CLOSED FOR TWO WEEKS IN AN EFFORT TO GET RID OF THOUSANDS OF **RABBITS** THAT HAVE OVERRUN THE ISLAND AND PRISON...
©RAPID PHASE · 2008
www.madamandeve.co.za
IT SAYS HERE: "ROBBEN ISLAND WAS DECLARED A WORLD HERITAGE SITE IN 1999."
WHERE'S MANDELA'S CELL?! I WANT TO SEE MANDELA'S CELL!!
TAKE A PHOTO OF ME AND THE JAIL!
HOLD STILL, DAMMIT!

WHAT'S THAT?
A QUARTER LOAF OF BREAD, PINK POLONY AND SAUSAGE, PROCESSED CHEESE, FRIED EGG... AND COVERED IN TOMATO SAUCE AND BUTTER.
www.madamandeve.co.za
...WANT A BITE? IT'S CALLED "THE QUARTER" -- THE "SOUTH AFRICAN BIG MAC!"
...ONLY WITH WAY MORE FAT, CARBS AND CHOLESTEROL.
©RAPID PHASE · 2008
THIS IS A TRADITIONAL FOOD! MY ANCESTORS ATE THIS!
...AND THAT'S WHY THEY'RE NOW YOUR ANCESTORS!
SLAM!!
SHE DOESN'T KNOW WHAT SHE'S MISSING.
...GOT ANY CHILI SAUCE?

--NEXT!
...I'LL HAVE TWO QUARTER LOAVES OF BREAD, PINK POLONY AND SAUSAGE, PROCESSED CHEESE, FRIED EGG AND SLAP CHIPS, SMOTHERED WITH TOMATO SAUCE AND BUTTER.
www.madamandeve.co.za
©RAPID PHASE · 2008
COMING UP!
...YOU WANT ANYTHING?
EXCUSE ME... WHAT KIND OF SALADS DO YOU HAVE?
SALAD?! ...YOU MEAN, LIKE... WITH LETTUCE?!
HEE HEE SHE WANTS SALAD!! HA-HA-HA! HOO-HOO!! ...WITH LETTUCE!!
SHE DOESN'T GET OUT MUCH.

HERE YOU GO, SON. TWO QUARTER LOAVES OF BREAD, POLONY AND SAUSAGE, PROCESSED CHEESE AND FRIED EGG, CHIPS, TOMATO SAUCE AND BUTTER!
...AND A LARGE COLA!
WHAT?! ...THIS HAS SOMETHING FROM EACH OF THE FIVE DIFFERENT FOOD GROUPS!
DO YOU HAVE ANY IDEA HOW UNHEALTHY THAT IS?! YOU REALLY NEED TO CUT DOWN ON ALL THOSE CALORIES!
YOU'RE RIGHT!
©RAPID PHASE · 2008
www.madamandeve.co.za
MAKE THAT A LARGE DIET COLA!

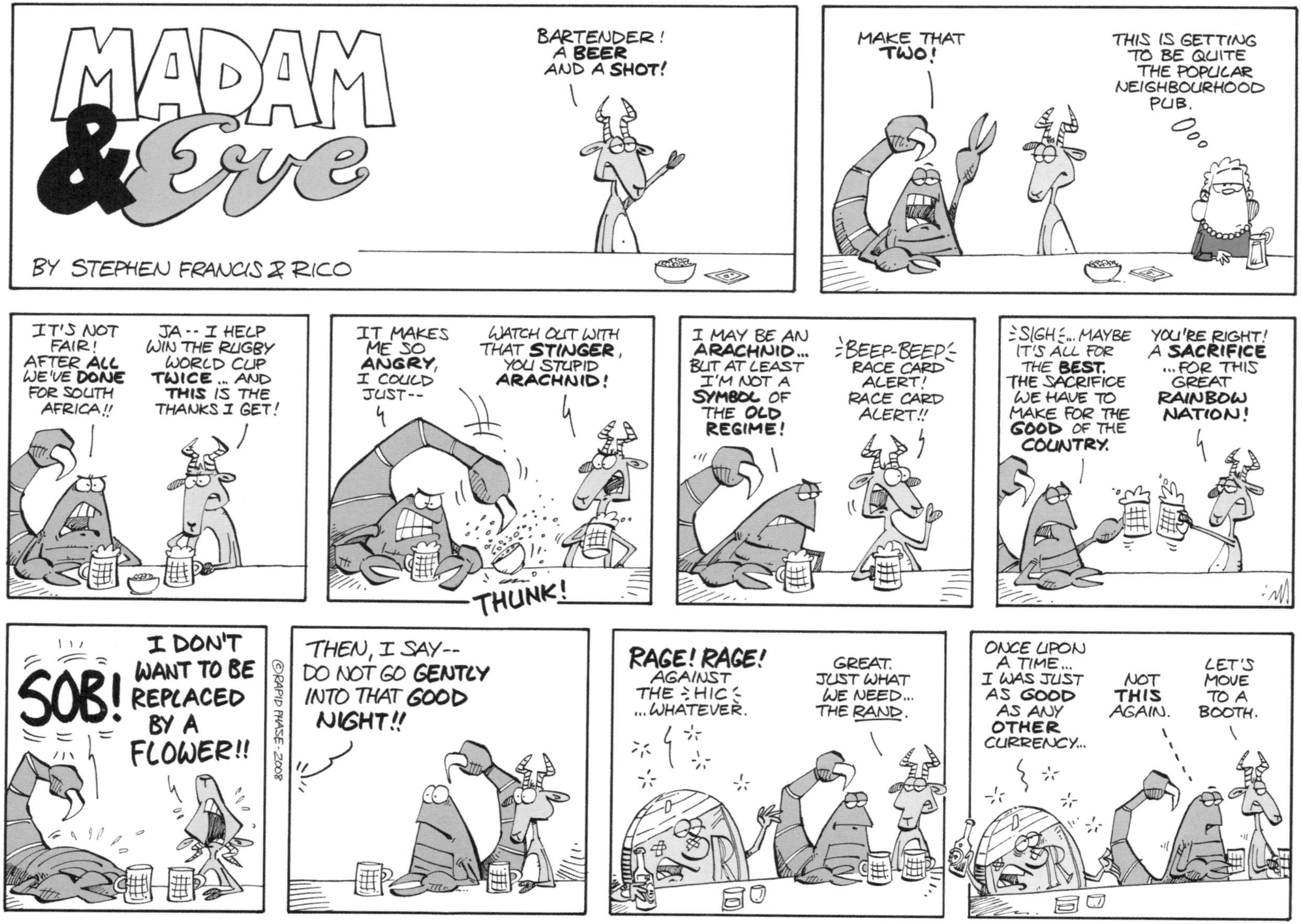
MADAM & Eve
BY STEPHEN FRANCIS & RICO
BARTENDER! A BEER AND A SHOT!
MAKE THAT TWO!
THIS IS GETTING TO BE QUITE THE POPULAR NEIGHBOURHOOD PUB.
IT'S NOT FAIR! AFTER ALL WE'VE DONE FOR SOUTH AFRICA!!
JA -- I HELP WIN THE RUGBY WORLD CUP TWICE ... AND THIS IS THE THANKS I GET!
IT MAKES ME SO ANGRY, I COULD JUST--
WATCH OUT WITH THAT STINGER, YOU STUPID ARACHNID!
THUNK!
I MAY BE AN ARACHNID... BUT AT LEAST I'M NOT A SYMBOL OF THE OLD REGIME!
BEEP-BEEP RACE CARD ALERT! RACE CARD ALERT!!
SIGH ... MAYBE IT'S ALL FOR THE BEST. THE SACRIFICE WE HAVE TO MAKE FOR THE GOOD OF THE COUNTRY.
YOU'RE RIGHT! A SACRIFICE ...FOR THIS GREAT RAINBOW NATION!
SOB!
I DON'T WANT TO BE REPLACED BY A FLOWER!!
©RAPID PHASE · 2008
THEN, I SAY-- DO NOT GO GENTLY INTO THAT GOOD NIGHT!!
RAGE! RAGE! AGAINST THE HIC ...WHATEVER.
GREAT. JUST WHAT WE NEED... THE RAND.
ONCE UPON A TIME... I WAS JUST AS GOOD AS ANY OTHER CURRENCY...
NOT THIS AGAIN.
LET'S MOVE TO A BOOTH.

NO JOB
NO MONEY
NO FOOD
©RAPID PHASE-2008 www.madamandeve.co.za

IT WAS ONLY WHEN THE SPRINGBOK SAW SARAH PALIN STARING AT HIM IN MOOSE-HUNTING GEAR ... THAT HE REALISED HIS DAYS MIGHT BE TRULY NUMBERED.
©RAPID PHASE-2008

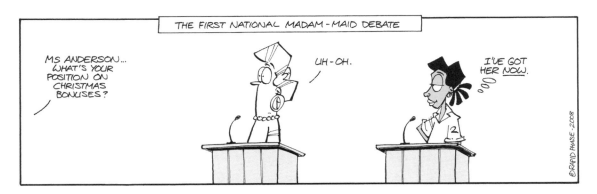

THE FIRST NATIONAL MADAM-MAID DEBATE
MS ANDERSON... WHAT'S YOUR POSITION ON CHRISTMAS BONUSES?
UH-OH.
I'VE GOT HER NOW.
©RAPID PHASE-2008

SHOULDN'T YOU BE STUDYING FOR YOUR EXAMS?
NAH. GRADES AND SYMBOLS AREN'T THAT IMPORTANT.
www.madamandeve.co.za
WHAT?! WHO SAID THAT?
OUR EDUCATION MINISTER.
©RAPID PHASE-2008
UH, I THINK SHE WAS DEFENDING THE ANC YOUTH LEAGUE PRESIDENT'S LOW MATRIC RESULTS.
EXACTLY MY POINT!
JULIUS HAD LOUSY GRADES AND LOOK HOW HE TURNED OUT!!
MOM!! I'M LISTENING TO THIS!

...THE PRESIDENT OF THE ANC WOMEN'S LEAGUE SAID THE ANC IS NOT GOING TO THE DOGS... "BECAUSE ALL THE DOGS HAVE LEFT!"
THE DOGS HAVE LEFT?! THEN WHO LET THEM OUT?
©RAPID PHASE-2008
WHO LET THE DOGS OUT?! WHO?! WHO?! WHO LET THE DOGS OUT?! WHO?! WHO?!
www.madamandeve.co.za
...METAPHORICALLY SPEAKING, OF COURSE.

CHECK IT OUT. A BRAND NEW BE MY WIFE.
HUH?
©RAPID PHASE-2008
"BE MY WIFE." --TOWNSHIP SLANG FOR A BMW.
OH. I SEE. TOWNSHIP SLANG.
www.madamandeve.co.za
SCREECH!!
VROOOM!!
--BUT THE GUY DRIVING IT LOOKS LIKE A TOTAL "MALEMA."

WHILE IT'S TRUE THE RAIN CLOUDS MAY HAVE FOUND US AND SUNNY SKIES HAVE TEMPORARILY GONE AWAY...
WE ARE CURRENTLY ON COURSE TO RIDE OUT THE STORM.
©RAPID PHASE · 2008
TRUST ME, THIS THUNDER WILL PASS.
IS THIS THE WEATHER CHANNEL?
TREVOR MANUEL.

HAPPY HALLOWEEN.
THANKS.
www.madamandeve.co.za
WHY ARE YOU LOOKING AT ME LIKE THAT?
©RAPID PHASE · 2008
... NO REASON.

AND IN OTHER NEWS, LOCAL MANUFACTURERS BELIEVE THAT, THANKS TO THE 2010 WORLD CUP, THE VUVUZELA COULD CATCH ON INTERNATIONALLY.
...PRESIDENT BUSH? HAVE YOU EVER SEEN A SOUTH AFRICAN VUVUZELA?
...YEAH.
www.madamandeve.co.za
...BUT I WAS PRETTY DRUNK AT THE TIME AND IT COST ME FIFTY BUCKS!
UH, SIR...
©RAPID PHASE · 2008
AND FOR GOODNESS SAKE -- DON'T TELL MY WIFE!
UH, SIR...

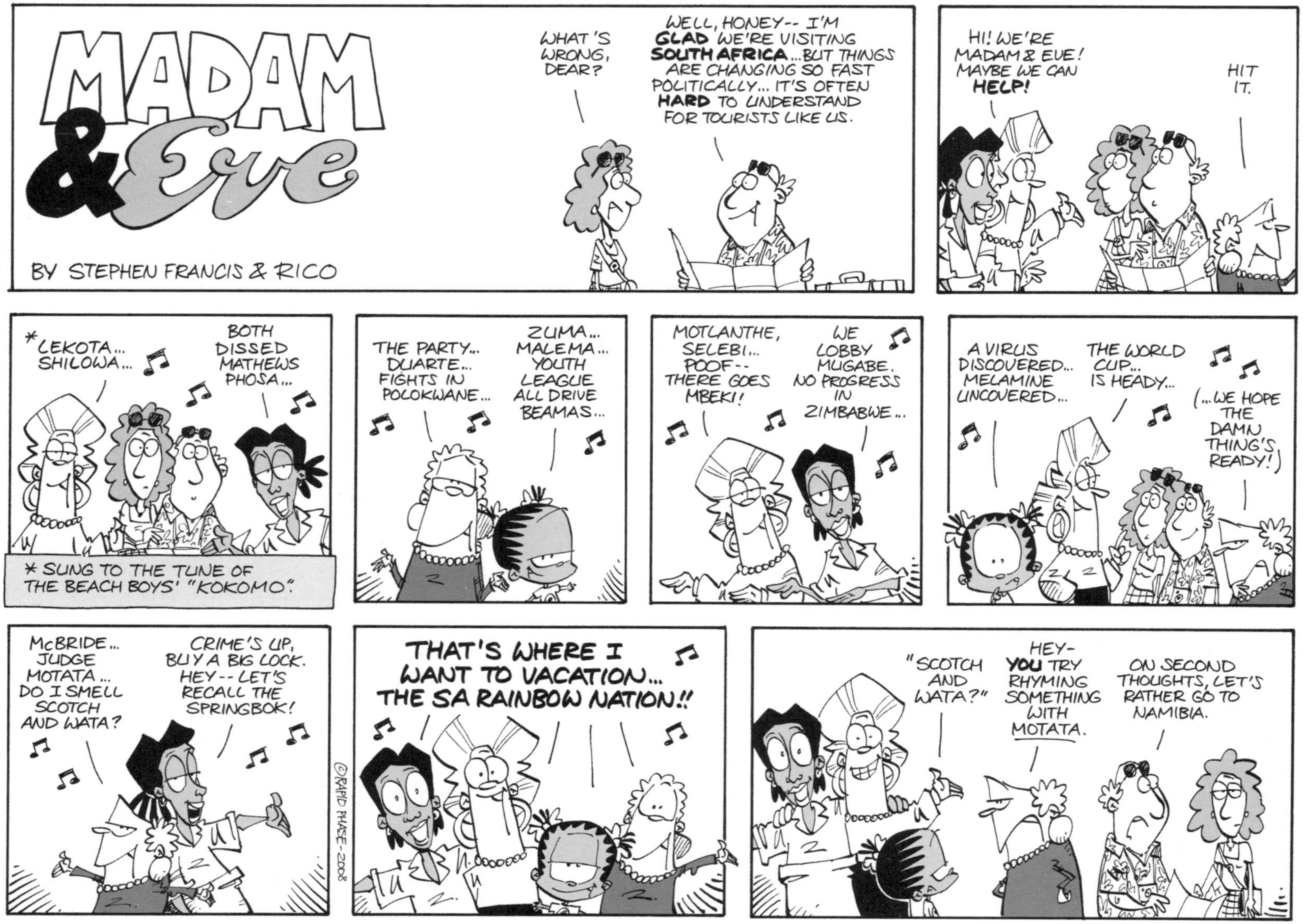
MADAM & Eve
BY STEPHEN FRANCIS & RICO
WHAT'S WRONG, DEAR?
WELL, HONEY-- I'M GLAD WE'RE VISITING SOUTH AFRICA...BUT THINGS ARE CHANGING SO FAST POLITICALLY... IT'S OFTEN HARD TO UNDERSTAND FOR TOURISTS LIKE US.
HI! WE'RE MADAM & EVE! MAYBE WE CAN HELP!
HIT IT.
*LEKOTA... SHILOWA...
BOTH DISSED MATHEWS PHOSA...
* SUNG TO THE TUNE OF THE BEACH BOYS' "KOKOMO".
THE PARTY... DUARTE... FIGHTS IN POLOKWANE...
ZUMA... MALEMA... YOUTH LEAGUE ALL DRIVE BEAMAS...
MOTLANTHE, SELEBI... POOF-- THERE GOES MBEKI!
WE LOBBY MUGABE. NO PROGRESS IN ZIMBABWE...
A VIRUS DISCOVERED... MELAMINE UNCOVERED...
THE WORLD CUP... IS HEADY...
(...WE HOPE THE DAMN THING'S READY!)
McBRIDE... JUDGE MOTATA... DO I SMELL SCOTCH AND WATA?
CRIME'S UP, BUY A BIG LOCK. HEY-- LET'S RECALL THE SPRINGBOK!
©RAPID PHASE-2008
THAT'S WHERE I WANT TO VACATION... THE SA RAINBOW NATION!!
"SCOTCH AND WATA?"
HEY-- YOU TRY RHYMING SOMETHING WITH MOTATA.
ON SECOND THOUGHTS, LET'S RATHER GO TO NAMIBIA.

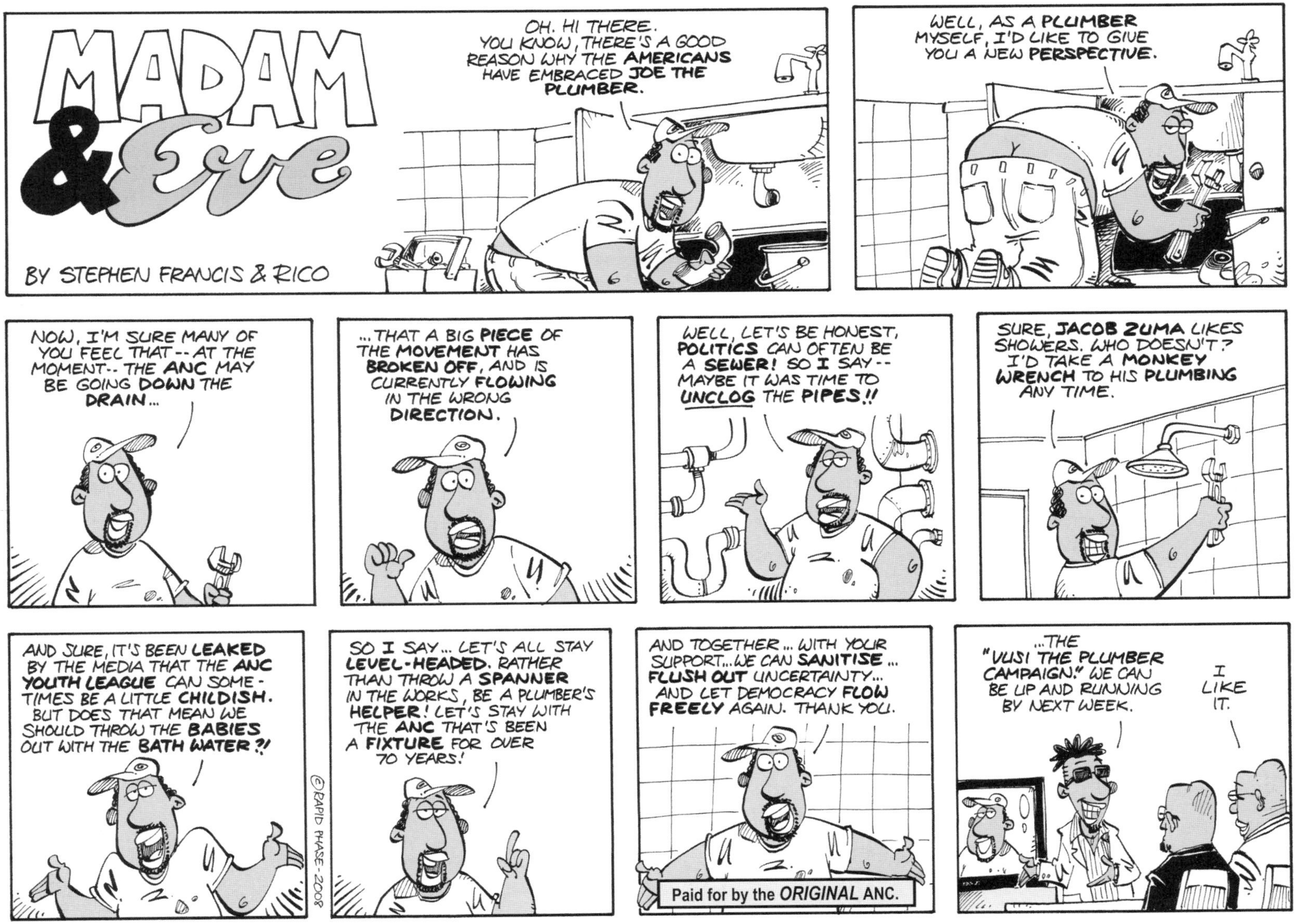
MADAM & Eve
BY STEPHEN FRANCIS & RICO
OH. HI THERE. YOU KNOW, THERE'S A GOOD REASON WHY THE AMERICANS HAVE EMBRACED JOE THE PLUMBER.
WELL, AS A PLUMBER MYSELF, I'D LIKE TO GIVE YOU A NEW PERSPECTIVE.
NOW, I'M SURE MANY OF YOU FEEL THAT -- AT THE MOMENT -- THE ANC MAY BE GOING DOWN THE DRAIN...
...THAT A BIG PIECE OF THE MOVEMENT HAS BROKEN OFF, AND IS CURRENTLY FLOWING IN THE WRONG DIRECTION.
WELL, LET'S BE HONEST, POLITICS CAN OFTEN BE A SEWER! SO I SAY -- MAYBE IT WAS TIME TO UNCLOG THE PIPES!!
SURE, JACOB ZUMA LIKES SHOWERS. WHO DOESN'T? I'D TAKE A MONKEY WRENCH TO HIS PLUMBING ANY TIME.
AND SURE, IT'S BEEN LEAKED BY THE MEDIA THAT THE ANC YOUTH LEAGUE CAN SOMETIMES BE A LITTLE CHILDISH. BUT DOES THAT MEAN WE SHOULD THROW THE BABIES OUT WITH THE BATH WATER?!
© RAPID PHASE - 2008
SO I SAY... LET'S ALL STAY LEVEL-HEADED. RATHER THAN THROW A SPANNER IN THE WORKS, BE A PLUMBER'S HELPER! LET'S STAY WITH THE ANC THAT'S BEEN A FIXTURE FOR OVER 70 YEARS!
AND TOGETHER... WITH YOUR SUPPORT... WE CAN SANITISE... FLUSH OUT UNCERTAINTY... AND LET DEMOCRACY FLOW FREELY AGAIN. THANK YOU.
Paid for by the ORIGINAL ANC.
...THE "VUSI THE PLUMBER CAMPAIGN." WE CAN BE UP AND RUNNING BY NEXT WEEK.
I LIKE IT.

WE WOULD KILL FOR ZUMA!!
KILL SHILOWA!! KILL LEKOTA!!
©RAPID PHASE - 2008
BAD NEWS, JULIUS! A SPOKESPERSON FOR UNISA ISSUED A STATEMENT DENYING YOU EVER REGISTERED FOR A LAW OR ANY OTHER DEGREE!
KILL UNISA!! KILL THE SPOKESPEOPLE!!

BRAINSTORMING
OKAY. WHAT WAS THE LAST ONE AGAIN?
THE "SOUTH AFRICAN DEMOCRATIC CONGRESS." -- IT'S ARLREADY REGISTERED.
G#$G!!
HOW ABOUT... "THE SOUTH AFRICAN BREAKAWAY CONGRESS?"
...THAT WOULD MAKE US THE SABC.
I'VE GOT IT! "THE CONGRESS OF NATIONAL AFRICANS!"
I LIKE IT!
ME TOO!
THAT'S IT!!
©RAPID PHASE - 2008
WAIT A MINUTE! THEN WE'D BE THE CNA!
DAMN! ALL THE GOOD ACRONYMS ARE ALREADY TAKEN!
LET'S BREAKAWAY FOR LUNCH.

I'VE GOT IT! THE NAME OF THE NEW BREAKAWAY PARTY!
WHAT IS IT?
THE A.N.C-N PARTY.
ANC-N?
THE AFRICAN NATIONAL CONGRESS - NOT!!
©RAPID PHASE - 2008
FINE! LET'S SEE WHAT SHIKOTA THINK!!

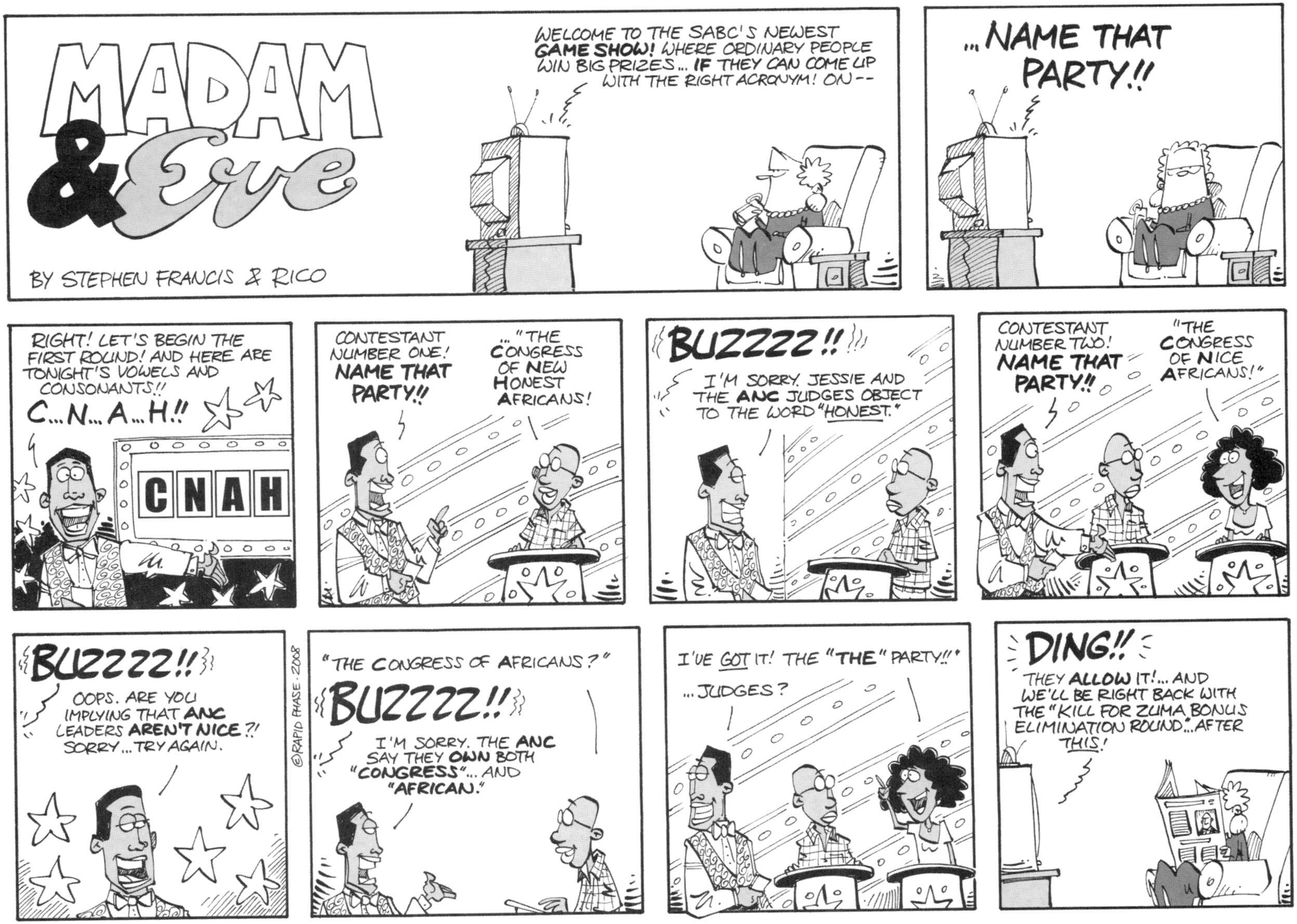
MADAM & Eve
BY STEPHEN FRANCIS & RICO
WELCOME TO THE SABC'S NEWEST GAME SHOW! WHERE ORDINARY PEOPLE WIN BIG PRIZES... IF THEY CAN COME UP WITH THE RIGHT ACRONYM! ON --
...NAME THAT PARTY!!
RIGHT! LET'S BEGIN THE FIRST ROUND! AND HERE ARE TONIGHT'S VOWELS AND CONSONANTS!!
C...N...A...H!!
CNAH
CONTESTANT NUMBER ONE! NAME THAT PARTY!!
..."THE CONGRESS OF NEW HONEST AFRICANS!
BUZZZZ!!
I'M SORRY. JESSIE AND THE ANC JUDGES OBJECT TO THE WORD "HONEST."
CONTESTANT NUMBER TWO! NAME THAT PARTY!!
"THE CONGRESS OF NICE AFRICANS!"
BUZZZZZ!!
OOPS. ARE YOU IMPLYING THAT ANC LEADERS AREN'T NICE?! SORRY... TRY AGAIN.
©RAPID PHASE · 2008
"THE CONGRESS OF AFRICANS?"
BUZZZZZ!!
I'M SORRY. THE ANC SAY THEY OWN BOTH "CONGRESS"... AND "AFRICAN."
I'VE GOT IT! THE "THE" PARTY!!"
...JUDGES?
DING!!
THEY ALLOW IT!... AND WE'LL BE RIGHT BACK WITH THE "KILL FOR ZUMA BONUS ELIMINATION ROUND"... AFTER THIS!

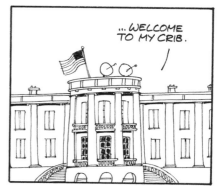

MADAM & Eve

BY STEPHEN FRANCIS & RICO

PRESIDENT BUSH!

PRESIDENT-ELECT OBAMA! GREAT TO SEE YOU!

...WELCOME TO MY CRIB.

JUST THINK, BARRACK! IN A FEW SHORT MONTHS ALL **THIS** WILL BE **YOURS**!

I KNOW. A NEW CHAPTER IN AMERICAN HISTORY...

...IT'S ALL VERY EXCITING.

YOU GOT **THAT** RIGHT! SO WHILE I GIVE YOU THE **TOUR**...JUST MAKE YOURSELF AT **HOME**!...RELAX! ...BE YOURSELF!

I CAN BE **MYSELF**?

SURE!

THANKS, BIG G!! YO -- YOU MY **MAIN MAN**, AW-ITE?! YOU A **PLAYA**! SHOW ME SOME **LOVE**, HOMEY!!

I KNEW IT!

YOU RIGHT! I'VE BEEN "TALKING THE TALK" **24-7**! NOW THAT MY **PEEPS** ARE GETTING **PAID**...I'M ABOUT TO BUST A MOVE AS **COMMANDER IN CHIEF**... I CAN FINALLY BE CHILLIN'.

I KNEW IT!!

WELL, I GOT A **BOOTYCALL** IN HALF AN HOUR, IT'S ALL ABOUT THE **BLING** AND **BENJAMINS**, SO LET'S GET DOWN TO BIZNESS. WHERE THE TOUR AT?!

I KNEW IT!!

YO MAN! WHY YOU **CLOCKIN'** ME?...DUDE TRIPPIN'!

I'M **RECORDING** THIS **ENTIRE** CONVERSATION!

DID YOU JUST CALL ME "**WHITEBOY**?!"

CODE RED! THE PRESIDENT'S HAVING ANOTHER OBAMA-MARE!!

©RAPID PHASE - 2008

34

JUST THINK. AMERICA HAS A BLACK PRESIDENT.
...COPYCATS.
©RAPID PHASE · 2008

AND COMING UP... MORE COVERAGE OF THE **AMERICAN ELECTION**.
...I'M REALLY GLAD **OBAMA** GOT **ELECTED**... BUT I'M ALSO VERY **SURPRISED**.
AND WHY IS THAT?
©RAPID PHASE · 2008
FRANKLY, HIS SUPPORT BASE WASN'T VERY LOYAL.
WHY?
...I DIDN'T HEAR **ONE PERSON** OFFER TO **KILL** FOR HIM.

AMERICA...WE HAVE COME SO FAR. BUT THERE IS SO MUCH MORE TO DO -- **YES WE CAN!**

TO THOSE WHO SAY WE **CAN'T** ... WE RESPOND WITH THE **SPIRIT** OF THE AMERICAN PEOPLE -- **YES WE CAN!!**

IT'S AFTER FIVE!! COULD **SOMEONE** POSSIBLY BRING ME MY **GIN & TONIC** ... TODAY ?!!

YES WE CAN!! ...BUT ONLY AFTER OUR **TEA BREAK!**

©RAPID PHASE - 2008

PRESIDENT **BUSH**... I'M SURE PRESIDENT-ELECT **OBAMA** DIDN'T STEAL YOUR SLOGAN!

HE DID **TOO!** I WAS SAYING **"YES WE CAN!"** YEARS AGO!

"CAN WE RIG THE FLORIDA VOTING RECOUNT?! YES WE CAN!"

"CAN WE INVADE IRAQ? YES WE CAN!"

"CAN WE SPEND A TRILLION DOLLARS? YES WE CAN!"

AT LEAST NOBODY'S MADE A **MOVIE** ABOUT OBAMA, SIR.

GOOD POINT.

www.madamandeve.co.za

©RAPID PHASE - 2008

YES, PRESIDENT **BUSH**?

UNTIL MY TERM IS **OVER**, I DON'T WANT ANYONE **MENTIONING** THE "O-WORD" IN THE **WHITE HOUSE!**

I DON'T WANT TO SEE ANY OF HIS PHOTOS, INTERVIEWS, QUOTES, U-TUBE CLIPS ...

EXCUSE ME, SIR. THE DEMOCRATS ARE ON LINE TWO ...

...THEY WANT TO KNOW IF YOU AND YOUR FAMILY CAN **MOVE OUT** BY JANUARY 10th.

TELL 'EM **"YES WE CAN."**

-- OOPS!! @#X G#!!

HE'LL CALL YOU BACK.

www.madamandeve.co.za

©RAPID PHASE - 2008

OKAY. CHECK THIS OUT. ...HIT IT, GUYS.

www.madamandeve.co.za

CAN WE BRING HIM HIS MACHINE GUN?! YES WE CAN!!

ANC YOUTH LEAGUE

CAN WE LAY DOWN OUR LIVES FOR ZUMA?! YES WE CAN!!

ANC YOUTH LEAGUE

©RAPID PHASE · 2008

...WELL?

I DON'T KNOW, JULIUS. THE BOSS SAYS WE KEEP A LOW PROFILE.

ANC YOUTH LEAGUE

AND IN OTHER NEWS, ACCORDING TO POLITICAL ANALYSTS, ANC YOUTH LEAGUE PRESIDENT **JULIUS MALEMA** HAS BECOME A **LIABILITY** TO THE ANC.

...AND AN **ASSET** TO THE BREAKAWAY PARTY, COPE.

DID YOU HEAR THAT? JULIUS IS MAKING A REAL **ASSET** OF HIMSELF.

©RAPID PHASE · 2008

OLD NEWS, DEAR. OLD NEWS.

MOM!!

www.madamandeve.co.za

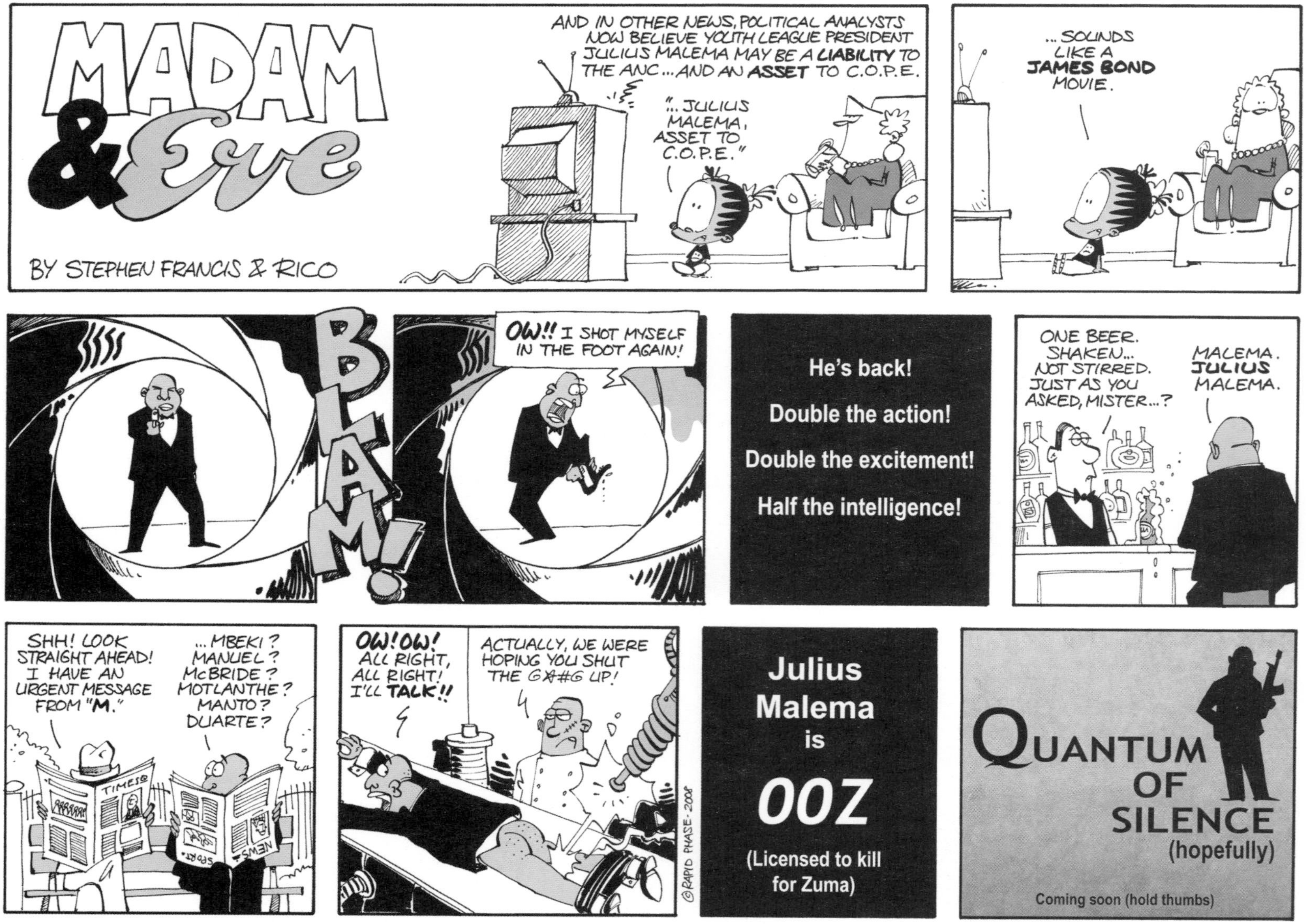
MADAM & Eve
BY STEPHEN FRANCIS & RICO
AND IN OTHER NEWS, POLITICAL ANALYSTS NOW BELIEVE YOUTH LEAGUE PRESIDENT JULIUS MALEMA MAY BE A **LIABILITY** TO THE ANC... AND AN **ASSET** TO C.O.P.E.
"... JULIUS MALEMA, ASSET TO C.O.P.E."
... SOUNDS LIKE A **JAMES BOND** MOVIE.
BLAM!
OW!! I SHOT MYSELF IN THE FOOT AGAIN!
He's back!
Double the action!
Double the excitement!
Half the intelligence!
ONE BEER. SHAKEN... NOT STIRRED. JUST AS YOU ASKED, MISTER...?
MALEMA. **JULIUS** MALEMA.
SHH! LOOK STRAIGHT AHEAD! I HAVE AN URGENT MESSAGE FROM "**M.**"
... MBEKI? MANUEL? McBRIDE? MOTLANTHE? MANTO? DUARTE?
OW! OW! ALL RIGHT, ALL RIGHT! I'LL **TALK!!**
ACTUALLY, WE WERE HOPING YOU SHUT THE G✗#G UP!
©RAPID PHASE · 2008
Julius Malema is 00Z
(Licensed to kill for Zuma)
QUANTUM OF SILENCE
(hopefully)
Coming soon (hold thumbs)

FATIMA!
WAIT!
COME BACK!!

I CAN'T **BELIEVE** IT!
WE'RE LEAKING LIKE
A SIEVE! EVERY TIME
I TURN AROUND,
ANOTHER ANC MEMBER
DEFECTS TO JOIN THE
NEW PARTY!!

WE'VE GOT TO <u>DO</u>
SOMETHING BEFORE
IT'S TOO **LATE!**
...RIGHT, COMRADE?

©RAPID PHASE - 2008
www.madamandeve.co.za

...COMRADE?

AND, WITH **ANC** MEMBERS
NOW JOINING **COPE**
AND THE STRENGTHENING
OF THE **DA**...

...THE SOUTH AFRICAN
POLITICAL LANDSCAPE
IS RAPIDLY **CHANGING.**
WHERE WE **END UP**... IS
ANYONE'S GUESS.

www.madamandeve.co.za
©RAPID PHASE - 2008

WHY DON'T
WE JUST
GET A
GPS UNIT?

FINE!!
YOU GOT A
BETTER
IDEA?!

DOES THE
PROSECUTION
REST?

NO,
YOUR
WORSHIP.

THE PROSECUTION
CALLS TWO
SURPRISE REBUTTAL
WITNESSES!

OBJECTION!

©RAPID PHASE - 2008

-- JACK DANIELS AND
JOHNNY WALKER BLACK!

YES!!

... AND WE'LL BE BACK...
WITH **MORE** ON THE
JUDGE MOTATA
DRUNK DRIVING TRIAL
... AFTER <u>THIS</u>.

MADAM & EVE
SCREECH!! SCREECH!!

BY STEPHEN FRANCIS & RICO

GET OUT OF THE WAY!! WE'RE TRANSPORTING AN IMPORTANT GOVERNMENT VIP TO A MEETING!!

YOU GET OUT OF THE WAY! WE'RE TRANSPORTING AN IMPORTANT GOVERNMENT VIP!!

OUR VIP IS MORE IMPORTANT THAN YOUR VIP!!

SAYS WHO?! YOU DON'T EVEN KNOW WHO OUR VIP IS!!

OKAY. WHO IS IT?

WELL, IF YOU DON'T KNOW, WE'RE NOT GOING TO TELL YOU!!

FINE! DON'T TELL US! ...I GUESS WE'LL ALL JUST SIT HERE ALL DAY!

FINE WITH US!!

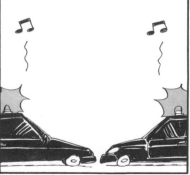

©RAPID PHASE · 2008

...AND THAT'S WHAT HAPPENS WHEN AN IRRESISTABLE FORCE MEETS AN IMMOVABLE OBJECT.

...SHE GAVE YOU AN "F"?

NOBODY APPRECIATES ORIGINAL THINKING ANY MORE!!

WOOOOOO!!
GET OUT OF THE WAY! VERY IMPORTANT PEOPLE -- MUCH MORE IMPORTANT THAN YOU -- ARE COMING THROUGH!!
www.madamandeve.co.za
WOOOOOO!!
©RAPID PHASE - 2008
VIP BLUE LIGHTS
Only 10 Rand

BLUE LIGHT ENVY
THIS IS GETTING RIDICULOUS.
©RAPID PHASE - 2008

MISTER ZUMA-- PEOPLE SAY YOU'RE TRYING TO CURRY FAVOUR WITH EVERYONE!... THAT YOU TELL EACH GROUP WHAT THEY WANT TO HEAR!
I KNOW.
©RAPID PHASE - 2008
www.madamandeve.co.za
... AND YOU'RE ABSOLUTELY RIGHT.
I... AM?
YES... WHICH IS WHY I ALWAYS SUPPORT THE BIASED LIBERAL MEDIA!
YOU DO?
VIVA!! FREEDOM OF THE PRESS! VIVA!!
YOU HAVE TO ADMIT -- THE GUY MAKES A LOT OF SENSE.

WELL?
GREAT NEWS, COMRADES! COMRADE MALEMA HAS AGREED TO STAY AWAY FROM THE MEDIA AND NOT MAKE ANY MORE CONTROVERSIAL STATEMENTS!
CONGRATULATIONS!
YES!
YEBO! IT'S SMOOTH SAILING FROM NOW ON!
AND IN OTHER NEWS... AN ANC FREE STATE LEADER HAS JUST COMPARED JACOB ZUMA TO JESUS.
© RAPID PHASE · 2008
D'OH!!

AND IN OTHER NEWS, OVER 6.5 MILLION RAND HAS GONE MISSING FROM THE GAUTRAIN BUDGET.
ISN'T THERE ANYONE LEFT WITH INTEGRITY ANY MORE?! I'D GIVE A MILLION BUCKS JUST TO FIND ONE HONEST PERSON!!
© RAPID PHASE · 2008
www.madamandeve.co.za
I JUST FOUND 50 CENTS BEHIND THE COUCH. IS IT YOURS?
NO.
...AND NICE TRY!!

FROM NOW ON, EVERY BRANCH OFFICE MUST TAKE THE ANC PLEDGE OF LOYALTY! RAISE YOUR RIGHT HAND AND REPEAT AFTER ME!
I, STATE YOUR NAME --
I STATE YOUR NAME --
© RAPID PHASE · 2008
NO, INSERT YOUR OWN NAME --
NO, INSERT YOUR OWN NAME --
www.madamandeve.co.za
CONGRATULATIONS. YOU PASSED. NEXT!!
CONGRATULATIONS. YOU PASSED. NEXT!!

MADAM & Eve

BY STEPHEN FRANCIS & RICO

Panel 1: AND IN OTHER NEWS... THE ENVIRONMENTAL AFFAIRS AND TOURISM DEPARTMENT SAYS SOUTH AFRICAN SERVICE DELIVERY STANDARDS HAVE BEEN RANKED AS ONE OF THE LOWEST IN THE WORLD.

Panel 2: UNBELIEVABLE.

Panel 3: Hello. You've reached the **SA Tourism Automated Holiday** Service. For airline reservations, say "ONE." For hotel information, say "TWO."

Panel 4: TWO.

Panel 5: Thank you. You just said "TWO." ... is that correct?

YES DAMMIT!

Panel 6: "Yes, dammit." Very good. Now please state your **QUESTION** slowly and clearly.

I'D LIKE INFORMATION. SOME PLACE WITH SUN ... AND OCEAN.

Panel 7: You would like some information on **"SUNTAN LOTION"**. Is that correct?

NO! I SAID "SUN... AND OCEAN!!

Panel 8: ... did you just say "LOTION?"

OCEAN!! "OCEAN!!" YOU BUNCH OF @*#'G IDIOTS! ...AND WHY DON'T YOU GO **JUMP IN** ONE?!

Panel 9: Let me see if I understand you. "WE ARE A BUNCH OF @#%# **IDIOTS** AND SHOULD GO **JUMP** IN THE **OCEAN!**" Is that correct?

YES!! YES!!

©RICO PHASE-2008

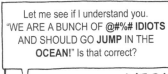

Panel 10: Thank you. Please **hold on** while I ask a **supervisor** if this is **possible**.

Panel 11: SO, MOM! DID YOU BOOK OUR HOLIDAY YET? WHERE ARE WE STAYING?

HOME!!

43

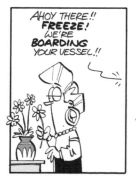

AHOY THERE!! **FREEZE!** WE'RE **BOARDING** YOUR VESSEL!!
GASP! ...**AUTOMATIC WEAPONS?!** WHAT DO YOU WANT?!
©RAPID PHASE · 2008
www.madamandeve.co.za
HAND OVER YOUR **VALUABLES!** ARRR!! WE'RE TAKING **CONTROL** OF YOUR **SHIP!!**
...**SOMALI** PIRATES OF THE CARIBBEAN.

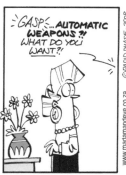

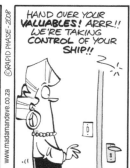

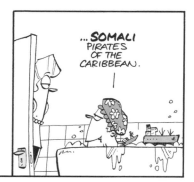

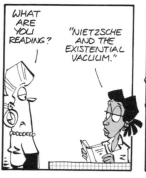

WHAT ARE YOU READING?
"NIETZSCHE AND THE EXISTENTIAL VACUUM."
©RAPID PHASE · 2008
ACCORDING TO NIETZSCHE, THE "EXISTENTIAL VACUUM" IS A REAL PROBLEM.
GOOD. BECAUSE THERE'S NOTHING WRONG WITH THE **VACUUM** WE ALREADY HAVE.

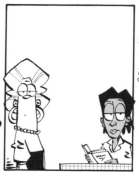

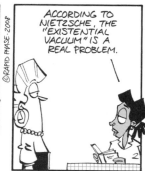

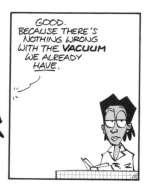

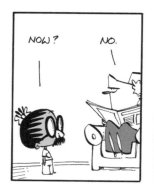

NOW?
NO.
...NOW?
NO.
www.madamandeve.co.za
©RAPID PHASE · 2008
HOW ABOUT NOW?
SLAM!!
I'M JUST TRYING TO GET A JUMP ON THE "**SILLY SEASON.**"

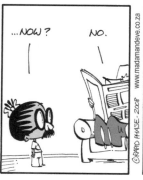

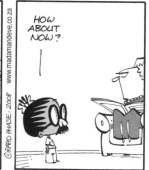

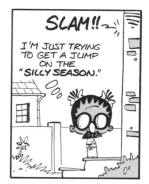

AND WE'LL BE BACK WITH MORE FINANCIAL AND BUSINESS NEWS... AFTER THIS.

IT'S NOT EASY TO UNDERSTAND ALL THESE **BUSINESS** BUZZ-PHRASES!

IT'S EASY. YOU HAVE "MERGERS" AND "AQUISITIONS." YOU NEED "CAPITAL", "CREDIT"... COMPANY "EQUITY"... AND ALWAYS KEEP YOUR EYE ON THE "BOTTOM LINE."

BUT THE MOST **IMPORTANT** THING OF ALL... IS TO ALWAYS HAVE AN **"EXIT STRATEGY."**

EXIT STRATEGY? WHAT'S AN **"EXIT STRATEGY?"**

©RAPID PHASE - 2008

SLAM!

OKAY... CLOSE YOUR EYES, GET IN TOUCH WITH THE UNIVERSE... AND **VISUALISE** WHAT YOU THINK IS A FAIR ANNUAL **WAGE INCREASE.**

OMMMMM!!

©RAPID PHASE - 2008

OMMMMM!!

WHO'S THAT GUY?

HE'S A LABOUR GURU.

...THEY'RE TRYING **TRANSCENDENTAL MEDIATION.**

TWENTY PERCENT?! ...ARE YOU **CRAZY?!**

OMMMM!

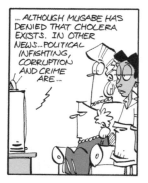

...ALTHOUGH MUGABE HAS DENIED THAT CHOLERA EXISTS. IN OTHER NEWS... POLITICAL INFIGHTING, CORRUPTION AND CRIME ARE...
AAAAH!!
...I FEEL A LITTLE BETTER.
SO DO I.
ME TOO.
©RAPID PHASE · 2008 www.madamandeve.co.za
THIS GATVOL MOMENT HAS BEEN BROUGHT TO YOU BY
MADAM & Eve
HAPPY HOLIDAYS!!

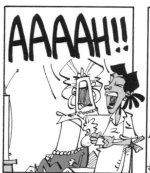

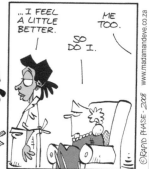

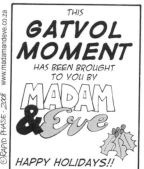

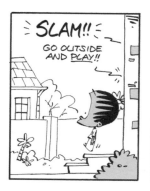

SLAM!!
GO OUTSIDE AND PLAY!!
WHATEVER HAPPENED TO "TIS THE SEASON TO BE JOLLY?!"
GO OUTSIDE AND PLAY!!
©RAPID PHASE · 2008
...HO, HO, HO.

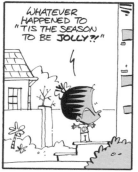

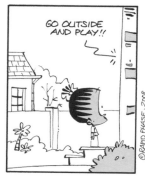

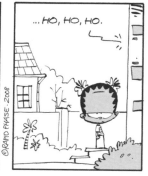

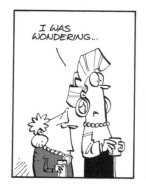

I WAS WONDERING...
WHY DO YOU THINK THEY CALL THIS THE "SILLY SEASON?"
HI. AM I GETTING A BIG BONUS THIS CHRISTMAS.
DON'T BE SILLY!
©RAPID PHASE · 2008 www.madamandeve.co.za
SORRY. WHAT WERE YOU SAYING?

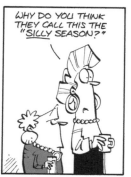

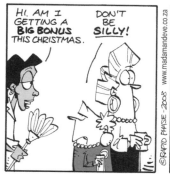

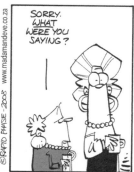

SOMEONE'S AT THE DOOR ASKING ABOUT A CHRISTMAS BONUS!!

KLOMP! KLOMP! KLOMP! KLOMP! KLOMP! KLOMP!

CREAK

www.madamandeve.co.za

IMPRESSIVE RESPONSE TIME.

© RAPID PHASE - 2008

BEEP! BEEP! BEEP! BEEP!

DUSTBIN MEN APPROACHING FROM NORTH-EAST SECTOR!

www.madamandeve.co.za

EVERYBODY! GET DOWN! NOW!!

© RAPID PHASE - 2008

KNOCK KNOCK!

EARLY CHRISTMAS BONUS WARNING ALARM.

CRASH!

© RAPID PHASE - 2008

"FORGETTING" TO PAY CHRISTMAS BONUSES GETS HARDER EVERY YEAR.

www.madamandeve.co.za

WHAT'S WRONG?

FATHER CHRISTMAS! THAT'S WHAT'S WRONG!!

"HE KNOWS WHEN I AM SLEEPING! HE KNOWS WHEN I'M AWAKE!"

"HE KNOWS IF I'VE BEEN BAD OR GOOD!"

... HOW DOES HE KNOW THESE THINGS?! I'LL TELL YOU!!

LIVE VIDEO STREAMING CAMERA!

www.madamandeve.co.za

© RAPID PHASE - 2008

THAT'S THE PROBLEM WITH THIS TIME OF YEAR!

EVERYBODY, BUT EVERYBODY EXPECTS AN EARLY CHRISTMAS BONUS!!

GET REAL!!

www.madamandeve.co.za

... WHERE WAS I?

© RAPID PHASE - 2008

HO HO HO! AND WHAT DO YOU WANT FOR CHRISTMAS, LITTLE GIRL? HOW ABOUT A NICE DOLL?

COOL. BUT LET'S START WITH THE "A's" BEFORE WE GET TO THE "D's" ... OKAY?

www.madamandeve.co.za © RAPID PHASE - 2008

≟ GASP! ≟ AN ALPHABETISED LIST OF EVERY PRESENT?!

DUH.

... NEW GUY.

GO EASY.

48

©RAPID PHASE · 2008
... AND I WANT A MACHINE GUN ...
AND I WANT TO BE PRESIDENT...
AND I WANT COPE TO GO
TO THE NORTH POLE ...

CHEERS!
www.madamandeve.co.za ©RAPID PHASE · 2008
HAPPY
NEW YEAR!!
MOM! NEW YEAR'S
ISN'T FOR ANOTHER
WEEK!!
PRACTICE
MAKES
PERFECT.

SILENT NIGHT...
HOLY NIGHT...
ALL IS CALM...
HOOT! HOOT! HOOT!
BLAM! BLAM!
MIELLLIES!
WHOOO! WHOO! WHOO!
Woof! Woof! Woof!
ALL IS
BRIGHT...
www.madamandeve.co.za ©RAPID PHASE · 2008
I'LL
CHECK
THE
FUSES.
@#☆#.!!
NOT THAT
AGAIN.
SIGH.
WHERE
ARE THE
CANDLES?

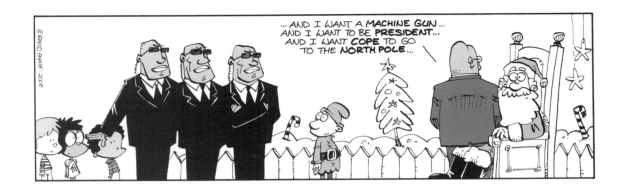

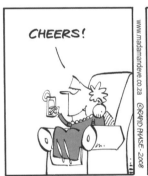

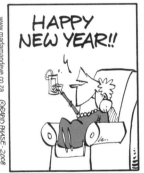

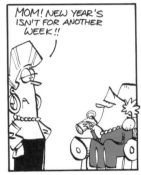

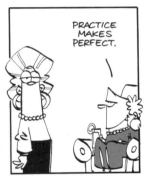

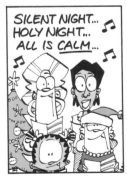

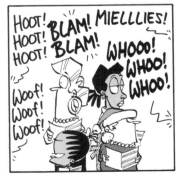

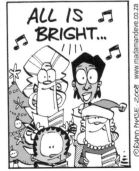

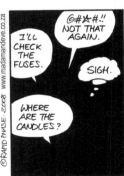

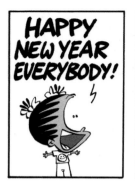

HAPPY NEW YEAR EVERYBODY!
ONE MORE YEAR ...AND THEN IT'S 2010!!
©RAPID PHASE · 2008
DID YOU HEAR ME?! ONE MORE YEAR AND THEN IT'S 2010!!
I HEARD. DO YOU MIND IF I GET THROUGH THIS YEAR FIRST?

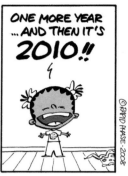

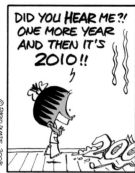

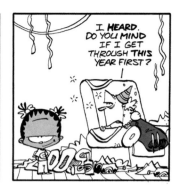

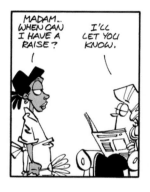

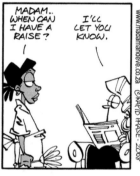

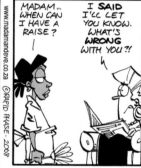

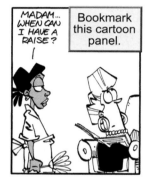

MADAM.. WHEN CAN I HAVE A RAISE?
I'LL LET YOU KNOW.
MADAM.. WHEN CAN I HAVE A RAISE?
I'LL LET YOU KNOW.
www.madamandeve.co.za ©RAPID PHASE · 2008
MADAM... WHEN CAN I HAVE A RAISE?
I SAID I'LL LET YOU KNOW. WHAT'S WRONG WITH YOU?!
MADAM... WHEN CAN I HAVE A RAISE?
Bookmark this cartoon panel.

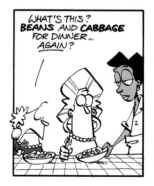

WHAT'S THIS? BEANS AND CABBAGE FOR DINNER... AGAIN?
YOU TOLD ME TIMES WERE TOUGH AND TO CUT COSTS. BEANS AND BOILED CABBAGE MAKE A STATEMENT!
©RAPID PHASE · 2008
www.madamandeve.co.za
IT'S NOT THE STATEMENT I'M WORRIED ABOUT. IT'S THE PUNCTUATION.

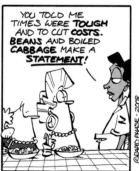

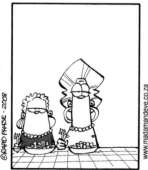

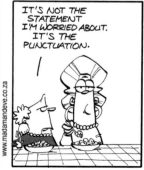

AND, IN OTHER NEWS... POLITICAL ANALYSTS SAY THAT THE IRAQI JOURNALIST WHO THREW A SHOE AT PRESIDENT BUSH, MAY HAVE STARTED A DISTURBING NEW TREND...
www.madamandeve.co.za ©RAPID PHASE - 2008
WE WILL KILL FOR...
UH-OH.

I'M WORRIED, GRACE. OUR BELOVED ZIMBABWE IS IN TROUBLE.
YOU CAN SAY THAT AGAIN, ROBERT.
MAYBE IT'S MY FAULT. MAYBE I SHOULD'VE BEEN MORE HANDS-ON!
"HANDS-ON?" THERE'S A CHOLERA EPIDEMIC!!
www.madamandeve.co.za
I DON'T CARE! MY NEW YEAR'S RESOLUTION IS TO BE MORE IN TOUCH WITH MY PEOPLE!
VERY WISE, ROBERT.
©RAPID PHASE - 2008
OF COURSE... IT'S NOT GOING TO BE EASY WEARING THIS ANTI-CHOLERA BIO-HAZARD SUIT.
YOU KNOW HOW HARD IT IS TO TRY ON NEW SHOES IN THIS THING?

AND IN OTHER NEWS... THIS WEEK'S DECISIVE ELECTIONS IN CAPE TOWN CONFIRM THAT MANY VOTERS HAVE ABANDONED THE ANC IN FAVOUR OF COPE.
...MAYBE WE SHOULD CALL CAPE TOWN "COPE TOWN" NOW.
GET IT?! COPE TOWN!! ...THERE'S THE WESTERN COPE! THE COPE OF GOOD HOPE...
www.madamandeve.co.za ©RAPID PHASE - 2008
SOME PEOPLE HAVE TROUBLE COPING WITH PUNS.

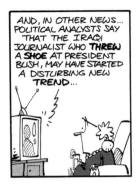

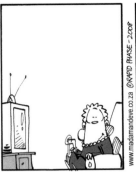

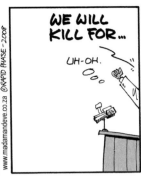

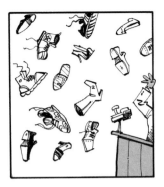

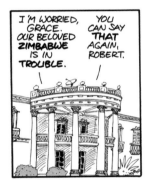

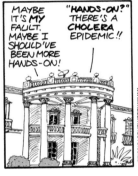

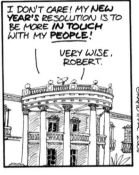

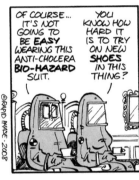

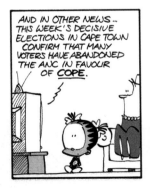

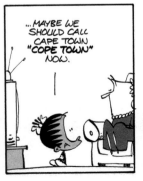

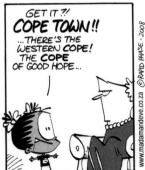

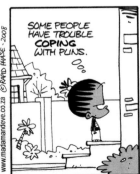

IN AN EFFORT TO WEED OUT DISLOYAL PARTY MEMBERS,... ARE YOU READY TO BEGIN YOUR "ANC PSYCHOLOGICAL LOYALTY EVALUATION?"
SIGH YES.
QUESTION ONE: WHAT DOES THIS INKBLOT LOOK LIKE TO YOU?
IT LOOKS LIKE... A GROUP OF WORTHY COMRADES NOW TAINTED BY GREED AND POWER... WHO OFTEN PLACE PARTY POLITICS OVER THE INTERESTS OF THE PEOPLE.
www.madamandeve.co.za ©RAPID PHASE - 2008
ER... I MEAN... IT'S A BUTTERFLY.
GOOD! NEXT QUESTION.

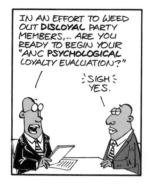

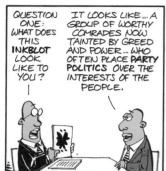

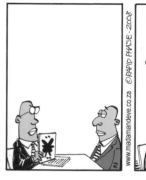

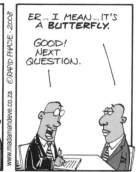

RIGHT! LET'S CONTINUE WITH YOUR ANC PSYCHOLOGICAL EVALUATION TO ASSESS YOUR PARTY LOYALTY... READY?
READY.
QUESTION # 2: "JULIUS MALEMA IS ... BLANK."
TRUE! I AGREE. HE'S TOTALLY BLANK!
...UH, NO... I MEANT "JULIUS MALEMA IS... FILL IN THE BLANK."
OHH!
www.madamandeve.co.za ©RAPID PHASE - 2008
... I'LL STICK WITH MY FIRST ANSWER.

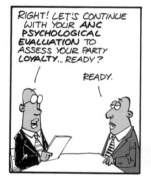

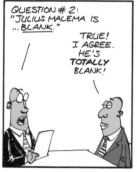

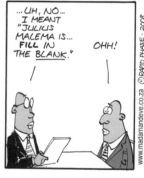

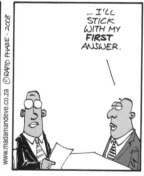

CONGRATULATIONS. YOU'RE DOING FINE! YOU'RE ALMOST DONE WITH YOUR ANC LOYALTY TEST!
QUESTION NUMBER THREE: AS A LOYAL ANC MEMBER, WOULD YOU DO ANYTHING YOUR PARTY ASKED YOU TO DO?
YES.
...INCLUDING, BUT NOT LIMITED TO, HITTING YOUR HEAD REPEATEDLY WITH A CRICKET BAT IF SO ORDERED?
UH...
www.madamandeve.co.za ©RAPID PHASE - 2008
QUESTION NUMBER FOUR: ARE YOU RIGHT-HANDED OR LEFT-HANDED?
CAN I GET BACK TO YOU ON THAT?

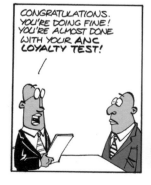

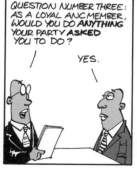

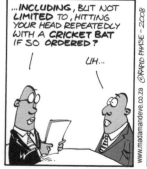

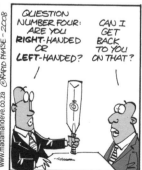

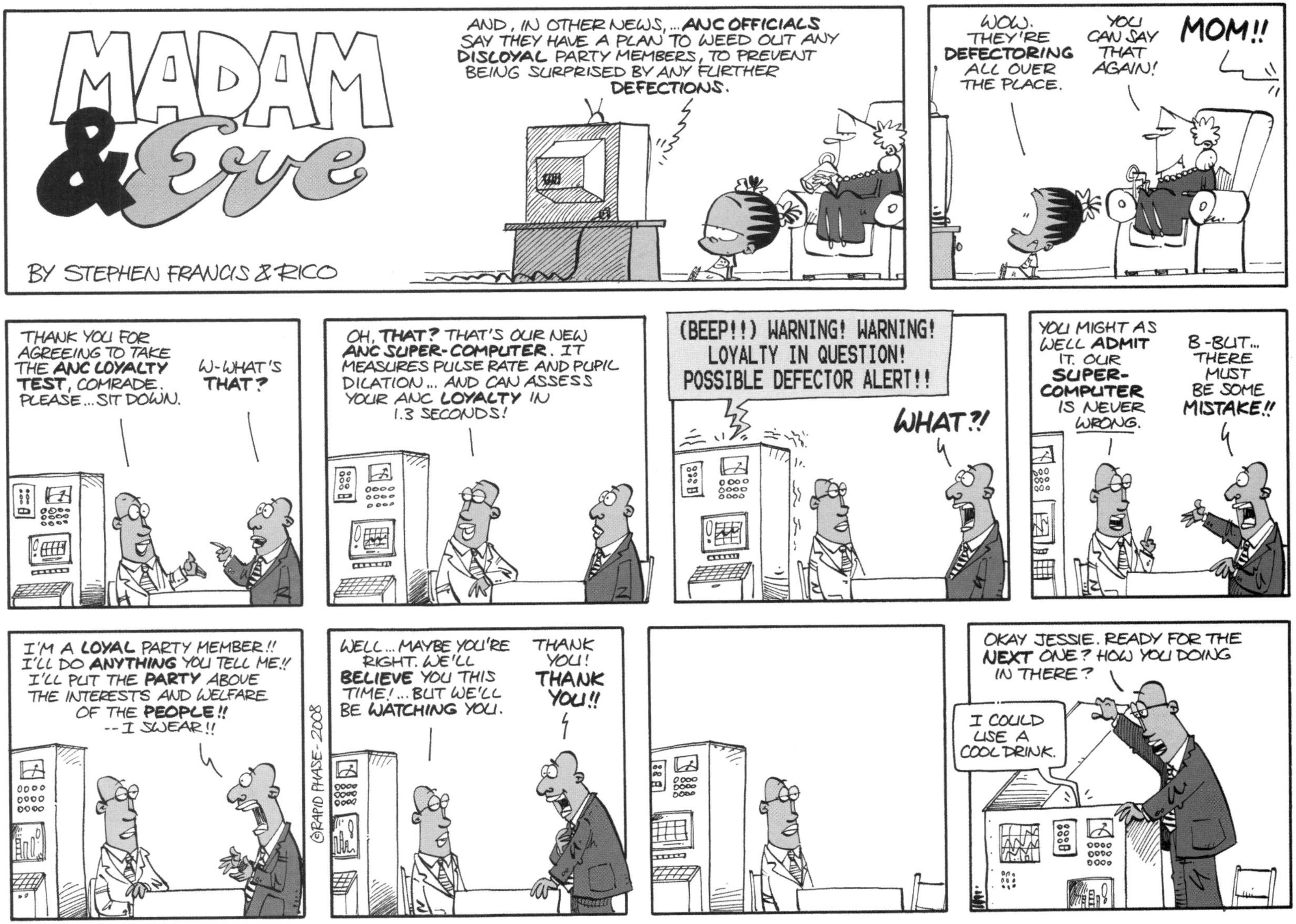
MADAM & Eve
BY STEPHEN FRANCIS & RICO
AND, IN OTHER NEWS, ... ANC OFFICIALS SAY THEY HAVE A PLAN TO WEED OUT ANY DISLOYAL PARTY MEMBERS, TO PREVENT BEING SURPRISED BY ANY FURTHER DEFECTIONS.
WOW. THEY'RE DEFECTORING ALL OVER THE PLACE.
YOU CAN SAY THAT AGAIN!
MOM!!
THANK YOU FOR AGREEING TO TAKE THE ANC LOYALTY TEST, COMRADE. PLEASE... SIT DOWN.
W-WHAT'S THAT?
OH, THAT? THAT'S OUR NEW ANC SUPER-COMPUTER. IT MEASURES PULSE RATE AND PUPIL DILATION... AND CAN ASSESS YOUR ANC LOYALTY IN 1.3 SECONDS!
(BEEP!!) WARNING! WARNING! LOYALTY IN QUESTION! POSSIBLE DEFECTOR ALERT!!
WHAT?!
YOU MIGHT AS WELL ADMIT IT. OUR SUPER-COMPUTER IS NEVER WRONG.
B-BUT... THERE MUST BE SOME MISTAKE!!
I'M A LOYAL PARTY MEMBER!! I'LL DO ANYTHING YOU TELL ME!! I'LL PUT THE PARTY ABOVE THE INTERESTS AND WELFARE OF THE PEOPLE!! --I SWEAR!!
©RAPID PHASE-2008
WELL... MAYBE YOU'RE RIGHT. WE'LL BELIEVE YOU THIS TIME!... BUT WE'LL BE WATCHING YOU.
THANK YOU! THANK YOU!!
OKAY JESSIE. READY FOR THE NEXT ONE? HOW YOU DOING IN THERE?
I COULD USE A COOL DRINK.

MADAM!! I'M BACK FROM MY HOLIDAYS!!
©RAPID PHASE · 2007
WHO'S BEEN SLEEPING ON MY IRONING BOARD?!
YOU'VE BEEN CHEATING ON ME WITH ANOTHER MAID, HAVEN'T YOU?!
IT MEANT NOTHING, I SWEAR!!

LET ME GET THIS STRAIGHT: WHILE I WAS AWAY ON HOLIDAY, YOU HIRED ANOTHER MAID?!
I-- IT WAS JUST FOR A FEW DAYS!
WE THOUGHT OF YOU THE WHOLE TIME SHE WAS HERE! I PROMISE!!
©RAPID PHASE · 2008
WAIT A MINUTE!! WHOSE FEATHER DUSTER IS THIS?!!
UH-OH.

SO. YOU ADMIT YOU HIRED ANOTHER MAID WHILE I WAS AWAY ON HOLIDAY!
AND THIS IS HER FEATHER DUSTER!
...WELL?
©RAPID PHASE · 2008
IT WAS HER IDEA! I WAS AGAINST IT!!
LIAR!!

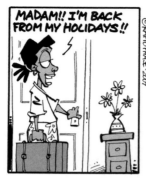

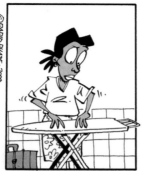

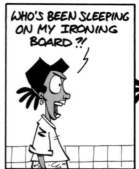

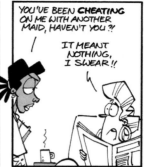

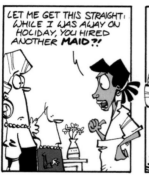

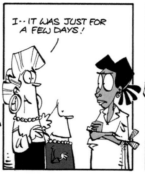

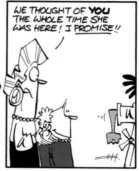

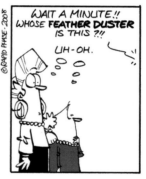

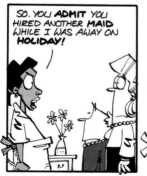

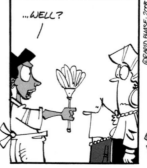

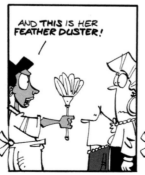

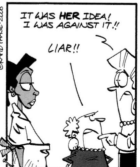

SOMEBODY'S BEEN SLEEPING ON MY IRONING BOARD!!

OKAY. SO WE HIRED A TEMPORARY MAID FOR A FEW DAYS. BIG DEAL.

WHAT'S THIS?

"ROSES ARE RED VIOLETS ARE BLUE YOU'RE A GREAT MADAM IT WAS NICE WORKING FOR YOU! ALL THE BEST, SIGNED PRECIOUS."

SHE LEFT YOU A CARD?!!

SHE DID WINDOWS TOO!

MOM!!

©RAPID PHASE - 2008

WELL...THAT'S IT, THEN. NO MORE POSTPONING! HOLIDAY'S OVER. LET'S GET BACK TO WORK!

SIGH.

©RAPID PHASE - 2009

www.madamandeve.co.za

BEEP   BEEP

WAS IT 2811 OR 1128?

...1128.

BEEP   BEEP

I JUST TRIED 1128!!

THEN ...2811? I CAN'T REMEMBER.

www.madamandeve.co.za

BEEPBEEPBEEPBEEPBEEP

WHAT DO YOU MEAN "YOU CAN'T REMEMBER?!"

WELL, YOU CAN'T EITHER!!

©RAPID PHASE - 2009

WHEEEEOOO!!

@#*#@.!!

POST-HOLIDAY ALARM CODE AMNESIA.

GASP
© RAPID PHASE · 2009 www.madamandeve.co.za
MMPH!!
DON'T BLAME ME. THREE WEEKS OF HOLIDAY LAUNDRY TAKES ON A LIFE OF ITS OWN.
SOMEBODY GET THIS OFF ME!!

GO AHEAD.
YOU GO AHEAD.
NO, YOU GO AHEAD.
NO, I INSIST! AFTER YOU.
© RAPID PHASE · 2009
POST-HOLIDAY REFRIGERATOR AROMA CHECK.

I DON'T BELIEVE THIS! WE'VE BEEN ON HOLIDAY FOR ONLY THREE WEEKS ... AND ALREADY I'VE FORGOTTEN MY PIN CODE!
ATM
IT'S 3643.
THANK YOU.
© RAPID PHASE · 2009 www.madamandeve.co.za

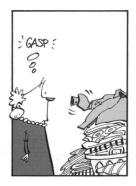

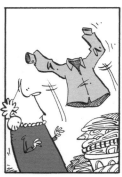

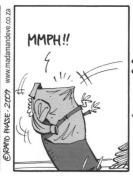

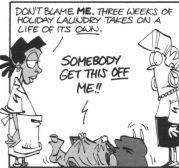

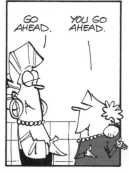

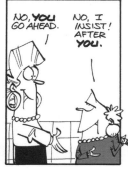

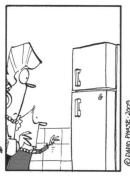

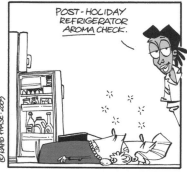

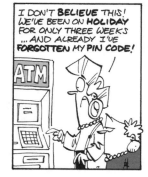

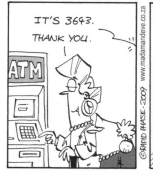

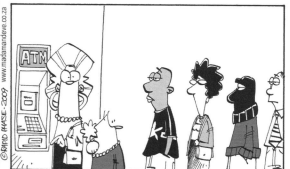

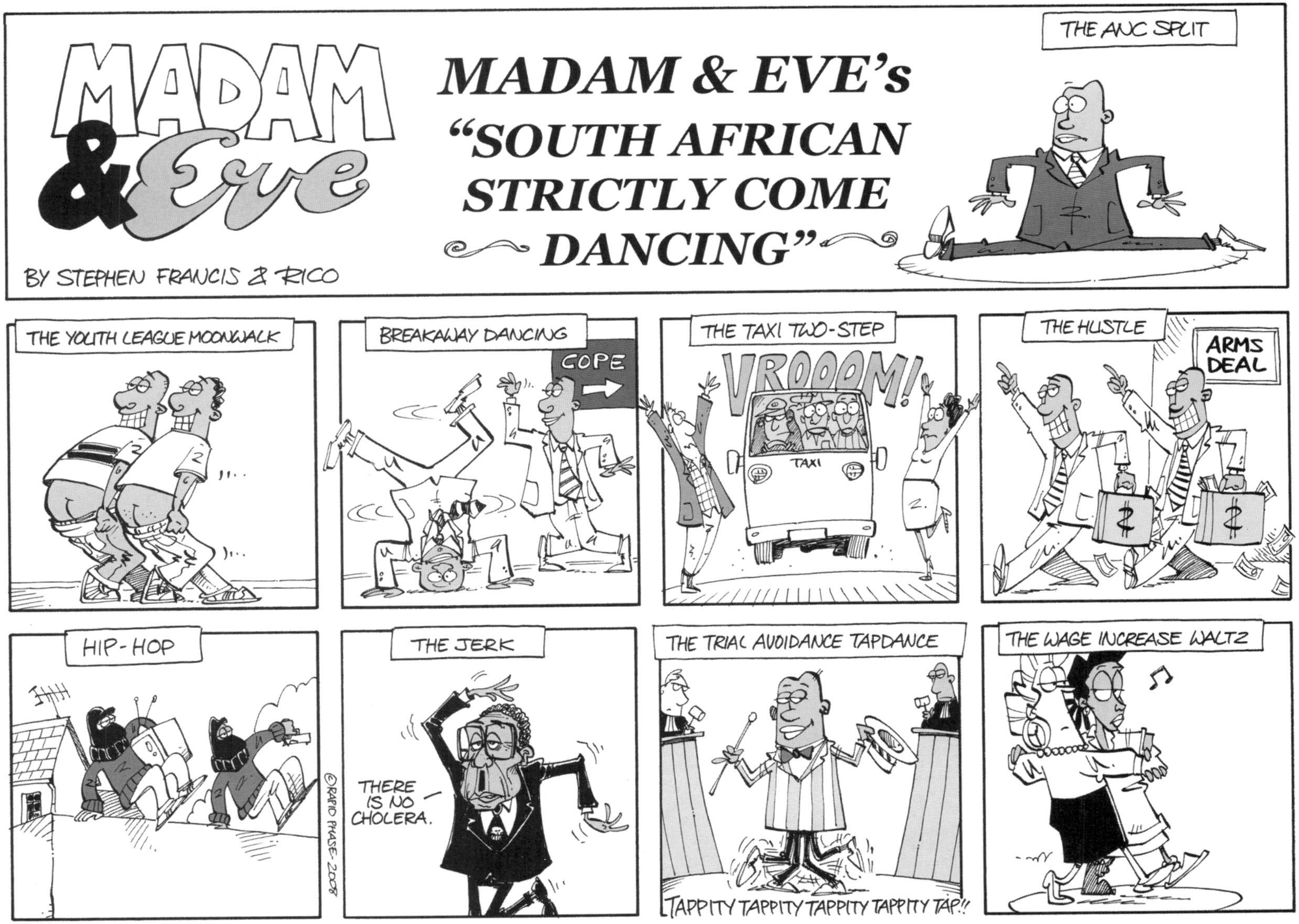
MADAM & Eve
MADAM & EVE's "SOUTH AFRICAN STRICTLY COME DANCING"
BY STEPHEN FRANCIS & RICO
THE ANC SPLIT
THE YOUTH LEAGUE MOONWALK
BREAKAWAY DANCING
COPE
THE TAXI TWO-STEP
VROOOM!
TAXI
THE HUSTLE
ARMS DEAL
HIP-HOP
THE JERK
THERE IS NO CHOLERA.
©RAPID PHASE-2008
THE TRIAL AVOIDANCE TAPDANCE
TAPPITY TAPPITY TAPPITY TAPPITY TAP!!
THE WAGE INCREASE WALTZ

AND, IN A HISTORIC MOMENT, **BARACK OBAMA** BECAME THE **44th PRESIDENT** OF THE **UNITED STATES.**
THE NEW PRESIDENT SAID HE'S LOOKING FORWARD TO RESTORING WORLD **CONFIDENCE** IN AMERICA.
BUT FIRST, OBAMA SAID THAT A NUMBER OF SERIOUS **DOMESTIC PROBLEMS** REQUIRE HIS IMMEDIATE ATTENTION!
SEE?!
©RAPID PHASE · 2009
...WE'RE NOT THE ONLY ONES WITH **DOMESTIC PROBLEMS!**

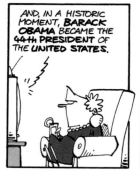

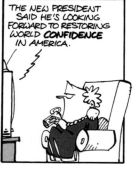

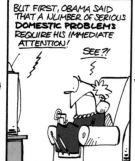

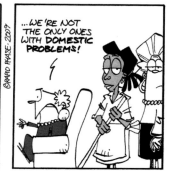

LOOK AT THIS ARTICLE: "PRESIDENT BARACK OBAMA GETS USED TO HIS NEW LIFE."
HE DOESN'T HAVE TO DO **ANYTHING** HIMSELF. TWENTY-FOUR-HOUR CHEF... WHATEVER OBAMA **WANTS** IS DONE FOR HIM... IT'S LIKE HE'S LIVING IN A **BUBBLE.**
©RAPID PHASE · 2009
COOL.
IS HE **LUCKY** OR WHAT?

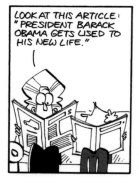

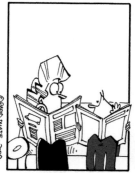

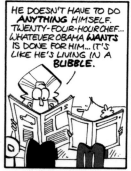

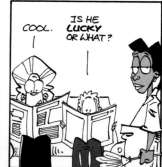

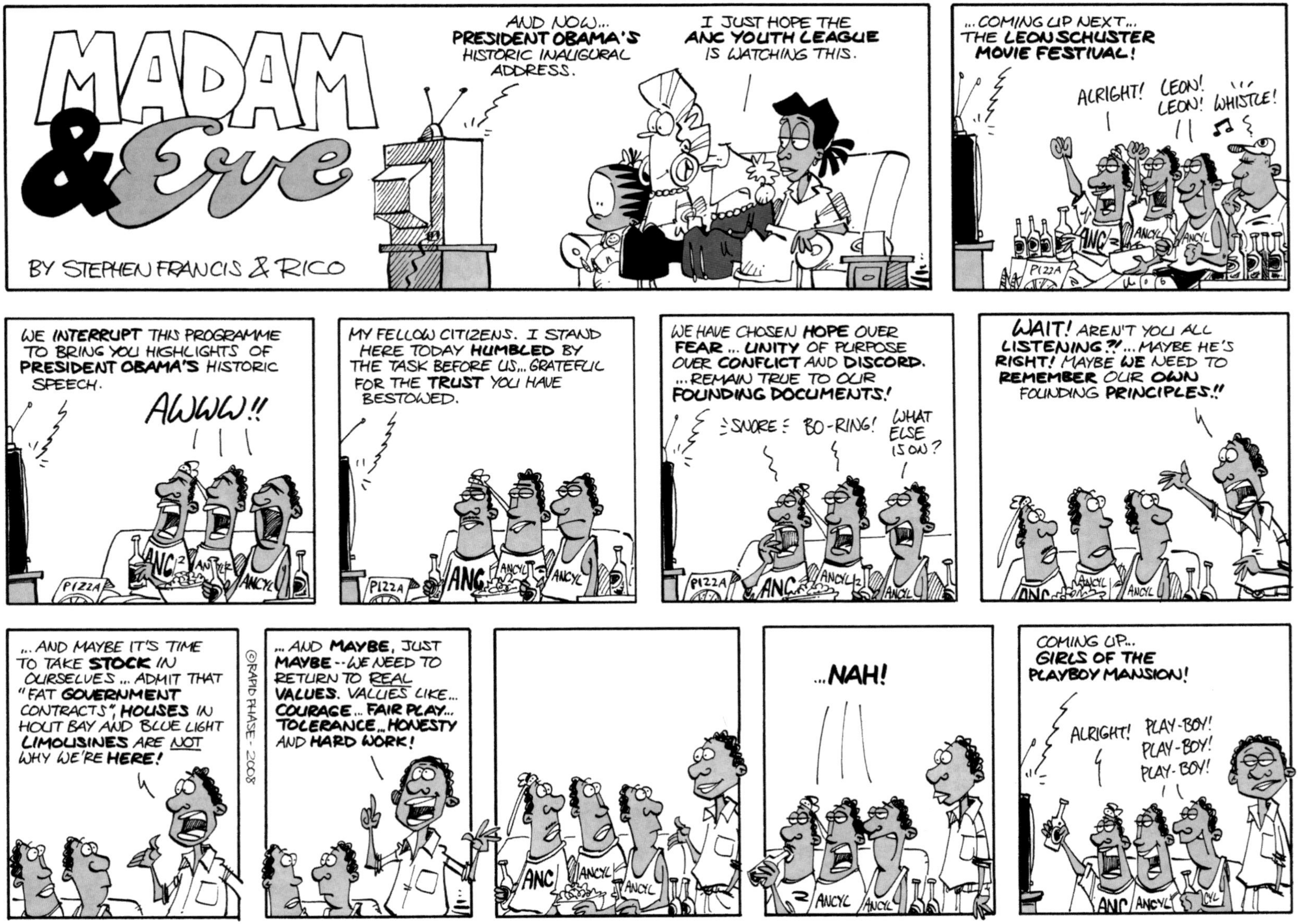
MADAM & Eve
BY STEPHEN FRANCIS & RICO
AND NOW... PRESIDENT OBAMA'S HISTORIC INAUGURAL ADDRESS.
I JUST HOPE THE ANC YOUTH LEAGUE IS WATCHING THIS.
...COMING UP NEXT... THE LEON SCHUSTER MOVIE FESTIVAL!
ALRIGHT!
LEON! LEON!
WHISTLE!
ANC
ANCYL
PIZZA
WE INTERRUPT THIS PROGRAMME TO BRING YOU HIGHLIGHTS OF PRESIDENT OBAMA'S HISTORIC SPEECH.
AWWW!!
MY FELLOW CITIZENS. I STAND HERE TODAY HUMBLED BY THE TASK BEFORE US... GRATEFUL FOR THE TRUST YOU HAVE BESTOWED.
WE HAVE CHOSEN HOPE OVER FEAR ... UNITY OF PURPOSE OVER CONFLICT AND DISCORD. ...REMAIN TRUE TO OUR FOUNDING DOCUMENTS!
SNORE
BO-RING!
WHAT ELSE IS ON?
WAIT! AREN'T YOU ALL LISTENING?!... MAYBE HE'S RIGHT! MAYBE WE NEED TO REMEMBER OUR OWN FOUNDING PRINCIPLES!!
...AND MAYBE IT'S TIME TO TAKE STOCK IN OURSELVES ... ADMIT THAT "FAT GOVERNMENT CONTRACTS", HOUSES IN HOUT BAY AND BLUE LIGHT LIMOUSINES ARE NOT WHY WE'RE HERE!
©RAPID PHASE · 2008
...AND MAYBE, JUST MAYBE -- WE NEED TO RETURN TO REAL VALUES. VALUES LIKE... COURAGE... FAIR PLAY... TOLERANCE... HONESTY AND HARD WORK!
...NAH!
COMING UP... GIRLS OF THE PLAYBOY MANSION!
ALRIGHT!
PLAY-BOY! PLAY-BOY! PLAY-BOY!

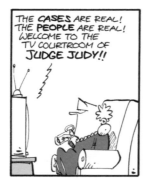

THE **CASES** ARE REAL! THE **PEOPLE** ARE REAL! WELCOME TO THE TV COURTROOM OF **JUDGE JUDY!!**
NEXT CASE!
JACOB ZUMA! ... STEP FORWARD.
YOU'VE BEEN ACCUSED OF **CORRUPTION!** HOW DO YOU--
YOUR HONOUR, IF I MAY--
©RAPID PHASE-2009
www.madamandeve.co.za
QUIET!! I'M TALKING!!
AT LEAST WE'LL KNOW THE **VERDICT** IN ABOUT 8 MINUTES.

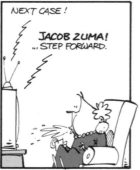

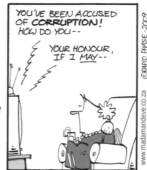

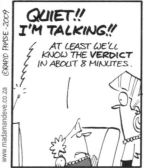

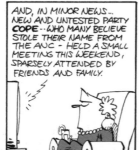

AND, IN MINOR NEWS... NEW AND UNTESTED PARTY **COPE**--WHO MANY BELIEVE STOLE THEIR NAME FROM THE ANC - HELD A SMALL MEETING THIS WEEKEND, SPARSELY ATTENDED BY FRIENDS AND FAMILY.
MANY FELT THE "EVENT," WHICH ANNOUNCED COPE'S SO-CALLED "MANIFESTO" AND TROTTED OUT GREEDY AND TRAITOROUS FORMER ANC MEMBERS, WAS DEFINITELY A DAMP SQUIB.
www.madamandeve.co.za
YOU'R WATCHING **SABC NEWS**-- A FAIR AND IMPARTIAL BROADCASTER.
©RAPID PHASE-2009
COMING UP-- AN EXCLUSIVE LOOK INSIDE JACOB ZUMA'S SOCK DRAWER.

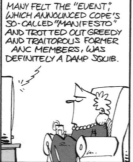

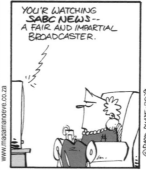

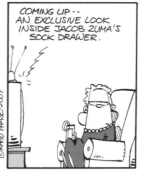

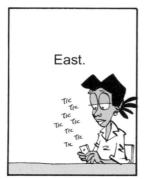

East.
Either.
www.madamandeve.co.za
©RAPID PHASE-2009
Eight.
WHAT ARE YOU DOING?
TEACHING MY CELLPHONE PREDICTIVE TEXT TO RECOGNISE "EISH."

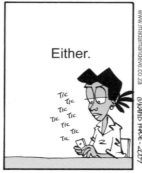

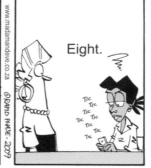

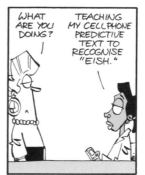

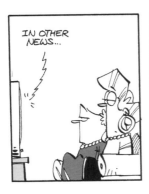

IN OTHER NEWS...
A GROUP OF SOUTH AFRICAN AIRWAYS EMPLOYEES WERE CAUGHT ALLEGEDLY TRYING TO SMUGGLE **DRUGS** ON AN OVERSEAS FLIGHT.
WHATEVER HAPPENED TO **"JUST SAY NO?"**
THEY REPLACED IT WITH **"YES, WE CAN!"**
© RAPID PHASE · 2009

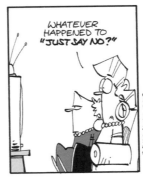

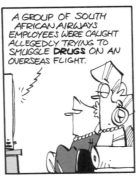

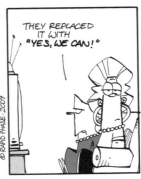

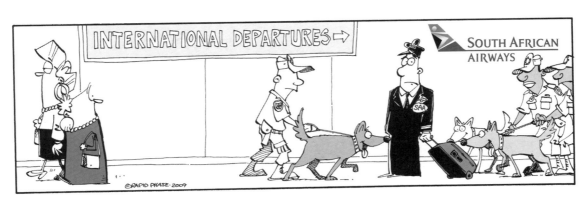

INTERNATIONAL DEPARTURES
SOUTH AFRICAN AIRWAYS
SAA
©RAPID PHASE · 2009

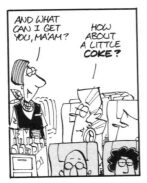

AND WHAT CAN I GET YOU, MA'AM?
HOW ABOUT A LITTLE **COKE?**
©RAPID PHASE · 2009
IT WASN'T **ME**, OKAY?! I DIDN'T **KNOW** IT WAS IN MY **LUGGAGE!!** I SWEAR! I'M INNOCENT, I TELL YOU! **INNOCENT!!**
www.madamandeve.co.za
THESE **SAA** CREW MEMBERS ARE REALLY TOUCHY LATELY.

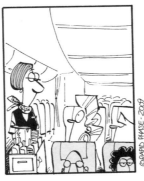

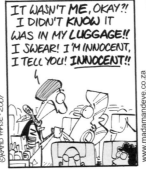

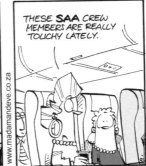

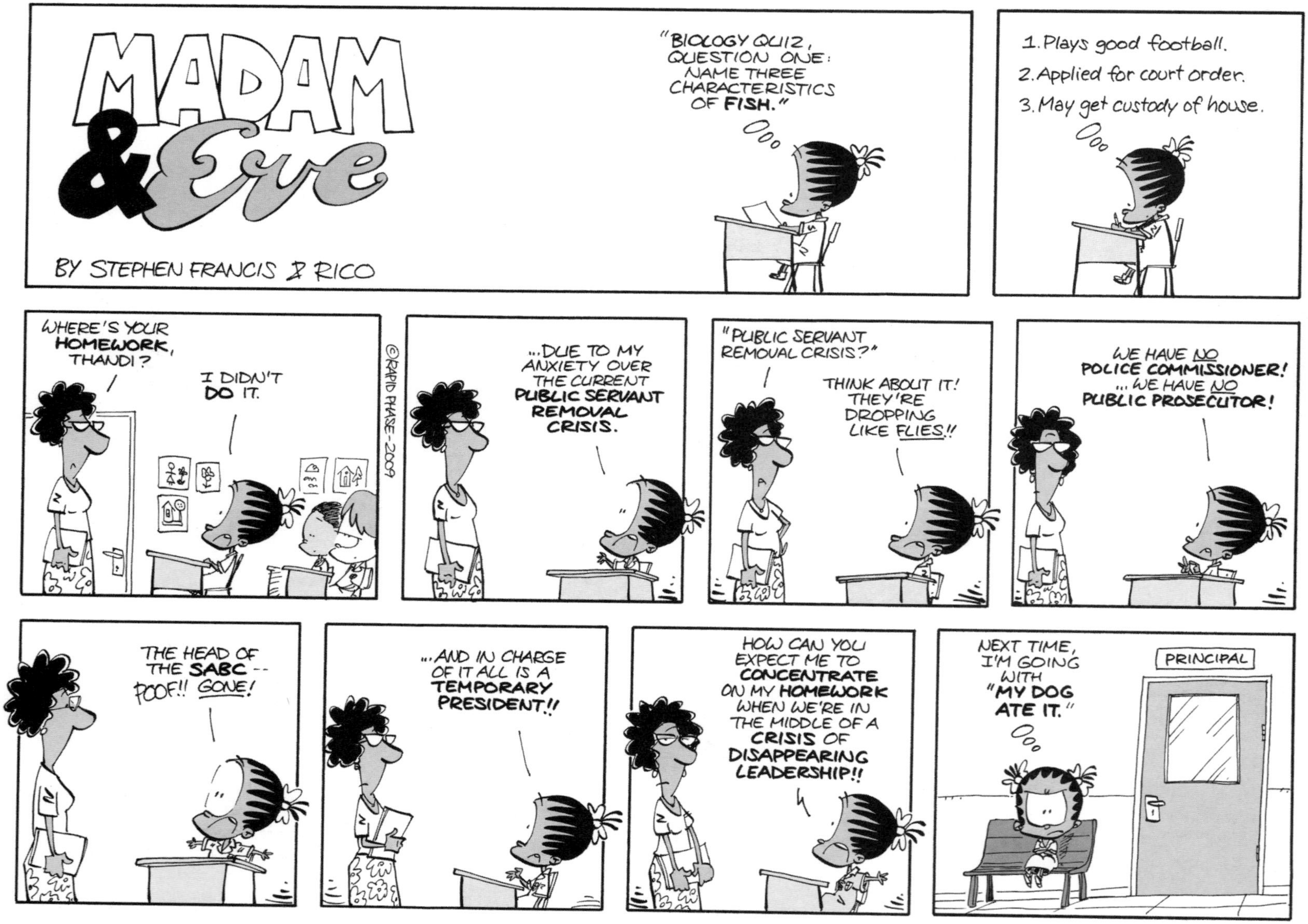
MADAM & Eve
BY STEPHEN FRANCIS & RICO
"BIOLOGY QUIZ, QUESTION ONE: NAME THREE CHARACTERISTICS OF FISH."
1. Plays good football.
2. Applied for court order.
3. May get custody of house.
WHERE'S YOUR HOMEWORK, THANDI?
I DIDN'T DO IT.
©RAPID PHASE-2009
...DUE TO MY ANXIETY OVER THE CURRENT PUBLIC SERVANT REMOVAL CRISIS.
"PUBLIC SERVANT REMOVAL CRISIS?"
THINK ABOUT IT! THEY'RE DROPPING LIKE FLIES!!
WE HAVE NO POLICE COMMISSIONER! ...WE HAVE NO PUBLIC PROSECUTOR!
THE HEAD OF THE SABC -- POOF!! GONE!
...AND IN CHARGE OF IT ALL IS A TEMPORARY PRESIDENT!!
HOW CAN YOU EXPECT ME TO CONCENTRATE ON MY HOMEWORK WHEN WE'RE IN THE MIDDLE OF A CRISIS OF DISAPPEARING LEADERSHIP!!
NEXT TIME, I'M GOING WITH "MY DOG ATE IT."
PRINCIPAL

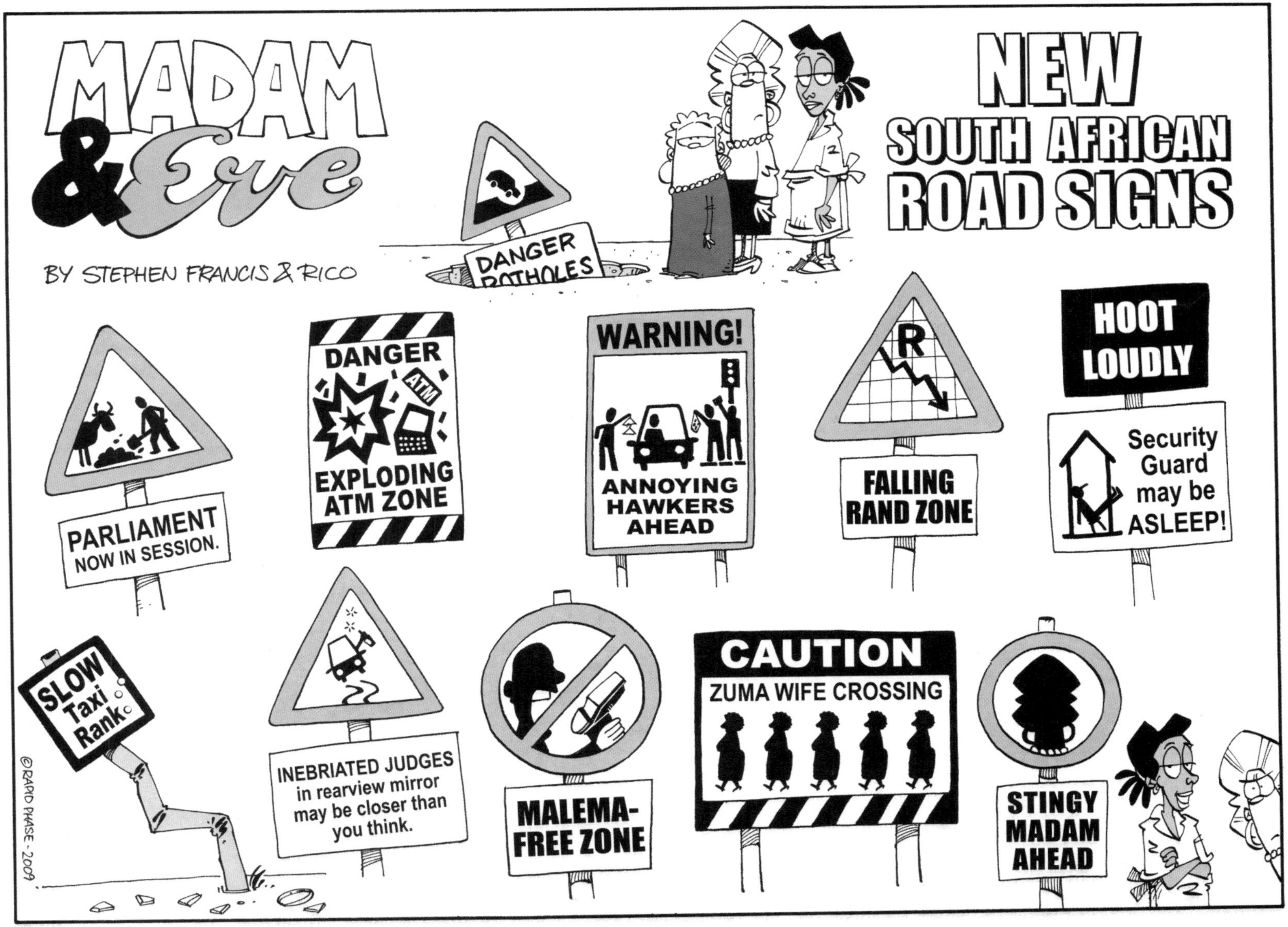
MADAM & Eve
BY STEPHEN FRANCIS & RICO
DANGER POTHOLES
NEW
SOUTH AFRICAN
ROAD SIGNS
PARLIAMENT
NOW IN SESSION.
DANGER
ATM
EXPLODING
ATM ZONE
WARNING!
ANNOYING
HAWKERS
AHEAD
R
FALLING
RAND ZONE
HOOT
LOUDLY
Security
Guard
may be
ASLEEP!
SLOW
Taxi
Rank
©RAPID PHASE - 2009
INEBRIATED JUDGES
in rearview mirror
may be closer than
you think.
MALEMA-
FREE ZONE
CAUTION
ZUMA WIFE CROSSING
STINGY
MADAM
AHEAD

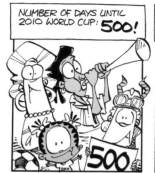

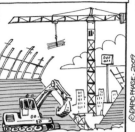

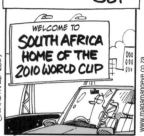

NUMBER OF DAYS UNTIL 2010 WORLD CUP: 500!
500
NUMBER OF DAYS UNTIL ALL STADIUMS ARE COMPLETED: 521
© RAPID PHASE · 2009
NUMBER OF DAYS UNTIL LAUNCH OF ADVERTISING AND PROMOTIONAL CAMPAIGN: 581
WELCOME TO SOUTH AFRICA HOME OF THE 2010 WORLD CUP
www.madamandeve.co.za
NUMBER OF DAYS UNTIL ALL POTHOLES FILLED: S.Q.

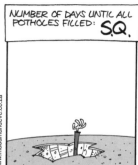

500 MORE DAYS UNTIL THE 2010 WORLD CUP!
© RAPID PHASE · 2009
499 MORE DAYS UNTIL THE 2010 WORLD CUP!
498...
NOTHING LIKE A LITTLE WORLD CUP SPIRIT.

MEN WORKING
© RAPID PHASE · 2009

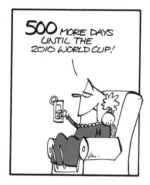

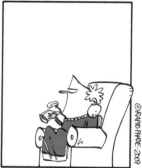

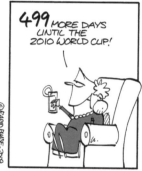

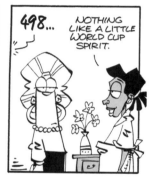

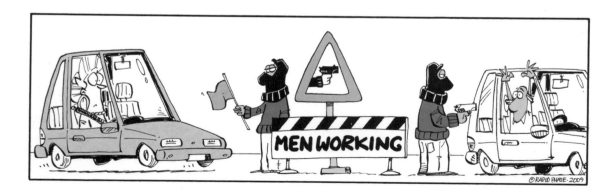

Panel 1:
WE'VE ASKED AROUND THE NEIGHBOURHOOD, EVE... AND FRANKLY, IN OUR OPINION, WE PAY YOU A VERY **FAIR WAGE** EACH MONTH!

Panel 2:
Google:
Domestic workers in this post code area that make more than I do.

TIC TIC TIC TIC

Panel 3:
BRRT. BRRT. DING.

Panel 4:
WAGE NEGOTIATIONS WERE MUCH EASIER BEFORE THE INTERNET.

©RAPID PHASE · 2009

Panel 5:
BY THE WAY... WHEN AM I GETTING A **WAGE** INCREASE?

WAGE INCREASE ?! WE SHOULD CHARGE **YOU** FOR THE NICE TIME YOU HAVE HERE.

Panel 6:
NICE TIME ?! I'M HAVING A **NICE TIME ?!**

DID YOU HAVE **BREAKFAST** THIS MORNING?

Panel 7:
YES.

DO YOU HAVE **TAXI** MONEY?

YES... SO?

Panel 8:
...SO, ACCORDING TO **JULIUS MALEMA**, YOU'RE HAVING A **NICE TIME.**

©RAPID PHASE · 2009

Panel 9:
THIS IS LIZZIE. SHE'S A **PROFESSIONAL PARTY SUPPORTER.**

Panel 10:
A "PROFESSIONAL PARTY SUPPORTER?"

FOR **100 BUCKS** (PLUS LUNCH) SHE'LL TRAVEL TO ANY RALLY AND PASSIONATELY **SUPPORT** THE PARTY OF YOUR **CHOICE.**

©RAPID PHASE · 2009

Panel 11:
VIVA ANC!! COPE-THE PARTY OF HOPE!! VOTE DP!! IFP!!

Panel 12:
SHE'S GOOD.

SHE GETS A **CASH BONUS** IF SHE GETS ON THE NEWS.

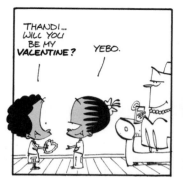

THANDI... WILL YOU BE MY VALENTINE?
YEBO.
WILL YOU BE MINE?
YEBO.
©RAPID PHASE-2009
...NOW WHAT HAPPENS?
YOU TELL ME YOU HAD A NICE TIME, I GIVE YOU TAXI FARE... AND THEN I TAKE A SHOWER.

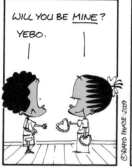

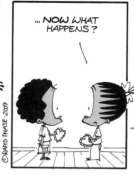

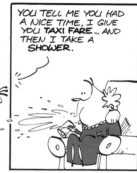

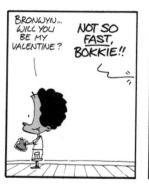

BRONWYN... WILL YOU BE MY VALENTINE?
NOT SO FAST, BOKKIE!!
I THOUGHT I WAS YOUR "VALENTINE!"
YOU ARE, THANDI.
...AND ALSO EIGHT OTHER GIRLS.
WHAT?! WHO TOLD YOU THAT YOU COULD HAVE MORE THAN ONE VALENTINE?!
©RAPID PHASE-2009
JACOB ZUMA.
GOOD COMEBACK.

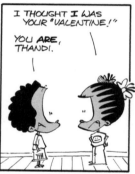

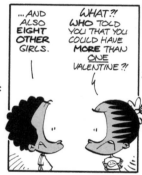

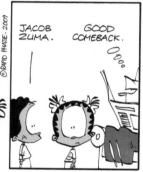

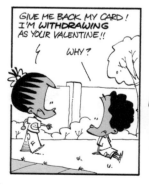

GIVE ME BACK MY CARD! I'M WITHDRAWING AS YOUR VALENTINE!!
WHY?
WHY???
BECAUSE YOU ALSO ASKED EIGHT OTHER GIRLS TO BE YOUR VALENTINE!!
SO?
©RAPID PHASE-2009
www.madamandeve.co.za
SO?! THAT MEANS YOU'RE -- YOU'RE --
--YOU'RE A VALENTINE'S DAY POLYGAMIST!!
...IT'S A CULTURAL THING.

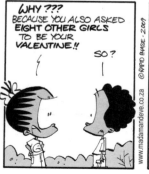

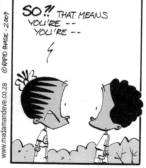

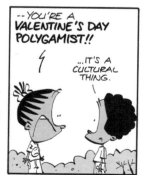

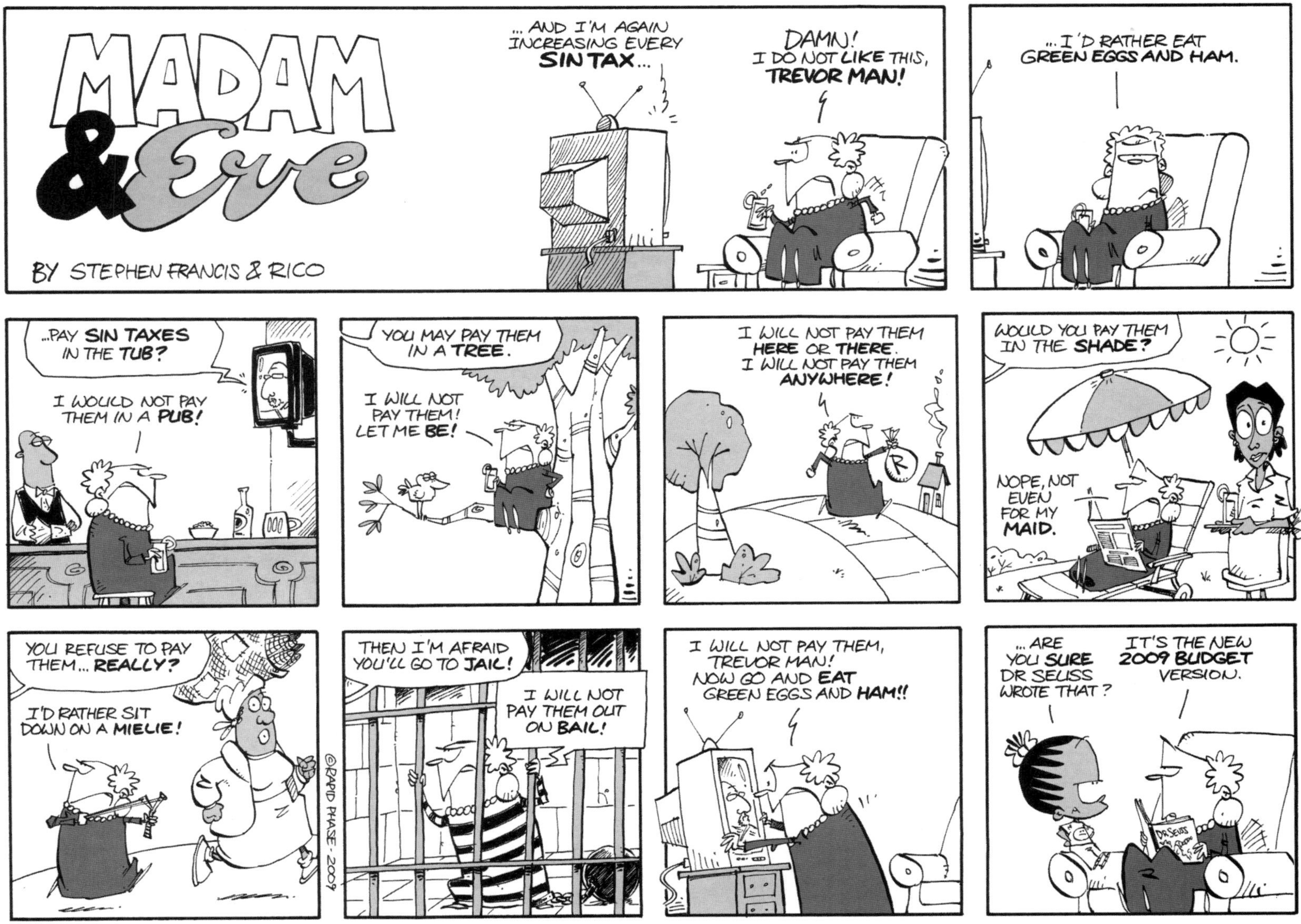
MADAM & Eve
BY STEPHEN FRANCIS & RICO
... AND I'M AGAIN INCREASING EVERY SIN TAX...
DAMN! I DO NOT LIKE THIS, TREVOR MAN!
... I'D RATHER EAT GREEN EGGS AND HAM.
...PAY SIN TAXES IN THE TUB?
I WOULD NOT PAY THEM IN A PUB!
YOU MAY PAY THEM IN A TREE.
I WILL NOT PAY THEM! LET ME BE!
I WILL NOT PAY THEM HERE OR THERE. I WILL NOT PAY THEM ANYWHERE!
WOULD YOU PAY THEM IN THE SHADE?
NOPE, NOT EVEN FOR MY MAID.
YOU REFUSE TO PAY THEM... REALLY?
I'D RATHER SIT DOWN ON A MIELIE!
©RAPID PHASE · 2009
THEN I'M AFRAID YOU'LL GO TO JAIL!
I WILL NOT PAY THEM OUT ON BAIL!
I WILL NOT PAY THEM, TREVOR MAN! NOW GO AND EAT GREEN EGGS AND HAM!!
... ARE YOU SURE DR SEUSS WROTE THAT?
IT'S THE NEW 2009 BUDGET VERSION.

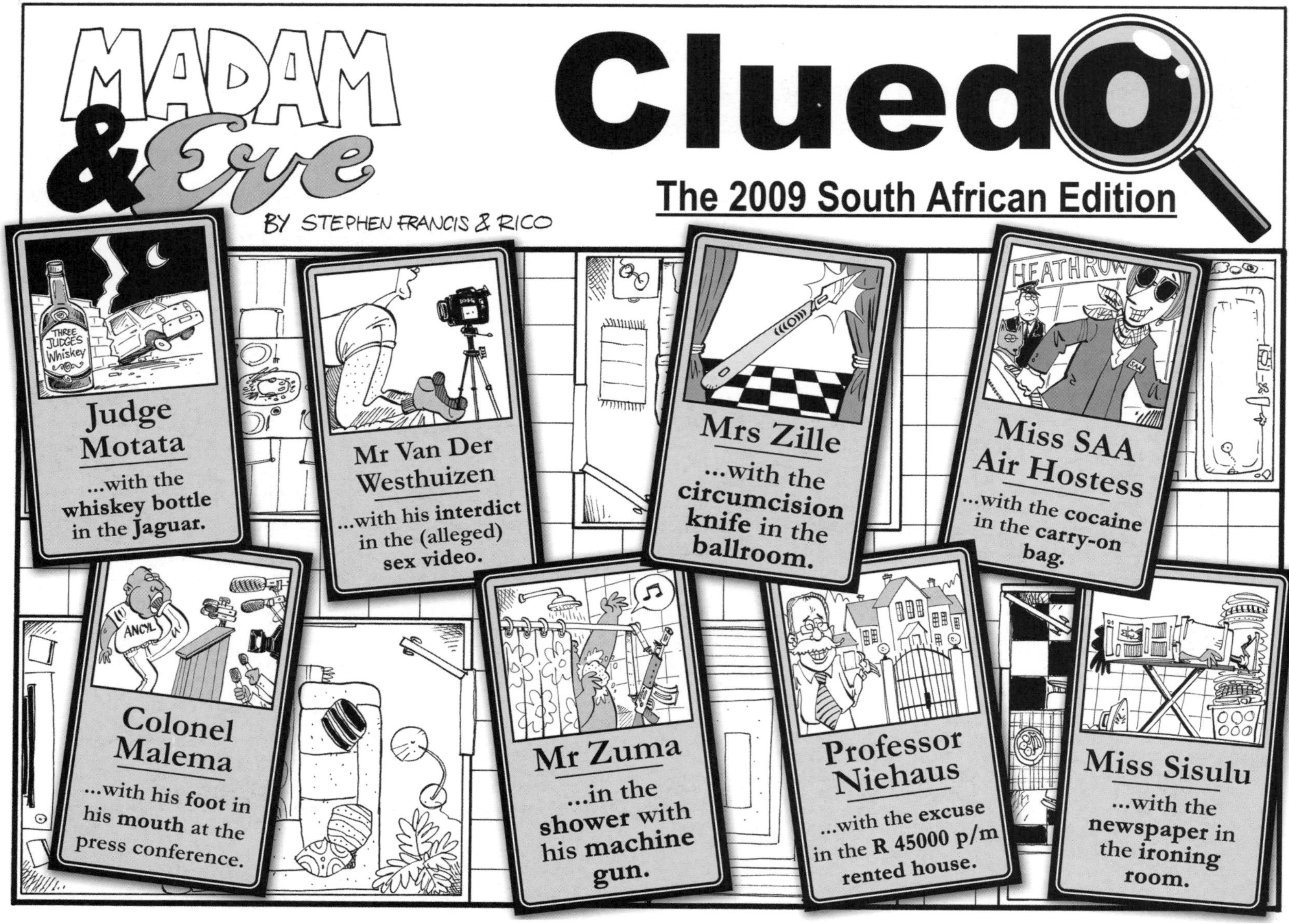
MADAM & Eve
BY STEPHEN FRANCIS & RICO
Cluedo
The 2009 South African Edition
THREE JUDGES Whiskey
Judge Motata
...with the whiskey bottle in the Jaguar.
Mr Van Der Westhuizen
...with his interdict in the (alleged) sex video.
Mrs Zille
...with the circumcision knife in the ballroom.
HEATHROW
SAA
Miss SAA Air Hostess
...with the cocaine in the carry-on bag.
ANCYL
Colonel Malema
...with his foot in his mouth at the press conference.
Mr Zuma
...in the shower with his machine gun.
Professor Niehaus
...with the excuse in the R 45000 p/m rented house.
Miss Sisulu
...with the newspaper in the ironing room.

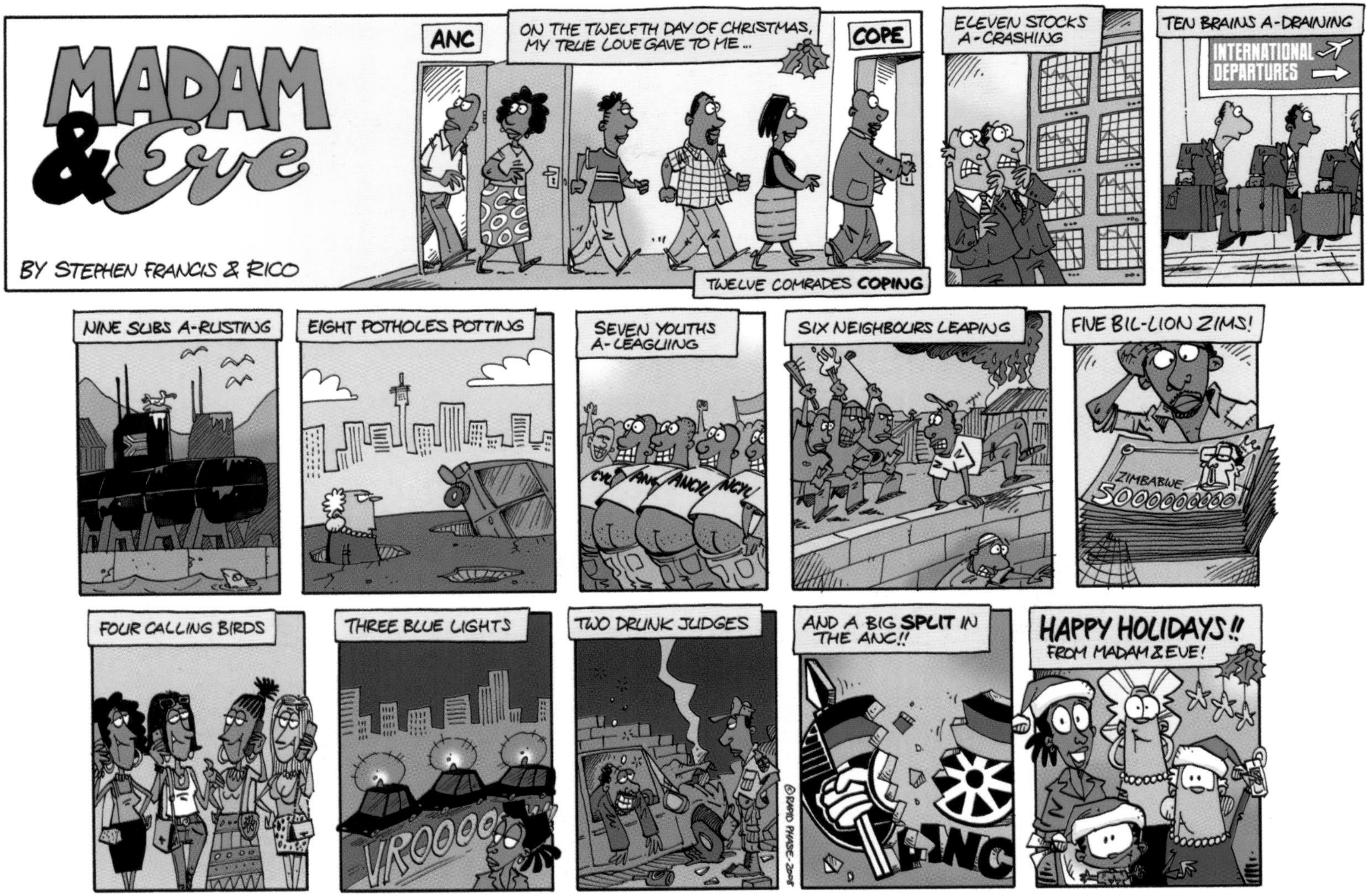
MADAM & Eve
BY STEPHEN FRANCIS & RICO
ANC
ON THE TWELFTH DAY OF CHRISTMAS, MY TRUE LOVE GAVE TO ME...
COPE
TWELVE COMRADES COPING
ELEVEN STOCKS A-CRASHING
TEN BRAINS A-DRAINING
INTERNATIONAL DEPARTURES
NINE SUBS A-RUSTING
EIGHT POTHOLES POTTING
SEVEN YOUTHS A-LEAGUING
SIX NEIGHBOURS LEAPING
FIVE BIL-LION ZIMS!
ZIMBABWE
5000000000
FOUR CALLING BIRDS
THREE BLUE LIGHTS
VROOOO
TWO DRUNK JUDGES
©RAPID PHASE-2008
AND A BIG SPLIT IN THE ANC!!
ANC
HAPPY HOLIDAYS!!
FROM MADAM & EVE!

BEEP BEEP Turn right now.
BEEP Left into second driveway. Approach front door.
STOP! Subject detected. Ring doorbell now.
DING DONG!
©RAPID PHASE-2008
"PORTABLE DUSTBIN MEN CHRISTMAS BONUS GPS."

LOOK MOM! IT'S SNOWING!! JUST IN TIME FOR CHRISTMAS!
©RAPID PHASE-2008
WAIT A SECOND! THIS ISN'T SNOW! ...THIS IS STYROFOAM!!
ACME STYROFOAM FACTORY
ATM
R
R

YOU KNOW... I WAS JUST THINKING.
EVE AND FATHER CHRISTMAS ACTUALLY HAVE A LOT IN COMMON.
A JOLLY NATURE? ...HOLIDAY SPIRIT?
©RAPID PHASE-2008
...BOTH ONLY WORK ABOUT ONE DAY A YEAR.
HA. HA. VERY FUNNY. PASS THE PINEAPPLE JUICE.

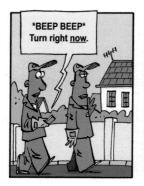

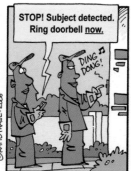

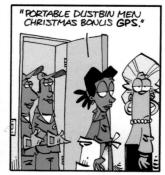

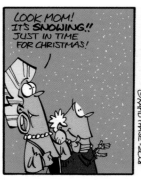

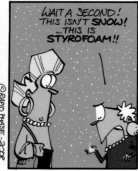

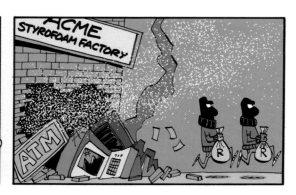

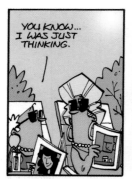

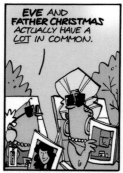

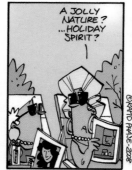

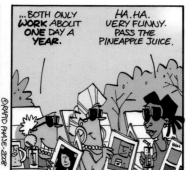

LEFTOVER FATHER CHRISTMAS HATS *Only* 10 RAND

© RAPID PHASE - 2009

EVERY TIME I SAY SOMETHING YOU **DISAGREE** WITH, YOU THROW ME OUT ON TO THE **FRONT STOEP!!**

WELL, I'VE **HAD** IT! NO MORE THROWING ME OUT ON TO THE FRONT STOEP!

AND THAT INCLUDES THE **BACK STOEP** TOO!!

© RAPID PHASE - 2008   www.madamandeve.co.za

x

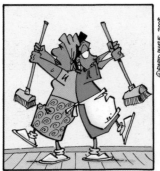

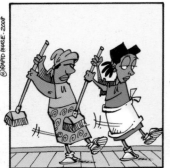

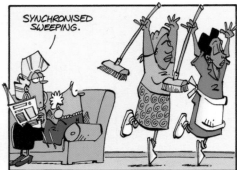

©RAPID PHASE - 2008
SYNCHRONISED SWEEPING.

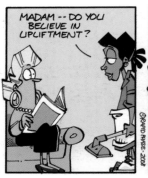

MADAM -- DO YOU BELIEVE IN UPLIFTMENT?
©RAPID PHASE - 2008
WHY, YES. YES I DO.
GOOD. THEN LIFT YOUR FEET UP.
www.madamandeve.co.za

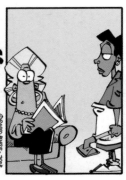

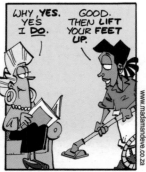

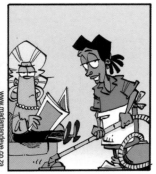

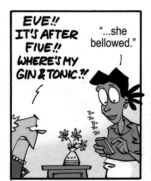

EVE!! IT'S AFTER FIVE!! WHERE'S MY GIN & TONIC?!
"...she bellowed."
TIC TIC TIC TIC
"Oh look. It's my 100 year-old vacuum cleaner."
TIC TIC TIC TIC
"...but I'm sure Madam will give me a wage increase if I ask nicely."
TIC TIC TIC TIC TIC
©RAPID PHASE - 2009
"NOT!!"
EVE'S DISCOVERED TWITTER.
TIC TIC TIC TIC TIC

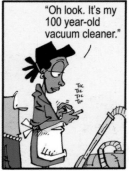

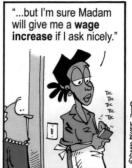

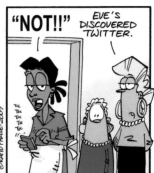

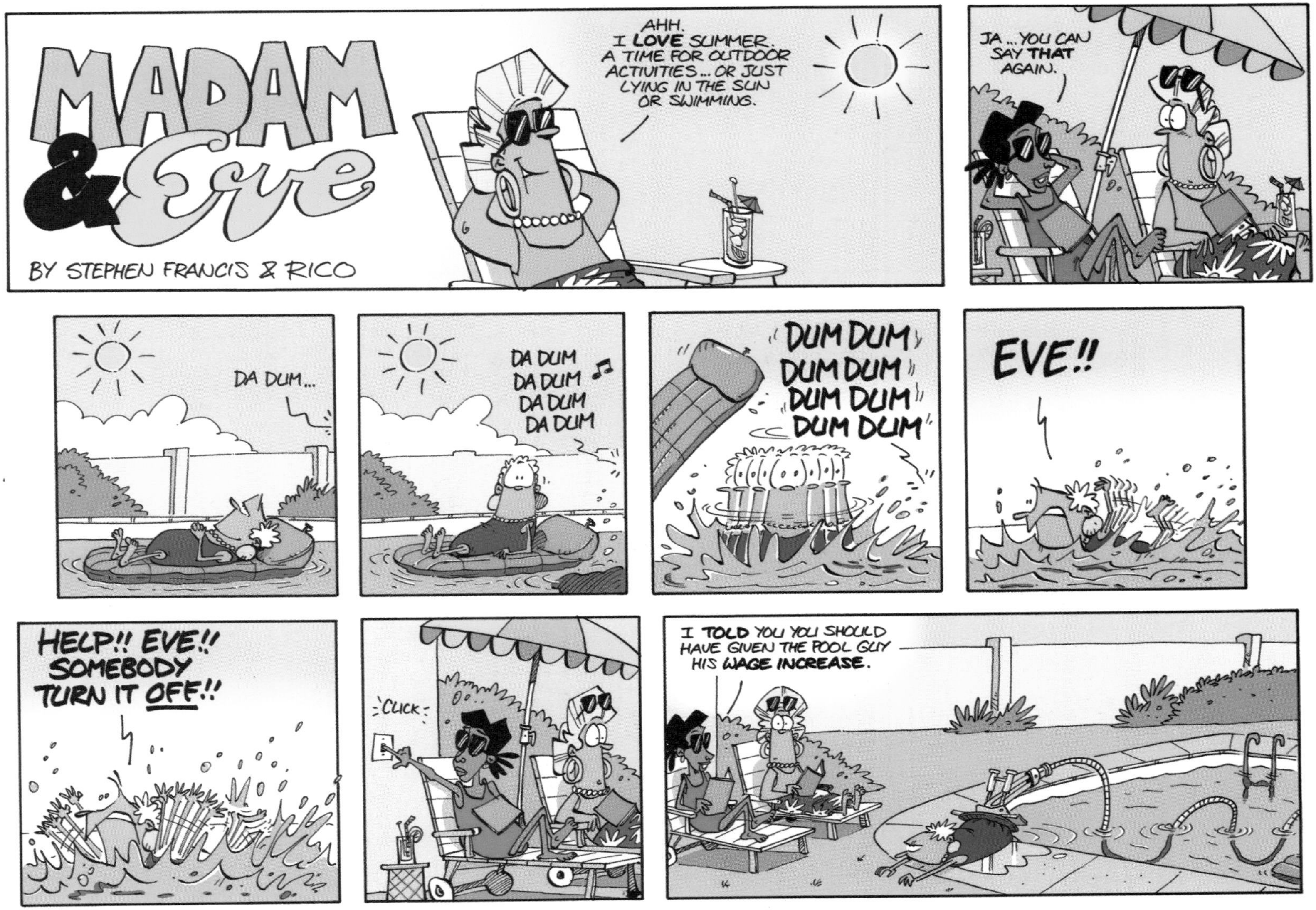
MADAM & Eve
BY STEPHEN FRANCIS & RICO
AHH. I LOVE SUMMER. A TIME FOR OUTDOOR ACTIVITIES... OR JUST LYING IN THE SUN OR SWIMMING.
JA ... YOU CAN SAY THAT AGAIN.
DA DUM...
DA DUM DA DUM DA DUM DA DUM
DUM DUM DUM DUM DUM DUM DUM DUM
EVE!!
HELP!! EVE!! SOMEBODY TURN IT OFF!!
CLICK
I TOLD YOU YOU SHOULD HAVE GIVEN THE POOL GUY HIS WAGE INCREASE.

LOOK AT THIS... ANOTHER LABOUR DISPUTE! ... ISN'T THERE ANYONE WHO HASN'T GONE ON STRIKE YET ?!
©RAPID PHASE - 2009
CARTOONISTS ON STRIKE!
MORE PAY!
BETTER WORKING CONDITIONS!

©RAPID PHASE - 2009
www.madamandeve.co.za
ZZZZZZZ
PiSSH!
WHO INSTALLED AN AIRBAG IN MY IRONING BOARD ?!!

EVE!!
IN HERE! I'M ONLINE!
"WELCOME TO THE DOMESTIC CHAT ROOM."
IT'S A NEW WEBSITE FOR DOMESTIC WORKERS EVERYWHERE!
©RAPID PHASE - 2009
... BUT WHERE IS EVERYBODY?! THE SCREEN IS BLANK AND THE CHATROOM'S EMPTY!!
WE'RE ALL ON A TEA BREAK.

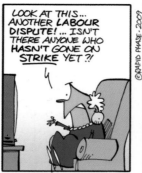

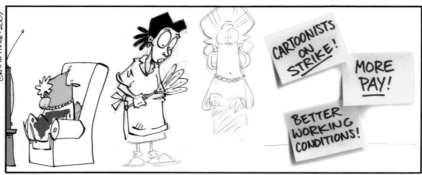

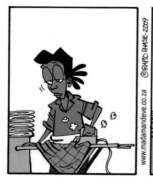

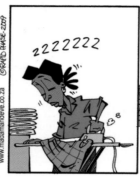

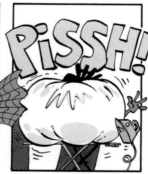

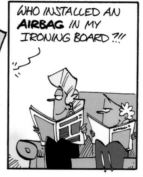

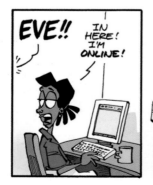

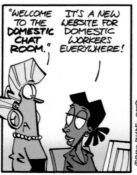

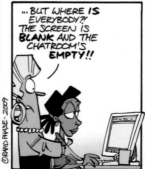

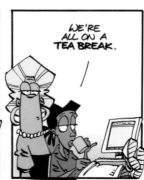

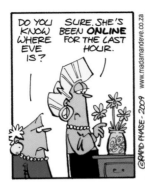

DO YOU KNOW WHERE EVE IS?
SURE. SHE'S BEEN ONLINE FOR THE LAST HOUR.
©RAPID PHASE - 2009 www.madamandeve.co.za

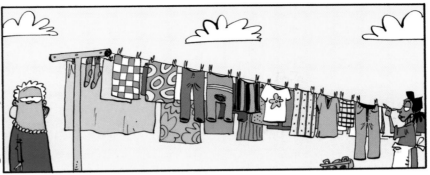

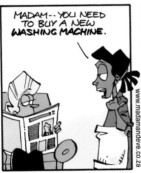

MADAM-- YOU NEED TO BUY A NEW WASHING MACHINE.
OH YEAH? WHO TOLD YOU THAT?
LET'S JUST SAY... THE INFORMATION WAS LEAKED TO ME.
www.madamandeve.co.za
©RAPID PHASE - 2009

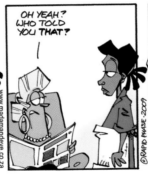

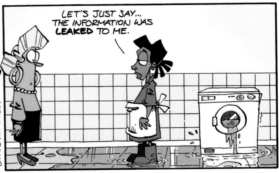

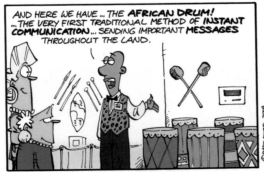

AND HERE WE HAVE ... THE AFRICAN DRUM! ...THE VERY FIRST TRADITIONAL METHOD OF INSTANT COMMUNICATION... SENDING IMPORTANT MESSAGES THROUGHOUT THE LAND.
TIC
©RAPID PHASE - 2009

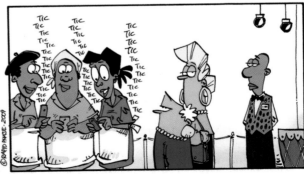

YO! WHAT UP, HOMIE?
YOU CHILLIN'? SHARP. I'M DOWN WITH THAT!!
BECAUSE I'M A PLAYA! UH, HUH. A BIG-TIME **PLAYA!!**
©RAPID PHASE-2008
SLAM!!
GO "PLAYA" OUTSIDE!
THAT'S SOOO FUNNY, I FORGOT TO BUST A MOVE.

SLAM!
OH, HI MOM. YOU'RE HOME EARLY. DID YOU WIN... OR LOSE?
www.madamandeve.co.za
©RAPID PHASE-2009
SLOT MACHINE NIGHT AT THE BINGO CLUB.

TIC
TIC TIC
TIC TIC
TIC
TIC TIC
TIC TIC
TIC TIC
TIC TIC
TIC
TIC TIC
TIC
©RAPID PHASE-2009
YOU KNOW... I KIND OF MISS THE **OLD** TEA BREAKS.
TIC
TIC
TIC
TIC
TIC

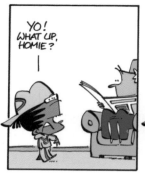

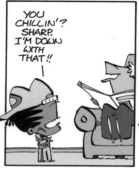

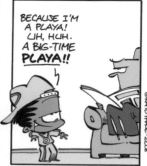

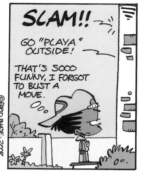

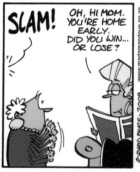

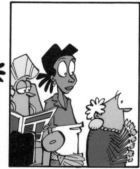

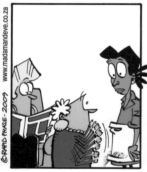

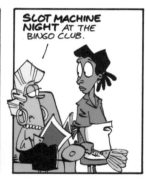

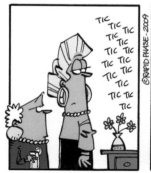

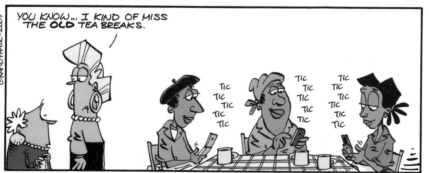

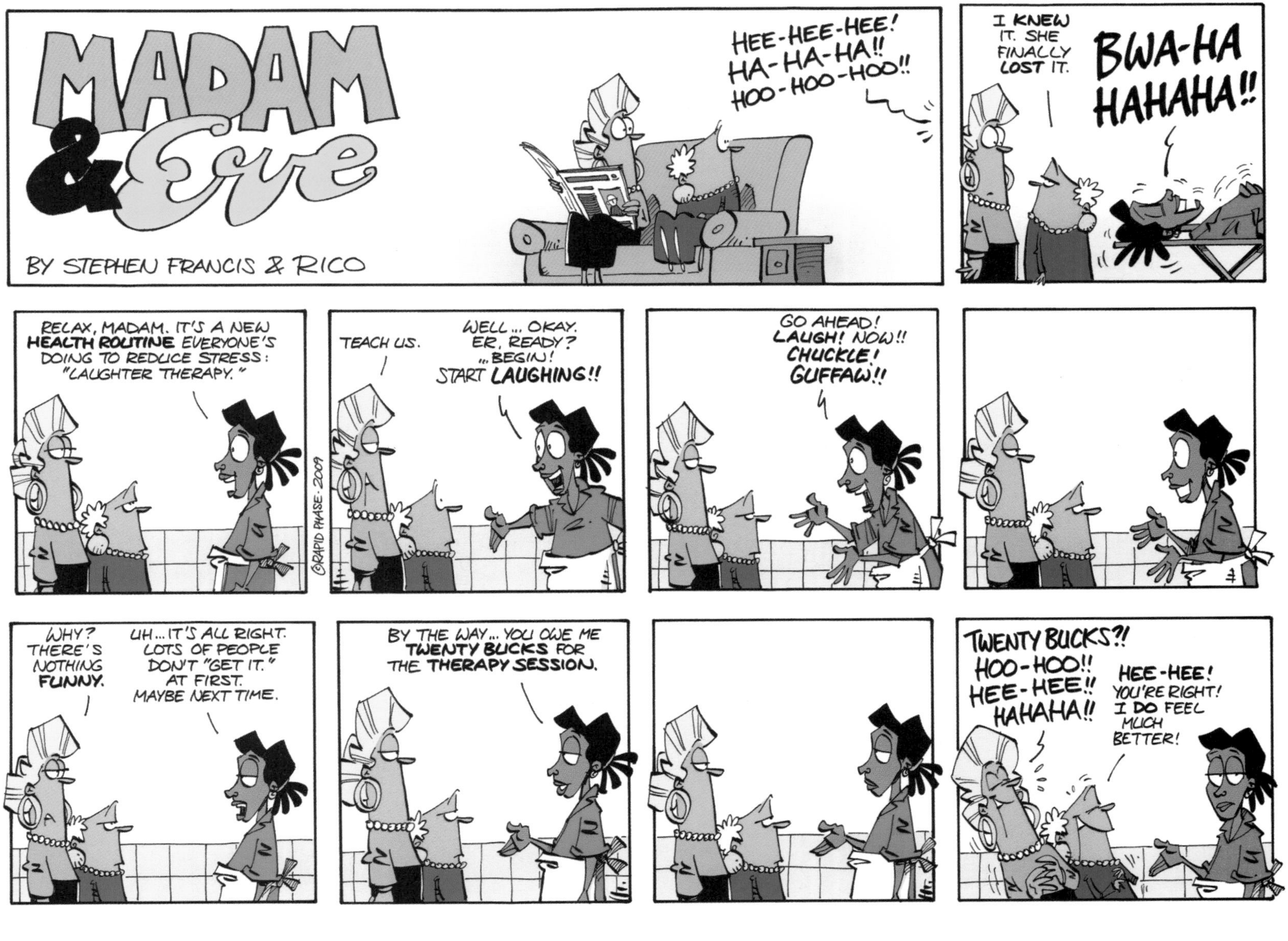
MADAM & Eve
BY STEPHEN FRANCIS & RICO
HEE-HEE-HEE! HA-HA-HA!! HOO-HOO-HOO!!
I KNEW IT. SHE FINALLY LOST IT.
BWA-HA HAHAHA!!
RELAX, MADAM. IT'S A NEW HEALTH ROUTINE EVERYONE'S DOING TO REDUCE STRESS: "LAUGHTER THERAPY."
©RAPID PHASE · 2009
TEACH US.
WELL... OKAY. ER, READY? ...BEGIN! START LAUGHING!!
GO AHEAD! LAUGH! NOW!! CHUCKLE! GUFFAW!!
WHY? THERE'S NOTHING FUNNY.
UH...IT'S ALL RIGHT. LOTS OF PEOPLE DON'T "GET IT." AT FIRST. MAYBE NEXT TIME.
BY THE WAY... YOU OWE ME TWENTY BUCKS FOR THE THERAPY SESSION.
TWENTY BUCKS?! HOO-HOO!! HEE-HEE!! HAHAHA!!
HEE-HEE! YOU'RE RIGHT! I DO FEEL MUCH BETTER!

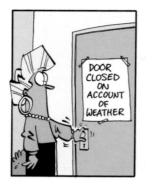

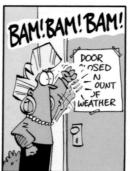

DOOR CLOSED ON ACCOUNT OF WEATHER
BAM! BAM! BAM!
WHAT'S THIS SIGN MEAN: "CLOSED ON ACCOUNT OF WEATHER?"
www.madamandeve.co.za ©RAPID PHASE · 2009
CLOSED ON ACCOUNT OF WEATHER EVE FEELS LIKE GETTING UP TO ANSWER IT OR NOT.

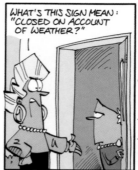

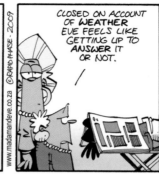

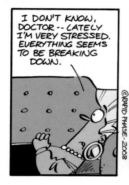

I DON'T KNOW, DOCTOR -- LATELY I'M VERY STRESSED. EVERYTHING SEEMS TO BE BREAKING DOWN.
©RAPID PHASE · 2008
...IT'S AS IF THE "RULES" DON'T APPLY ANY MORE. ...THERE'S NO RESPECT FOR PERSONAL BOUNDARIES. THERE'S NO --
www.madamandeve.co.za
OH. SORRY. ...YOU WERE SAYING?

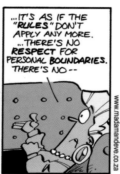

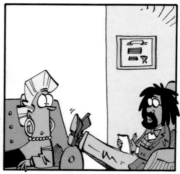

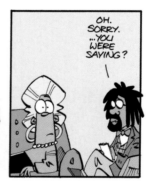

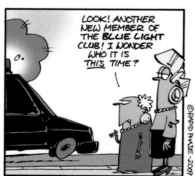

LOOK! ANOTHER NEW MEMBER OF THE BLUE LIGHT CLUB! I WONDER WHO IT IS THIS TIME?
©RAPID PHASE · 2009
MIELLIES!!

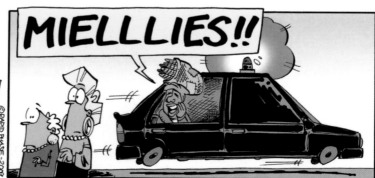

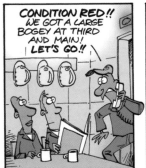

In a world where every step you take could be your last...
CONDITION RED!! WE GOT A LARGE BOGEY AT THIRD AND MAIN! LET'S GO!!
I'VE GOT A VISUAL!
WE'RE GONNA NEED A BIGGER SHOVEL!
SCREECH!!
©RAPID PHASE - 2009
POTHOLE SQUAD.
COMING SOON TO SABC.

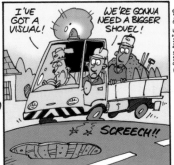

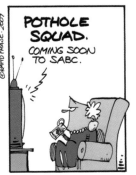

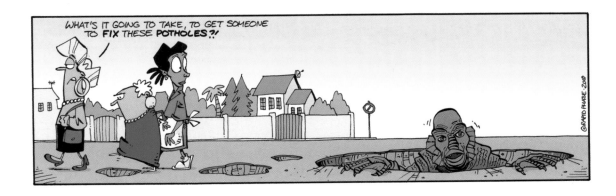

WHAT'S IT GOING TO TAKE, TO GET SOMEONE TO FIX THESE POTHOLES?!
©RAPID PHASE - 2009

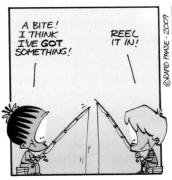

A BITE! I THINK I'VE GOT SOMETHING!
REEL IT IN!
©RAPID PHASE - 2009
EISH. IT'S JUST AN OLD TRAFFIC CONE.
...BETTER THROW IT BACK IN.
www.madamandeve.co.za
...POTHOLE FISHING. WANNA TRY?

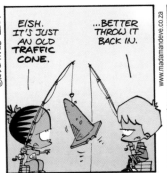

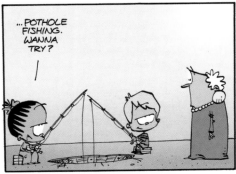

MADAM... I THINK IT'S TIME TO HAVE THE **ELECTRIFIED FENCE** SERVICED AGAIN.
REALLY? WHAT MAKES YOU SAY THAT?
©RAPID PHASE-2009
OH... JUST A FEELING.
SQUEAK SQUEAK SQUEAK SQUEAK

MIELLLIES!!
www.madamandeve.co.za
HARDEE DAH!!
©RAPID PHASE-2009
MIELLLIES!!
HARDEE DAH!!
MIELLLIES!
HARDEE DAH!!
SO MANY CHOICES, SO LITTLE TIME...

2010 WORLD CUP
OFFICIAL 3 GUYS ON THE BACK OF A BAKKIE
©RAPID PHASE-2009

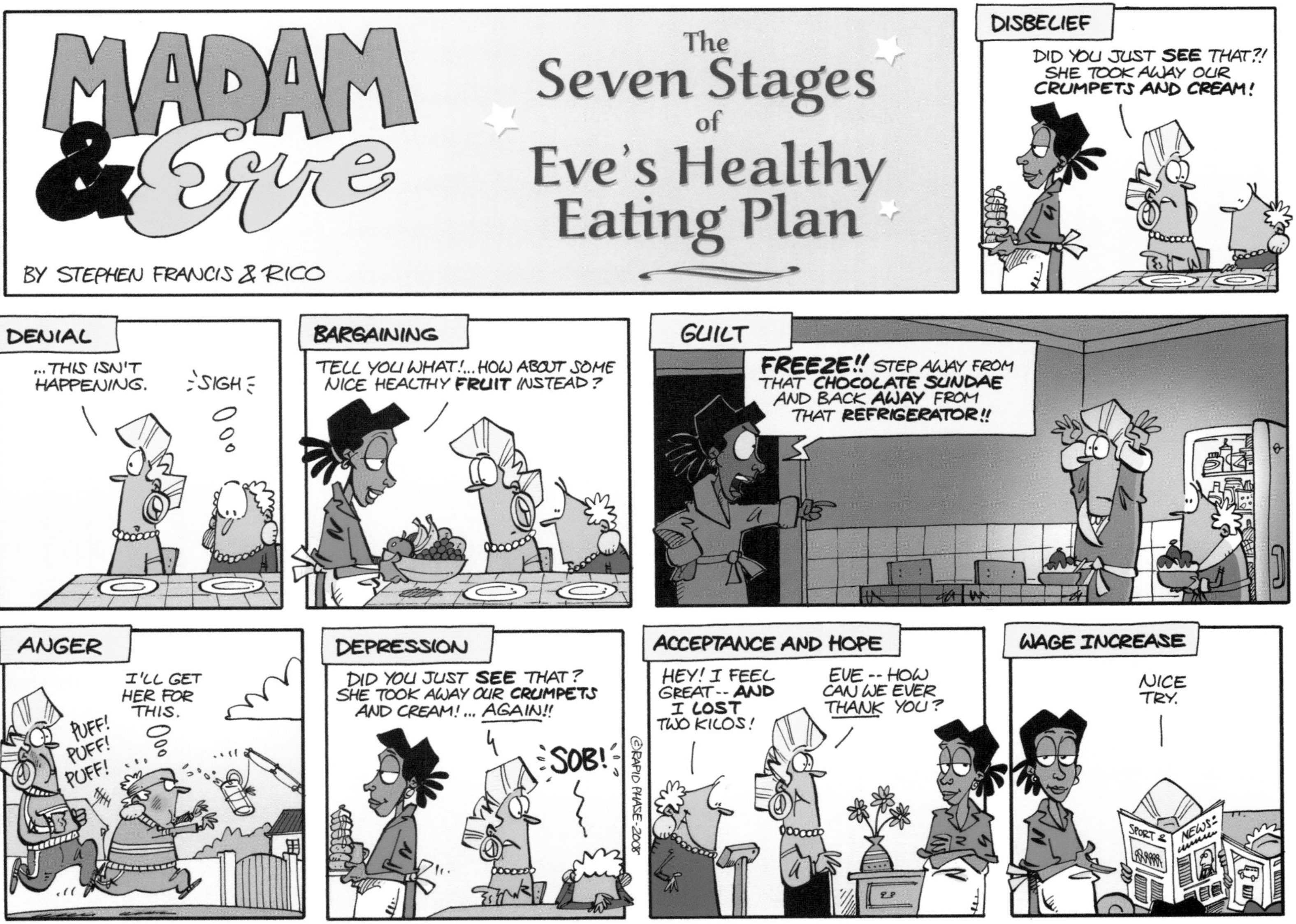
MADAM & Eve
The Seven Stages of Eve's Healthy Eating Plan
BY STEPHEN FRANCIS & RICO
DISBELIEF
DID YOU JUST SEE THAT?! SHE TOOK AWAY OUR CRUMPETS AND CREAM!
DENIAL
...THIS ISN'T HAPPENING.
SIGH
BARGAINING
TELL YOU WHAT!... HOW ABOUT SOME NICE HEALTHY FRUIT INSTEAD?
GUILT
FREEZE!! STEP AWAY FROM THAT CHOCOLATE SUNDAE AND BACK AWAY FROM THAT REFRIGERATOR!!
ANGER
PUFF! PUFF! PUFF!
I'LL GET HER FOR THIS.
DEPRESSION
DID YOU JUST SEE THAT? SHE TOOK AWAY OUR CRUMPETS AND CREAM! ... AGAIN!!
SOB!
©RAPID PHASE 2008
ACCEPTANCE AND HOPE
HEY! I FEEL GREAT -- AND I LOST TWO KILOS!
EVE -- HOW CAN WE EVER THANK YOU?
WAGE INCREASE
NICE TRY.
SPORT
NEWS

CLICK
WHAT'S GOING ON?
... IT'S THE NEIGHBOURHOOD MAIDS' ANNUAL SMS PHOTO CONTEST "MADAMS FROM HELL."
www.madamandeve.co.za
©RAPID PHASE - 2009
BEEP! BEEP!
YES!!
WE WON!!

www.madamandeve.co.za
©RAPID PHASE - 2009
THREE GIN & TONICS AND I GET AWAY WITH PRACTICALLY ANYTHING.

WHAT A MORNING! AS SOON AS I WOKE UP, I STARTED BLOGGING, GOOGLING, AND TWITTERING.
MAYBE YOU SHOULD SEE A DOCTOR.
I DID! HE TOLD ME I COULD HAVE A VIRUS, SO I NEED TO TAKE MYSELF OFFLINE, GO BACK TO EMBEDDING AND PUT MYSELF IN SLEEP MODE.
IT'S COMPUTER HUMOUR! "SLEEP MODE! GET IT?! GET IT?!!
www.madamandeve.co.za
©RAPID PHASE - 2009
I'VE BEEN PUT ON STANDBY.
YAHOO.

©RAPID PHASE · 2009
X-MAIDS
DOMESTIC ORIGINS
COMING SOON TO A THEATRE NEAR YOU

©RAPID PHASE · 2009
TAXI
BRT
BRT
TRANSFORMERS
REVENGE OF THE GOVERNMENT
Coming soon to a highway near you.

MORE PAY!
DARK SIDE PAYS PEANUTS!
ON STRIKE!
LIVING WAGE!
WE DEMAND FAIR PAY!!
©RAPID PHASE · 2009
THE EMPIRE STRIKES BACK - The South African Version

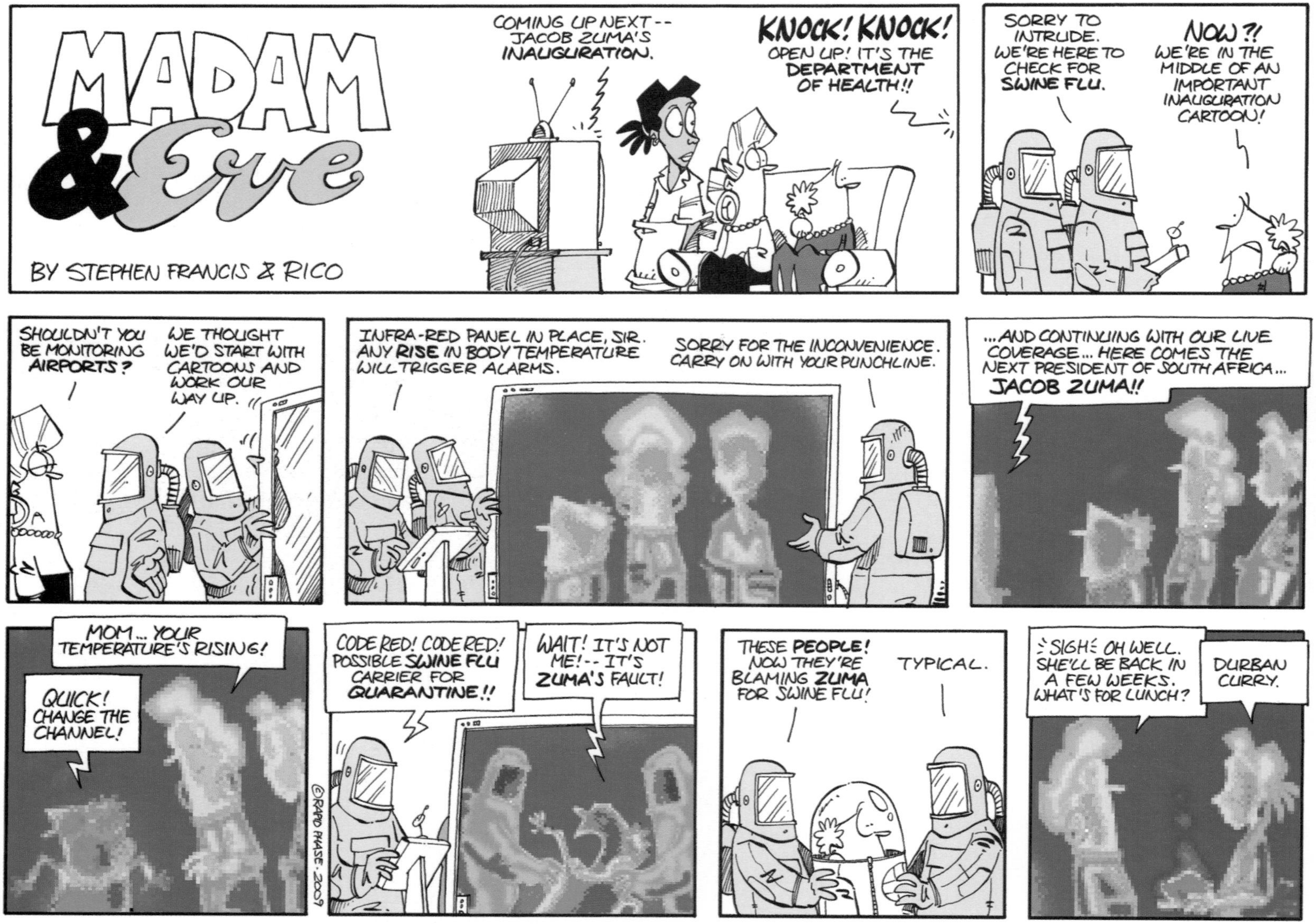
MADAM & Eve
BY STEPHEN FRANCIS & RICO
COMING UP NEXT -- JACOB ZUMA'S INAUGURATION.
KNOCK! KNOCK!
OPEN UP! IT'S THE DEPARTMENT OF HEALTH!!
SORRY TO INTRUDE. WE'RE HERE TO CHECK FOR SWINE FLU.
NOW?! WE'RE IN THE MIDDLE OF AN IMPORTANT INAUGURATION CARTOON!
SHOULDN'T YOU BE MONITORING AIRPORTS?
WE THOUGHT WE'D START WITH CARTOONS AND WORK OUR WAY UP.
INFRA-RED PANEL IN PLACE, SIR. ANY RISE IN BODY TEMPERATURE WILL TRIGGER ALARMS.
SORRY FOR THE INCONVENIENCE. CARRY ON WITH YOUR PUNCHLINE.
...AND CONTINUING WITH OUR LIVE COVERAGE... HERE COMES THE NEXT PRESIDENT OF SOUTH AFRICA... JACOB ZUMA!!
MOM... YOUR TEMPERATURE'S RISING!
QUICK! CHANGE THE CHANNEL!
©RAPID PHASE 2009
CODE RED! CODE RED! POSSIBLE SWINE FLU CARRIER FOR QUARANTINE!!
WAIT! IT'S NOT ME! -- IT'S ZUMA'S FAULT!
THESE PEOPLE! NOW THEY'RE BLAMING ZUMA FOR SWINE FLU!
TYPICAL.
SIGH OH WELL. SHE'LL BE BACK IN A FEW WEEKS. WHAT'S FOR LUNCH?
DURBAN CURRY.

LONG WALK TO FREEDOM.
LONG WALK TO AN EXTRAVAGANT LIFESTYLE, DEBT AND FORGERY.
LONG WALK TO MY OWN PRIVATE HELICOPTER.
LONG WALK TO HUGE KICKBACKS FOR MY FAMILY AND FRIENDS.
... AN ENTOURAGE AND A FLEET OF BLUE-LIGHT LIMOUSINES.
... A HOLIDAY HOME IN HOUT BAY.
©RAPID PHASE · 2009

CARL-- IF WE'RE GOING TO HIRE YOU AS ANC SPOKESPERSON... WE'LL NEED A FEW DETAILS ABOUT YOUR PERSONAL LIFE AND CHARACTER.
LET'S SEE... I HAVE AN EXTRAVAGANT LIFESTYLE, I LIKE TO PLUNGE MYSELF INTO HUGE DEBT, COMPROMISE MY PRINCIPLES AND FORGE SIGNATURES.
...I SEE.
©RAPID PHASE · 2009
"PRO-ACTIVE WITH NUMEROUS HOBBIES." ...FAVOURITE COLOUR?
I'LL TELL YOU IF YOU LEND ME A THOUSAND BUCKS.

©RAPID PHASE · 2009
FRIENDS OF JACOB ZUMA
FRIENDS OF JACOB ZUMA THAT CARL NIEHAUS OWES MONEY TO

I REALLY APPRECIATE YOU WATCHING MY CAR.
PARKING
UNFORTUNATELY, I'M HAVING CASH FLOW PROBLEMS ... I WAS ACTUALLY HOPING TO BORROW TEN BUCKS.
PARKING
www.madamandeve.co.za ©RAPID PHASE · 2009
THANKS, COMRADE. I WON'T FORGET THIS.
WHO WAS THAT?
CARL NIEHAUS.

THE ANC WISHES TO STATE THAT CARL NIEHAUS REMAINS A LOYAL AND VALUED CADRE.
AND ALTHOUGH HE WILL BE STEPPING DOWN AS MEDIA OFFICER, THE PARTY WILL FIND ALTERNATIVE EMPLOYMENT WITHIN THE ANC.
IN SHORT, CARL NIEHAUS ISN'T GOING ANYWHERE.
©RAPID PHASE · 2009 www.madamandeve.co.za
... AT LEAST UNTIL HE PAYS US ALL BACK.

"ECONOMICS POP QUIZ. QUESTION ONE:"
"IF A QUANTITATIVE SUMMARY OF YOUR BUSINESS REVEALS THAT EXPENDITURES FAR EXCEED INCOME, WHAT IS THE FIRST THING YOU MUST DO?"
www.madamandeve.co.za ©RAPID PHASE · 2009
FIRE CARL NIEHAUS.

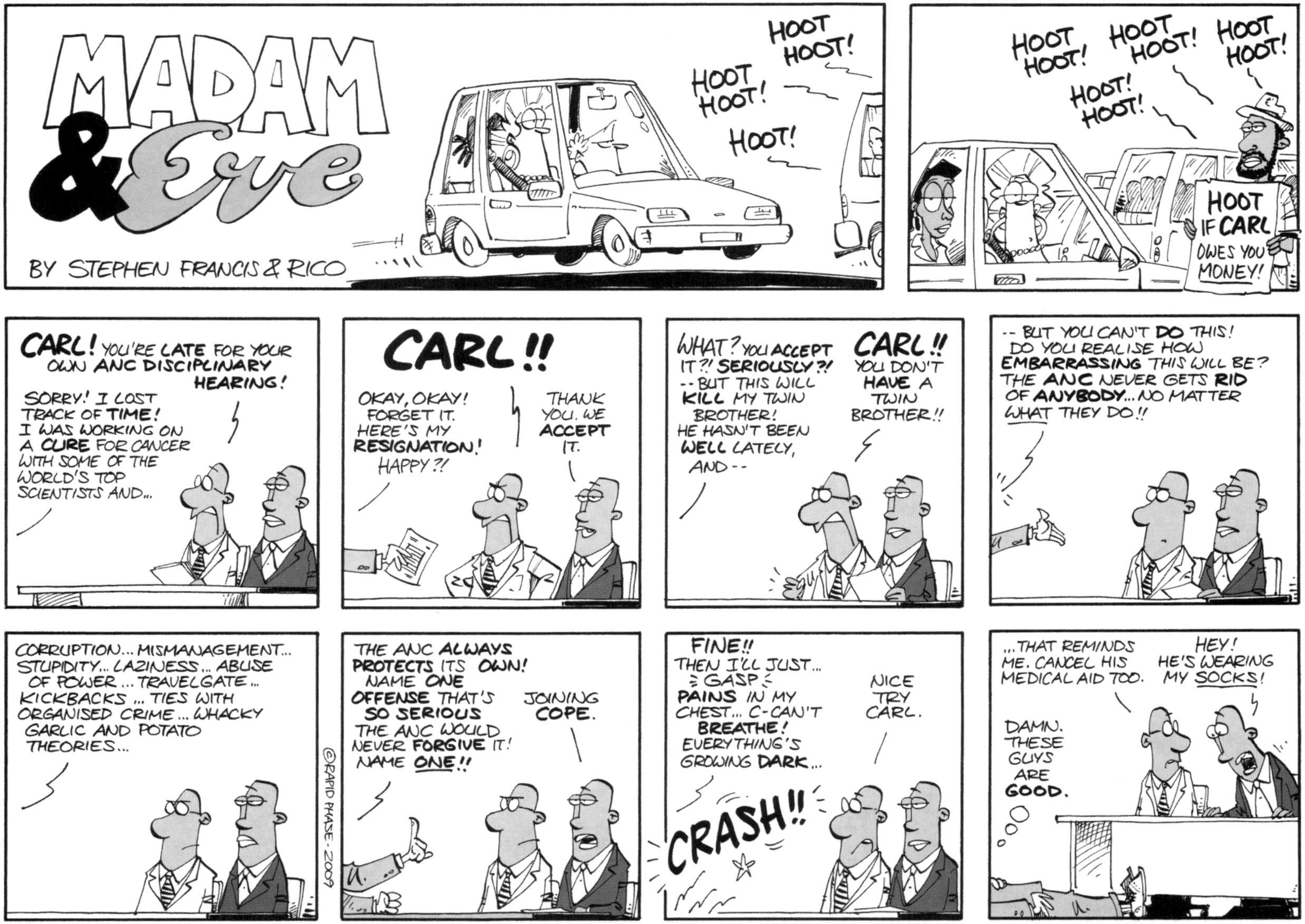
MADAM & Eve
BY STEPHEN FRANCIS & RICO
HOOT HOOT!
HOOT HOOT!
HOOT!
HOOT HOOT!
HOOT HOOT!
HOOT HOOT!
HOOT! HOOT!
HOOT IF CARL OWES YOU MONEY!
CARL! YOU'RE LATE FOR YOUR OWN ANC DISCIPLINARY HEARING!
SORRY! I LOST TRACK OF TIME! I WAS WORKING ON A CURE FOR CANCER WITH SOME OF THE WORLD'S TOP SCIENTISTS AND...
CARL!!
OKAY, OKAY! FORGET IT. HERE'S MY RESIGNATION! HAPPY?!
THANK YOU. WE ACCEPT IT.
WHAT? YOU ACCEPT IT?! SERIOUSLY?! --BUT THIS WILL KILL MY TWIN BROTHER! HE HASN'T BEEN WELL LATELY, AND--
CARL!! YOU DON'T HAVE A TWIN BROTHER!!
--BUT YOU CAN'T DO THIS! DO YOU REALISE HOW EMBARRASSING THIS WILL BE? THE ANC NEVER GETS RID OF ANYBODY... NO MATTER WHAT THEY DO!!
CORRUPTION... MISMANAGEMENT... STUPIDITY... LAZINESS... ABUSE OF POWER... TRAVELGATE... KICKBACKS... TIES WITH ORGANISED CRIME... WHACKY GARLIC AND POTATO THEORIES...
THE ANC ALWAYS PROTECTS ITS OWN! NAME ONE OFFENSE THAT'S SO SERIOUS THE ANC WOULD NEVER FORGIVE IT! NAME ONE!!
JOINING COPE.
©RAPID PHASE · 2009
FINE!! THEN I'LL JUST... GASP PAINS IN MY CHEST... C-CAN'T BREATHE! EVERYTHING'S GROWING DARK...
CRASH!!
NICE TRY CARL.
...THAT REMINDS ME. CANCEL HIS MEDICAL AID TOO.
HEY! HE'S WEARING MY SOCKS!
DAMN. THESE GUYS ARE GOOD.

IT IS.
NOPE. IT ISN'T.
©RAPID PHASE - 2009
IT IS. IT ISN'T. NO -- IT DEFINITELY ISN'T. BETTER RUN IT AGAIN.
www.madamandeve.co.za
DON'T TELL ME YOU'RE STILL WATCHING THE JOOST VIDEO?
DON'T YOU HAVE SOME WORK TO DO?!

419
NIGERIAN BUSINESS SCHOOL
GONE PHISHING
©RAPID PHASE - 2009 www.madamandeve.co.za

I SWEAR! I'M INNOCENT!
POLITICIANS! I'D PAY A HUNDRED BUCKS JUST TO HEAR SOMEONE ADMIT WRONGDOING AND TELL THE TRUTH!
©RAPID PHASE - 2009
MADAM ... I TOOK A THREE HOUR TEA BREAK THIS MORNING, I ATE ALL YOUR FAVOURITE BISCUITS ... AND BROKE YOUR GOOD VASE!
...THAT'LL BE ONE HUNDRED BUCKS.
OKAY! OKAY! HOW ABOUT FIFTY?!

GUESS WHAT?! **JULIUS MALEMA** VISITED OUR SCHOOL TODAY!

HE STRESSED THE IMPORTANCE OF A **GOOD EDUCATION** AND **HARD WORK** WHEN IT COMES TO FULFILLING THE **PROMISE** OF A **BRIGHTER FUTURE.**

www.madamandeve.co.za

..AND ALSO, THAT ANYONE WHO'S NOT **ANC** ARE **DOGS** AND **SNAKES** AND WILL INEVITABLY LEAD US ALL INTO A **SEA** OF **POVERTY.**

©RAPID PHASE·2009

THEN HE GAVE US **SWEETS,** POSED FOR THE MEDIA AND GOT BACK INTO HIS LIMO.

AND TO THINK ALL WE USED TO DO IS VISIT MUSEUMS.

WE'VE CALLED THIS PRESS CONFERENCE TO **VEHEMENTLY DENY** THAT WE "PARADED" MADIBA AROUND AT OUR ANC RALLY!

WE WOULD NEVER DO ANY-THING THAT **DESPERATE** AS TO ENDANGER HIS **SECURITY** OR **HEALTH** FOR THE SAKE OF CHEAP **ELECTIONEERING.**

BUT DON'T TAKE **MY** WORD FOR IT! ASK HIM **YOURSELF!** LOOK UP!! ...HERE HE COMES NOW!!

CONFETTI?

THAT'S **RIGHT!** IT'S THE **ANC HOT AIR BALLOON!!**

WATCH OUT, YOU **STUPID HEAD!**

ME?! **YOU'RE** THE STUPID HEAD!

©RAPID PHASE·2009

NO, **YOU** ARE!

ME?! NO, YOU ARE!

YOU ARE!

NO, **YOU** ARE!

COULD YOU TURN DOWN THE **ELECTION CANDIDATES'** PRESS **CONFERENCE?** WE'RE TRYING TO **PLAY.**

CLASS, TODAY WE'LL BE DISCUSSING THE UPCOMING ELECTION! HOW MANY OF THESE RETURNING ANC CANDIDATES CAN YOU IDENTIFY?
© RAPID PHASE - 2009
OH, COME ON! IT'S NOT THAT HARD! YOU'VE ALL SEEN THEIR PICTURES IN THE NEWSPAPER!
FRAUD AND THEFT! SUSPENDED SENTENCE!
TRAVELGATE! TRAVELGATE! TRAVELGATE!
FOURTH ROW! IMPLICATED IN ARMS DEAL SCANDAL!

GUESS WHAT'S COMING?! APRIL FOOL'S DAY!!
I LOVE APRIL FOOL'S DAY! JUST WHEN YOU START TO BELIEVE WHAT THEY TELL YOU... SURPRISE!! YOU'RE TRICKED, DUPED, AND TOTALLY SUCKERED!!
© RAPID PHASE - 2009
...WHEN IS APRIL FOOL'S DAY AGAIN?
www.madamandeve.co.za
APRIL 22nd, ELECTION DAY.
MOM!!

I'M BEING HAZED AND BULLIED AT SCHOOL! AND BY MY OWN TEACHER!!
WHAT?! HOW?!
FIRST, SHE FORCED ME TO STUDY TEXTBOOKS! THEN, SHE SMOTHERED ME WITH FACTS AND FIGURES! NOW... SHE'S MAKING ME DO "HOMEWORK" ... OUTSIDE OF SCHOOL!
I'M THINKING OF TAKING THE REST OF THE WEEK OFF IN PROTEST! CAN I COUNT ON YOUR SUPPORT?!
© RAPID PHASE - 2009
www.madamandeve.co.za
FINE! TOMORROW, WHEN SHE CRAMS MY BRAIN FULL OF PHOTOSYNTHESIS AND AZTEC HISTORY ... LET IT BE ON YOUR HEAD!!

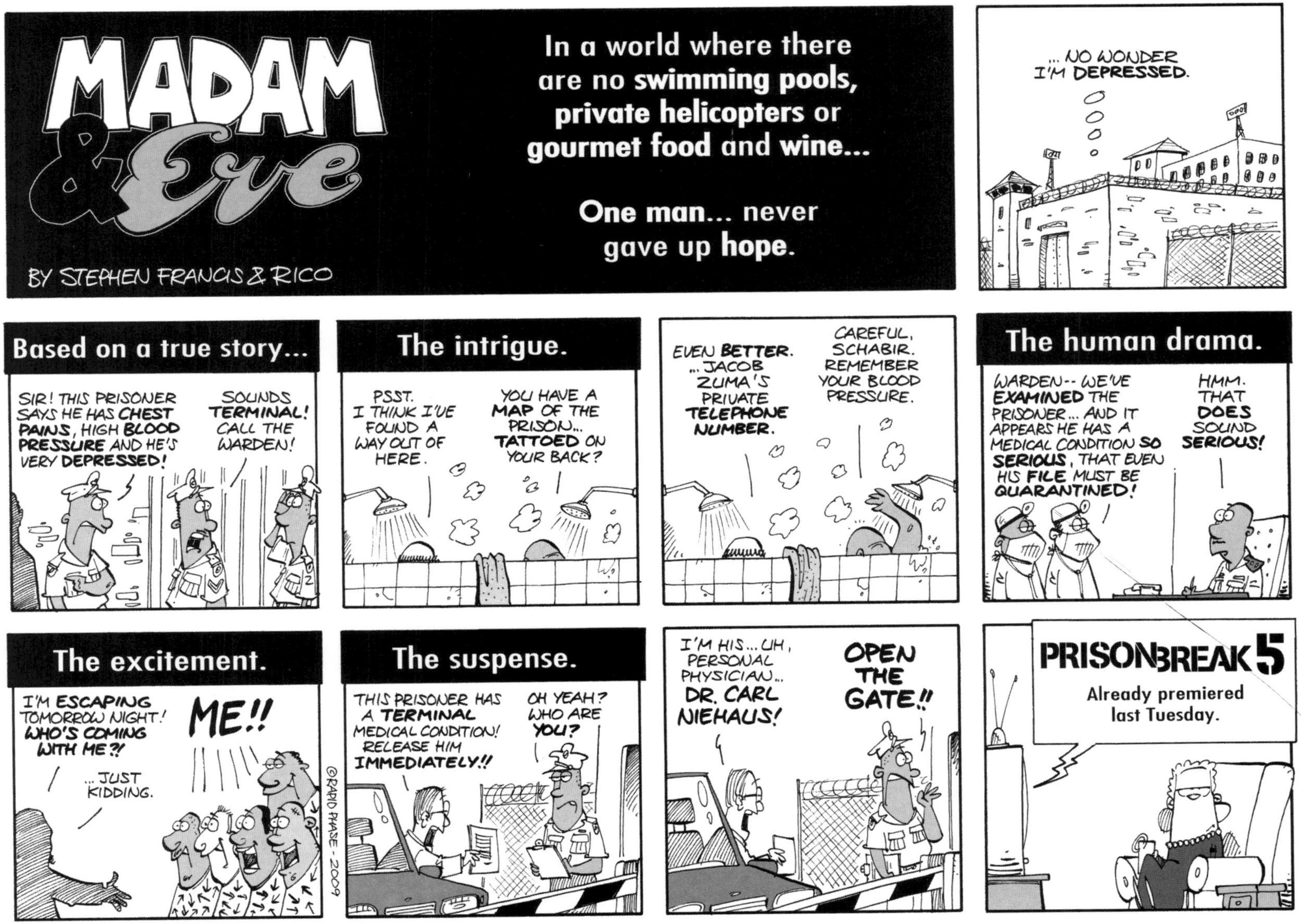
MADAM & Eve
BY STEPHEN FRANCIS & RICO
In a world where there are no swimming pools, private helicopters or gourmet food and wine...
One man... never gave up hope.
... NO WONDER I'M DEPRESSED.
Based on a true story...
SIR! THIS PRISONER SAYS HE HAS CHEST PAINS, HIGH BLOOD PRESSURE AND HE'S VERY DEPRESSED!
SOUNDS TERMINAL! CALL THE WARDEN!
The intrigue.
PSST. I THINK I'VE FOUND A WAY OUT OF HERE.
YOU HAVE A MAP OF THE PRISON... TATTOOED ON YOUR BACK?
EVEN BETTER. ...JACOB ZUMA'S PRIVATE TELEPHONE NUMBER.
CAREFUL, SCHABIR. REMEMBER YOUR BLOOD PRESSURE.
The human drama.
WARDEN-- WE'VE EXAMINED THE PRISONER... AND IT APPEARS HE HAS A MEDICAL CONDITION SO SERIOUS, THAT EVEN HIS FILE MUST BE QUARANTINED!
HMM. THAT DOES SOUND SERIOUS!
The excitement.
I'M ESCAPING TOMORROW NIGHT! WHO'S COMING WITH ME?!
ME!!
...JUST KIDDING.
©RAPID PHASE - 2009
The suspense.
THIS PRISONER HAS A TERMINAL MEDICAL CONDITION! RELEASE HIM IMMEDIATELY!!
OH YEAH? WHO ARE YOU?
I'M HIS... UH, PERSONAL PHYSICIAN... DR. CARL NIEHAUS!
OPEN THE GATE!!
PRISONBREAK 5
Already premiered last Tuesday.

©RAPID PHASE · 2009
Dear Thandi's Teacher,
Please release Thandi from School. She has a medical condition and could 'go' at any moment.
...So please let her go now.
Signed, Thandi's Doctor, M.D.
www.madamandeve.co.za
IF I WAS SHABIR SHAIK, I'D BE HOME BY NOW.
PRINCIPAL

BAD NEWS, SCHABIR. JACOB FEELS THAT THIS "PAROLE-GATE" THING IS NOW MAKING HIM LOOK BAD.
©RAPID PHASE · 2008
HE FEELS THAT -- FOR THE GOOD OF THE PARTY -- YOU NEED TO PROVE TO THE MEDIA THAT YOU REALLY DO HAVE A TERMINAL ILLNESS.
GOOD THINKING! BUT HOW?
www.madamandeve.co.za
WAIT A MINUTE!! ARE YOU SAYING I HAVE TO DIE?!!
...NOT RIGHT AWAY! JUST SOMETIME BEFORE APRIL 22nd.

YOU CAN'T BE SERIOUS! THE ANC WANTS ME TO KILL MYSELF?!
SCHABIR -- IT'S THE ONLY WAY TO CONVINCE EVERYONE THAT YOU REALLY DID HAVE A TERMINAL ILLNESS!
JACOB'S REALLY EXCITED ABOUT THIS! PICTURE IT: AFTER YOU PASS AWAY A FEW WEEKS AFTER BEING PAROLED... BOY, WILL THE MEDIA HAVE TO EAT CROW!!
IT'LL BE BEAUTIFUL!
...WE JUST WISH YOU COULD BE ALIVE TO SEE IT.
©RAPID PHASE · 2009
BUT, I DONT WANT TO DIIIIIIIIIE!!
WHERE'S YOUR PARTY LOYALTY?
LOOK! WE BROUGHT PIZZA!
PIZZA

COME ON, GUYS! YOU WANT ME TO **DIE** IN ORDER TO PROVE MY PARTY **LOYALTY**?!

IT'S THE ONLY WAY THE MEDIA WILL **BELIEVE** YOU'RE **TERMINALLY ILL**, SCHABIR.

YOU MEAN... I HAVE TO ACTUALLY... **EXPIRE**?!

DON'T BE SILLY! YOU'LL **FAKE** YOUR OWN **DEATH!** LIKE ELVIS!

AND **THEN** WHAT? THE **ANC** MIRACULOUSLY **RESURRECTS** ME?

UH, WE WERE THINKING MORE OF **COSMETIC SURGERY** AND A NEW **IDENTITY** IN GOVERNMENT.

OKAY, BUT I WANT A POSITION WITH **UNLIMITED ACCESS** TO LOTS OF **MONEY** AND I DON'T HAVE TO **ANSWER** TO ANYBODY!

GOTCHA. AN **SABC BOARD MEMBER!** LET ME RUN IT BY JACOB.

©RAPID PHASE - 2009
www.madamandeve.co.za

...SO YOU'RE SAYING...TO END "**PAROLE-GATE**"... YOU WANT ME TO **FAKE** MY OWN **DEATH** AND THE **ANC** WILL GIVE ME A NEW **IDENTITY**.

THAT'S RIGHT, SCHABIR.

YOU MUST BE **JOKING!** THE **SECRECY**...THE **COST**...WHY, IT WOULD PROBABLY BE **EASIER** AND **CHEAPER** JUST TO REALLY **KILL ME!!** HEE-HEE!!

...HA...HA...HA...

©RAPID PHASE - 2009

CALL **JACOB**. TELL HIM HIS **FINANCIAL ADVISOR** MAY BE ON TO SOMETHING.

NOW **HOLD ON** JUST A **MINUTE!!**

HELLO? MORNINGSIDE **PIZZA** DELIVERY! HOW CAN I HELP YOU?

IS THIS A SECURE LINE?

www.madamandeve.co.za

UH-OH.

...I'D LIKE A **LARGE ANCHOVY** AND ONION PIZZA WITH EXTRA CHILI AND GARLIC... DELIVERED IN AN **UNMARKED CAR**.

©RAPID PHASE - 2009

...NAME?

SHAIK! SAME ADDRESS AS YESTERDAY.

HEY VUSI! LOOK **OUTSIDE!** ARE THOSE **MEDIA TRUCKS?**

WHY **ME**?! WHY ON **MY** SHIFT?!

I KNOW HOW TO **END** POVERTY, CRIME, UNEMPLOYMENT AND **FIX** ALL POTHOLES IN ONLY **48** HOURS!

...HOW?

MAKE IT A CONDITION OF **SHABIR SHAIK'S** EARLY **PAROLE!**

...WHAT?

©RAPID PHASE - 2009

www.madamandeve.co.za

NOT ANOTHER **POTHOLE?!**

DON'T CALL THEM "**POTHOLES.**"

WHY NOT?

THEY'RE SYMPTOMS OF A **COLLAPSING** INFRASTRUCTURE...

...DUE TO **LAZINESS**, **CORRUPTION** AND/OR **INCOMPETENCE** ON BEHALF OF THE **GOVERNMENT.**

...SO THEY'RE **NOT** "**POTHOLES?**"

©RAPID PHASE - 2009

...THEY'RE A BUNCH OF **ANC-HOLES!**

www.madamandeve.co.za

CAN I HAVE THE **DAY OFF**, MADAM? I HAVE TO GO TO A **COPE** RALLY.

HOLD IT.

YESTERDAY... YOU TOOK THE WHOLE DAY **OFF** TO ATTEND AN **ANC** RALLY!

THAT'S RIGHT.

... AND TOMORROW I'M GOING TO LISTEN TO THE **DA!**

THEN WHICH PARTY ARE YOU SUPPORTING?!

©RAPID PHASE - 2009

DEPENDS. ...THE ONE WHICH GETS ME OUT OF **WORK.**

www.madamandeve.co.za

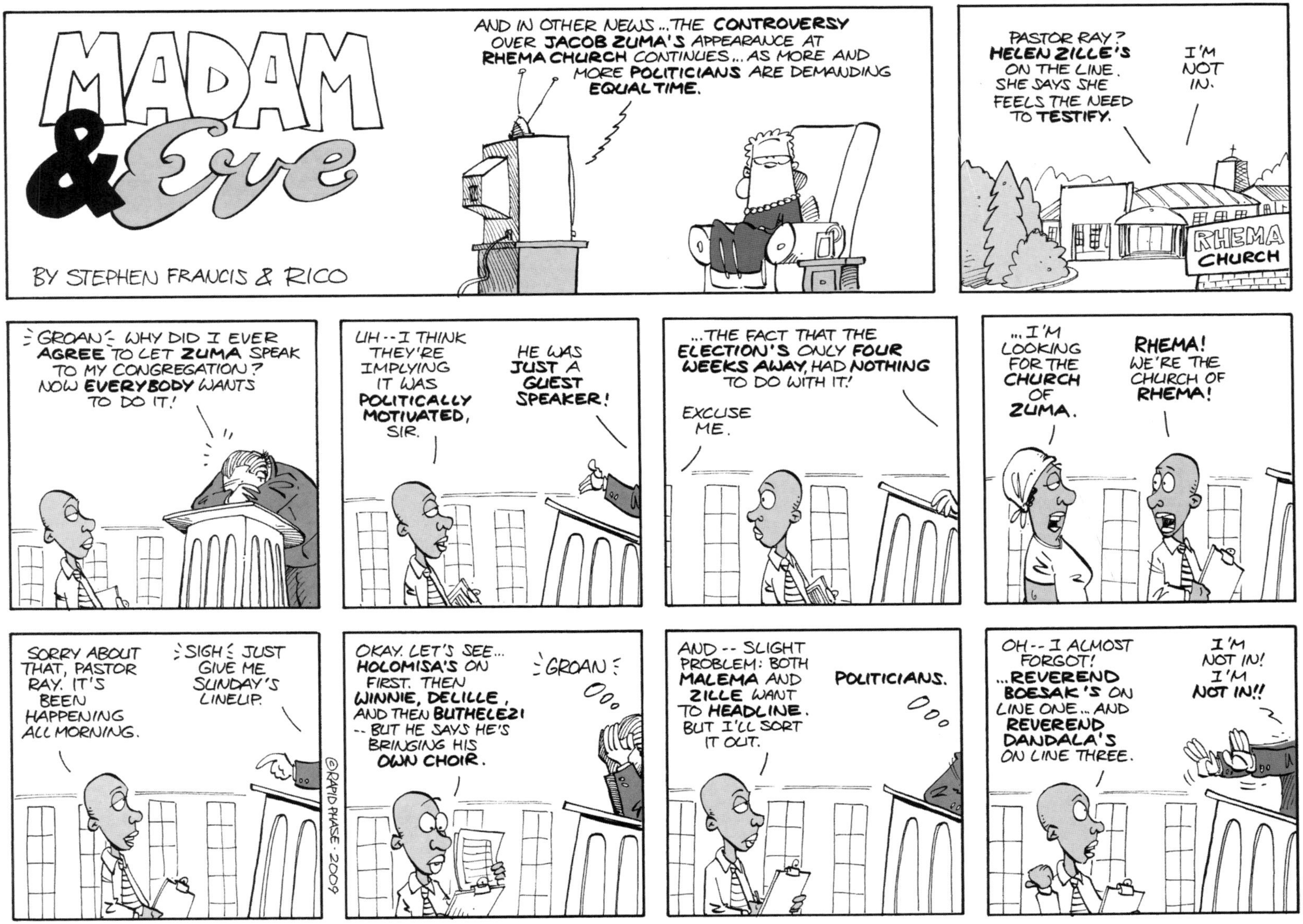

MADAM & Eve
BY STEPHEN FRANCIS & RICO
AND IN OTHER NEWS ... THE CONTROVERSY OVER JACOB ZUMA'S APPEARANCE AT RHEMA CHURCH CONTINUES ... AS MORE AND MORE POLITICIANS ARE DEMANDING EQUAL TIME.
PASTOR RAY? HELEN ZILLE'S ON THE LINE. SHE SAYS SHE FEELS THE NEED TO TESTIFY.
I'M NOT IN.
RHEMA CHURCH
GROAN WHY DID I EVER AGREE TO LET ZUMA SPEAK TO MY CONGREGATION? NOW EVERYBODY WANTS TO DO IT!
UH -- I THINK THEY'RE IMPLYING IT WAS POLITICALLY MOTIVATED, SIR.
HE WAS JUST A GUEST SPEAKER!
... THE FACT THAT THE ELECTION'S ONLY FOUR WEEKS AWAY, HAD NOTHING TO DO WITH IT!
EXCUSE ME.
... I'M LOOKING FOR THE CHURCH OF ZUMA.
RHEMA! WE'RE THE CHURCH OF RHEMA!
SORRY ABOUT THAT, PASTOR RAY. IT'S BEEN HAPPENING ALL MORNING.
SIGH JUST GIVE ME SUNDAY'S LINEUP.
©RAPID PHASE 2009
OKAY. LET'S SEE... HOLOMISA'S ON FIRST. THEN WINNIE, DELILLE, AND THEN BUTHELEZI -- BUT HE SAYS HE'S BRINGING HIS OWN CHOIR.
GROAN
AND -- SLIGHT PROBLEM: BOTH MALEMA AND ZILLE WANT TO HEADLINE. BUT I'LL SORT IT OUT.
POLITICIANS.
OH -- I ALMOST FORGOT! ... REVEREND BOESAK'S ON LINE ONE ... AND REVEREND DANDALA'S ON LINE THREE.
I'M NOT IN! I'M NOT IN!!

COMMUNITY CHEST! "YOU BANKRUPT PUBLIC COMPANY. RECEIVE 12 MILLION RAND BONUS."
MY TURN!
UTILITIES AND SERVICES! ...DO I WANT TO BUY TELKOM, ESKOM, SABC OR SAA?
...ARE YOU NUTS?
©RAPID PHASE·2009
WHAT ARE YOU PLAYING? "MONOPOLY" BY PARKER BROS.?
"ANC MONOPOLY." BY SHAIK BROS.
HA! I GOT THE "GET OUT OF JAIL FREE ON MEDICAL PAROLE" CARD!
LUCKY.

SO DON'T MISS IT! BE SURE TO JOIN US.
THE DECEPTION... THE NEPOTISM... THE BETRAYAL... THE GREED! ...CONTINUING NEXT WEEK ON SABC!
©RAPID PHASE·2009
...NEW SOAP OPERA?
...SABC JOB RECRUITMENT ADVERT.

AND, IN OTHER NEWS... A FORMER SABC EXECUTIVE IS UNDER INVESTIGATION FOR ALLEGEDLY WASTING OVER 50 MILLION RANDS.
ACCORDING TO SOURCES, THE HUGE SUMS WERE SPENT HANDING OUT LUCRATIVE CONTRACTS TO FRIENDS... OR BUYING HUNDREDS OF TOTALLY USELESS PROGRAMMES FOR BROADCAST.
www.madamandeve.co.za
HOWEVER, A SPOKESPERSON VIGOROUSLY DENIED THESE CHARGES.
©RAPID PHASE·2009
AND NOW, COMING UP NEXT ON SABC... "OUTER MONGOLIAN IDOLS", "PIMP MY GYM LOCKER" AND... "WHO WANTS TO BE A ZIMBABWEAN MILLIONAIRE?"

ALRIGHT, CLASS. YOU HAVE 45 MINUTES TO COMPLETE YOUR EXAM! READY? BEGIN!
"WHAT IS THE PURPOSE OF THE GREAT WALL OF CHINA?"
©RAPID PHASE · 2009
www.madamandeve.co.za
"TO KEEP OUT THE DALAI LAMA."

NOW THAT WAS GREAT CHINESE TAKEAWAY!
LET'S OPEN OUR FORTUNE COOKIES! ...GWEN?
"THE JOURNEY OF A THOUSAND MILES BEGINS WITH A SINGLE STEP."
MY TURN.
©RAPID PHASE · 2009
"YOUR EVERLASTING PATIENCE WILL BE REWARDED."
WHAT'S YOURS SAY, MOM?
"DON'T GIVE THE DALAI LAMA A VISA... OR ELSE."

GET OUT OF THE WAY!! VIP COMING THROUGH!!
GET OUT OF THE WAY!! VIP COMING THROUGH!!
©RAPID PHASE · 2009
GREAT. HE SPENDS ONE DAY IN SOUTH AFRICA AND NOW LOOK.

KLOMP! KLOMP! KLOMP! KLOMP!
SHH! DO YOU HEAR THAT?
WHAT?
www.madamandeve.co.za ©RAPID PHASE · 2009
KLOMP! KLOMP! KLOMP! KLOMP! KLOMP! KLOMP! KLOMP!
RUN FOR YOUR LIVES!!
KLOMP! KLOMP! KLOMP! KLOMP! KLOMP! KLOMP!
ZUMA BODYGUARD STAMPEDE!!

GET OUT OF THE WAY. VERY IMPORTANT PERSON COMING THROUGH.
MORNING, GWEN... EDITH.
MARGE.
©RAPID PHASE · 2009
GET OUT OF THE WAY. VERY IMPORTANT PERSON COMING THROUGH.
INFLATABLE TALKING BODYGUARDS
Only 10 Rand per hour

IT'S THE LATEST THING.
INFLATABLE TALKING BODYGUARDS
Only 10 Rand per hour
©RAPID PHASE · 2009
PULL THE RING AT THE BACK! THEY HAVE OVER A DOZEN DIFFERENT SAYINGS RECORDED FROM REAL BODYGUARDS!
...VIP COMING THROUGH! ...GET OUT OF THE WAY! ...GIVE ME THAT CAMERA!
...THANKS FOR THE JOB, COUSIN JACOB!
...WE'RE STILL WORKING OUT A FEW BUGS.

GET OUT OF THE WAY! VERY IMPORTANT PERSON COMING THROUGH!
INFLATABLE TALKING BODYGUARD
Only 10 Rand per Hour
OKAY, OKAY! HERE'S MY MONEY! I'LL TAKE ONE.
A WISE CHOICE.
©RAPID PHASE · 2009
...I'D CUT BACK A LITTLE ON THE **HELIUM**.

GET OUT OF THE WAY! **VERY** IMPORTANT PERSON COMING THROUGH!
...**YOU** GET OUT OF THE WAY! A **MORE** IMPORTANT PERSON COMING THROUGH!
OOMPH!!
UGH!
©RAPID PHASE · 2009
...INFLATABLE BODYGUARD GRIDLOCK.

HE **LOVES** ME...
HE LOVES
ME **NOT.**
HE LOVES ME...

...I'LL DROP THE
CHARGES...
I **WON'T** DROP
THE CHARGES...

©RAPID PHASE - 2009
www.madamandeve.co.za

I'LL **DROP** THE CHARGES...
I **WON'T** DROP THE CHARGES...
I'LL **DROP** THE CHARGES...
I **WON'T** DROP THE
CHARGES...

WHERE'S
THAT
GUY
FROM?

NATIONAL
PROSECUTING
AUTHORITY.

MISTER
ZUMA!

MISTER
ZUMA!

MISTER ZUMA!
CONGRATULATIONS
ON THE **DROPPED**
CHARGES...

THANK
YOU.

©RAPID PHASE - 2009

...BUT SIR,
WOULD YOU
CARE TO
COMMENT ON
THE **DARK**
CLOUD STILL
HANGING OVER
YOUR HEAD?

DARK
CLOUD?
WHAT
"DARK
CLOUD?"

THE... UH,
DARK
CLOUD.
IT'S **STILL**
THERE.
HOVERING
ABOVE
YOU.

WHAT ARE
YOU **TALKING**
ABOUT?!
I DON'T SEE
ANYTHING!

COULD
SOMEONE
PLEASE
GET
HIM A
MIRROR?!

MEDIA.
THEY ALWAYS
GIVE ME A
HEADACHE.

RUMBLE!
ZAP!

THABO --
ARE YOU
WATCHING
THE
NEWS?

OF **COURSE**
I'M
WATCHING
THE
NEWS!

:HEE-HEE: THEY MAY
HAVE DROPPED THE
CORRUPTION CHARGES
...BUT **ZUMA** STILL HAS
A DARK **CLOUD** HANGING
OVER HIM!

UH...

©RAPID PHASE - 2009
www.madamandeve.co.za

THABO...

I MAY HAVE
HAD **MY HEAD**
IN THE SAND...
BUT HE HAS
A **CLOUD**
HANGING OVER
HIS HEAD!

UH,
THABO...

--**WHAT**?!!

RUMBLE!

SAND

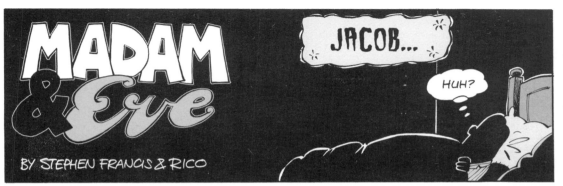

MADAM & Eve

BY STEPHEN FRANCIS & RICO

JACOB...

HUH?

THIS IS YOUR CONSCIENCE SPEAKING...

WAIT A MINUTE! I HAVE A **CONSCIENCE??**

FRANKLY, WE WERE SURPRISED ALSO! BUT, YOU'RE THE ONE WHO CLAIMED "MY CONSCIENCE IS CLEAR!"

I **KNEW** I NEVER SHOULD HAVE SAID THAT! ...WHY? WHAT ARE YOU SAYING? YOU'RE **NOT** CLEAR?

WELL... WHAT ABOUT THE **MILLIONS** SCHABIR GAVE YOU?

LOANS!

THE ILLEGAL TAPES?

THE ARMS DEAL?

LEAKS!

LIES!

YOU TOLD THE MEDIA YOU WANTED YOUR "DAY IN COURT."

I NEVER SAID THAT! I SAID... "I WANTED TO SPEND A **DAY** AT THE **FOOD COURT!** FOOD COURT!!"

...FOOD COURT!!

SHHH... JACOB! HONEY! WAKE UP!!

...HUH? WHAT?!

...YOU WERE HAVING ANOTHER NIGHTMARE ...JUST TRY AND REMEMBER: YOUR CONSCIENCE IS CLEAR!

IT IS? ¿WHEW¿ THANK GOODNESS! MY CONSCIENCE IS CLEAR!

©RAPID PHASE - 2009

WELL... SORRY I WOKE YOU UP. ...GOODNIGHT, DEAR.

GOOD-NIGHT, JACOB.

GOODNIGHT, DEAR.

GOODNIGHT, JACOB.

GOODNIGHT, DEAR.

GOODNIGHT, JACOB.

GOODNIGHT, DEAR.

GOODNIGHT, JACOB.

SIGH

WHAT'S **WRONG**, PRESIDENT MOTLANTHE?

I'LL BE **LEAVING** SOON... AND THIS PLACE HOLDS SO MANY MEMORIES. TRUE, I WAS PRESIDENT FOR ONLY **SEVEN** MONTHS.

...BUT I BELIEVE I WAS **BOLD**. I MADE **DECISIONS** ON MY **OWN**... AND I KNOW HISTORY AND THE PEOPLE, WILL ALWAYS **REMEMBER** ME.

© RAPID PHASE - 2009

...IS WHATSISNAME IN? ZUMA WANTS THE OFFICE REPAINTED.

SIGH I'M GOING TO HATE TO **GIVE UP** THIS OFFICE. SO MANY MEMORIES.

...WAXING NOSTALGIC, **PRESIDENT MOTLANTHE?**

THIS **DESK**...THAT I SAT BEHIND...TO **ALMOST** MAKE **DECISIONS**. THIS **PEN**... THAT I HELD...TO **ALMOST** SIGN LEGISLATION.

© RAPID PHASE - 2009

THIS **DOOR**...WITH MY **NAMEPLATE** THAT--

CLUNK!

PRESIDENT MOTLANTHE

HEY!! ALL THIS TIME -- IT WAS ONLY STUCK ON WITH **PRESSTICK?!**

UH-OH.

WHAT'S WRONG, PRESIDENT MOTLANTHE?

WELL,...FRANKLY, I HAVE TO SAY THAT **JACOB** ORDERING MY OFFICE REPAINTED... IS A LITTLE DISRESPECTFUL.

WELL...IT **IS** ONLY SEVEN DAYS UNTIL THE ELECTION.

...BUT TO HAVE THE OFFICE PAINTED WHILE I'M STILL **IN** IT?

POINT TAKEN, SIR. WOULD YOU LIKE YOUR TEA NOW?

SIGH JUST SLIP IT UNDER THE DROP SHEET.

© RAPID PHASE - 2009

AND IN OTHER NEWS... THE ANC SAID THEY'RE "CONFIDENT OF A HUGE VOTER TURNOUT... BECAUSE ZUMA IS A TSUNAMI."
© RAPID PHASE · 2009
WAIT A SECOND! ZUMA IS A TSUNAMI?!
...I THOUGHT HE WAS A ZULU!!
www.madamandeve.co.za
SLAM!!
EVERYONE GETS SO TENSE BEFORE ELECTIONS.

AND, IN OTHER NEWS.. AS APRIL 22nd DRAWS CLOSER, MORE AND MORE ELECTION POSTERS ARE BEING DEFACED BY GRAFITTI.
© RAPID PHASE · 2009
www.madamandeve.co.za
HOLD IT -- WHAT ARE YOU DOING WITH THAT CAN OF SPRAY PAINT?
...NOTHING.

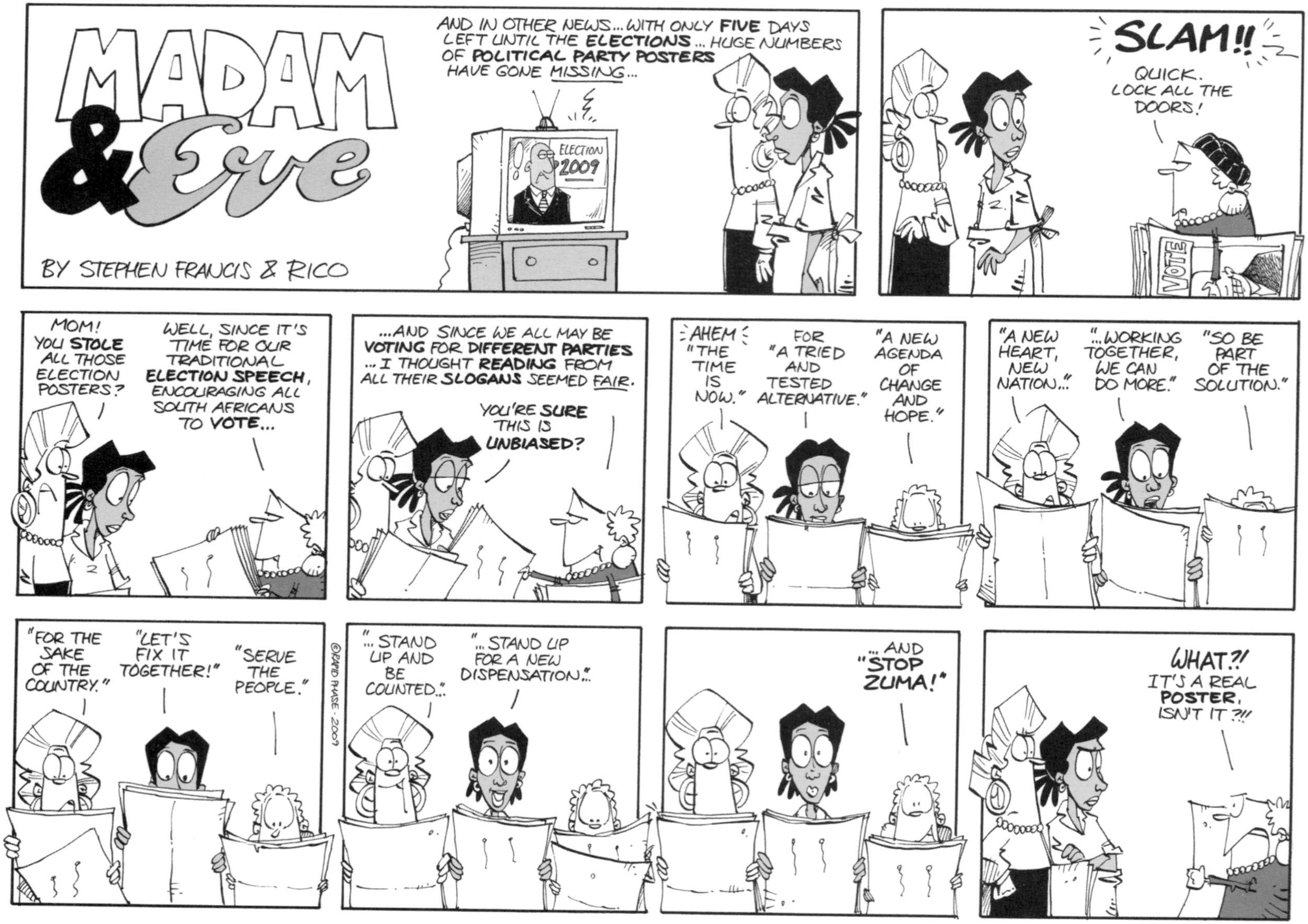
MADAM & Eve
BY STEPHEN FRANCIS & RICO
AND IN OTHER NEWS... WITH ONLY FIVE DAYS LEFT UNTIL THE ELECTIONS... HUGE NUMBERS OF POLITICAL PARTY POSTERS HAVE GONE MISSING...
ELECTION 2009
SLAM!!
QUICK. LOCK ALL THE DOORS!
VOTE
MOM! YOU STOLE ALL THOSE ELECTION POSTERS?
WELL, SINCE IT'S TIME FOR OUR TRADITIONAL ELECTION SPEECH, ENCOURAGING ALL SOUTH AFRICANS TO VOTE...
...AND SINCE WE ALL MAY BE VOTING FOR DIFFERENT PARTIES ... I THOUGHT READING FROM ALL THEIR SLOGANS SEEMED FAIR.
YOU'RE SURE THIS IS UNBIASED?
AHEM "THE TIME IS NOW."
FOR "A TRIED AND TESTED ALTERNATIVE."
"A NEW AGENDA OF CHANGE AND HOPE."
"A NEW HEART, NEW NATION..."
"...WORKING TOGETHER, WE CAN DO MORE."
"SO BE PART OF THE SOLUTION."
"FOR THE SAKE OF THE COUNTRY."
"LET'S FIX IT TOGETHER!"
"SERVE THE PEOPLE."
©RAPID PHASE · 2009
"... STAND UP AND BE COUNTED..."
"... STAND UP FOR A NEW DISPENSATION..."
... AND "STOP ZUMA!"
WHAT?! IT'S A REAL POSTER, ISN'T IT?!!

IT'S WINDY TODAY.
MOM! WATCH OUT FOR THAT ELECTION POSTER!!
CRASH!!
VOTE ANC
www.madamandeve.co.za ©RAPID PHASE - 2009
VOTE ANC
VOTE ANC

VOTE ANC
WORKING TOGETHER WE CAN DO MORE
©RAPID PHASE - 2009
www.madamandeve.co.za
NO WORK
NO FOOD
NO MONEY

VOTE ANC
MOM - WHAT ARE YOU DOING?! IT'S AGAINST THE LAW TO REMOVE ELECTION POSTERS!
©RAPID PHASE - 2009
IT'S ALL RIGHT. ...TOGETHER WE CAN DO MORE...
www.madamandeve.co.za
...ROAD REPAIRS.

YO! TAKE ONE!
YO! TAKE ONE!
©RAPID PHASE·2009
I HATE TO CRITICISE THE IEC…
www.madamandeve.co.za
…BUT MAYBE THIS ISN'T THE BEST WAY TO DISTRIBUTE BALLOT PAPERS.
YO! TAKE ONE.
YO! TAKE ONE!

VOTE ANC
STOP ZUMA
STEM DA
www.madamandeve.co.za
STEM DA
©RAPID PHASE·2009
POSTER TOKOLOSHES! SO THAT'S WHAT HAPPENS TO THEM AFTER THE ELECTIONS!!
MOM!
SHE ASKED.

YOU REALLY THINK THIS WILL WORK?
AT THIS POINT, I'LL TRY **ANYTHING!**
©RAPID PHASE · 2009 www.madamandeve.co.za
Neighbourhood BLOCK WATCHMEN

IF YOU ASK ME, OUR NEIGHBOURHOOD **SECURITY GUARD** IS GETTING **LAX.**
WHAT MAKES YOU SAY THAT?
©RAPID PHASE · 2009 www.madamandeve.co.za
DON'T FORGET TO FILL IN "PURPOSE OF VISIT."

THE NO QUESTIONS ASKED SHOP
WE BUY AND SELL
COPPER WIRE I PODS
Telephone cables
TELEVISIONS LAPTOPS
COMPUTERS Cell Phones
CAR RADIOS CD PLAYERS
DVD players ATM Machines

GUESS WHAT?! I KNOW WHAT I WANT TO BE WHEN I GROW UP!
...WHAT ?
©RAPID PHASE · 2009
A CRONY.
A WHAT?
www.madamandeve.co.za
COME ON -- IT'S IN THE NEWSPAPER COLUMNS ALMOST EVERY DAY--
" GOVERNMENT CRONIES RECEIVE ALL THE TOP JOBS."

THANDI - WHERE'S YOUR HOMEWORK ASSIGNMENT.
I DON'T HAVE IT. ...FRANKLY, I'M JUST AS SURPRISED AS YOU ARE.
...OBVIOUSLY, I'M THE VICTIM OF A POLITICALLY-MOTIVATED PLOT, ORCHESTRATED BY SHADOWY FORCES ATTEMPTING TO MALIGN MY FUTURE SCHOLASTIC ACHIEVEMENT.
©RAPID PHASE · 2008
MAYBE I CAN TALK HIM INTO DROPPING THE CHARGES.
PRINCIPAL

EVE!! YOU DIDN'T DO THE VACUUMING!!
I CAN'T! IT'S ELECTION DAY!!
...IT'S FREEDOM DAY!!
www.madamandeve.co.za
...IT'S WORKER'S DAY!!
©RAPID PHASE · 2009
HAPPY DAYS ARE HERE AGAIN.

CAN YOU HELP ME WITH MY HOMEWORK?

: SIGH :

"QUESTION ONE: GIVE ONE EXAMPLE OF AN OXYMORON."

©RAPID PHASE - 2009

FOLLOW ME.

...WORKER'S DAY.

: SIGH :
I DON'T KNOW, DOCTOR. IT'S ALL THESE LONG HOLIDAY WEEKENDS...

GO ON...

"FREEDOM DAY"... "WORKER'S DAY"... MY MAID'S HALFWAY OUT THE DOOR ALREADY.

GO ON...

NOBODY'S MIND IS ON THEIR WORK. EVERYONE TAKES OFF EARLY. RIGHT, DOCTOR? ...DOCTOR?

GO ON...

©RAPID PHASE - 2009

...BUT HURRY UP. MY WIFE AND I WANT TO BEAT THE TRAFFIC.

: SLAM! :

©RAPID PHASE - 2009

www.madamandeve.co.za

...YOU ASK HER HOW HER THREE-DAY WEEKEND WAS.

109

YOU OWE ME TEN BUCKS.
HOW DO YOU FIGURE?
WELL, YOU KNOW HOW -- WHENEVER I ASK IF I CAN **BORROW** TEN BUCKS, YOU ALWAYS SAY "YES -- WHEN PIGS FLY?"
...SO?
GUESS WHAT? THE **SWINE FLEW!** -- IT'S ALL OVER THE NEWS!
©RAPID PHASE · 2009
...MAYBE I'M MISSING SOMETHING HERE.

"Let me in!" cried the Wolf.
NOT BY THE HAIR OF MY CHINNY CHIN-CHIN!
©RAPID PHASE · 2009
"Then I'll HUFF and I'll PUFF... and... I'll..."
COUGH! COUGH!
COUGH!
COUGH!
ACHOO!!
HACK!
COUGH!
COUGH!
The wolf caught the SWINE FLU, the Three Little Pigs went "WEE WEE WEE ACHOO!" all the way to HONG KONG.
SOMEHOW I SEEM TO REMEMBER IT DIFFERENTLY.
MOM!!

KNOCK! KNOCK!
WHO'S THERE?
WE'RE FROM THE DEPARTMENT OF HEALTH! WE NEED TO CHECK YOUR HOUSE FOR **SWINE FLU**!
www.madamandeve.co.za
YEAH. SURE. NOW GO PUT AN **EGG** IN YOUR SHOES... AND **BEAT IT!!**
©RAPID PHASE · 2009
...**TOLD** YOU IT WOULDN'T WORK!

MEELEETH!!
"MEELEETH?"
MEELEETH!!
©RAPID PHASE · 2009
MEELEETH!!
www.madamandeve.co.za
SWINE FLU MASKS
Only 10 Rand

...BETTER ACT NOW. THEY'RE GOING FAST.
SWINE FLU MASKS
Only 10 Rand
©RAPID PHASE · 2009
SIGH OKAY. I'LL TAKE ONE.
WOULD YOU LIKE IT PERSONALLY CUSTOMISED? TWO BUCKS EXTRA.
PERSONALLY CUSTOMISED? WHAT DO YOU MEAN "PERSONALLY CUSTOMISED?"
www.madamandeve.co.za

DO YOU THINK I **OVER-PROMISED** DURING MY STATE OF THE NATION ADDRESS?
NOT AT ALL, PRESIDENT ZUMA.
©RAPID PHASE · 2009
...CREATING **500 000 NEW JOBS** BY DECEMBER IS A PIECE OF CAKE, SIR.
www.madamandeve.co.za
WITHOUT HIRING ANY **FRIENDS** OR **RELATIVES?**
WELL, SIR. THAT **DOES** COMPLICATE THINGS A LITTLE.

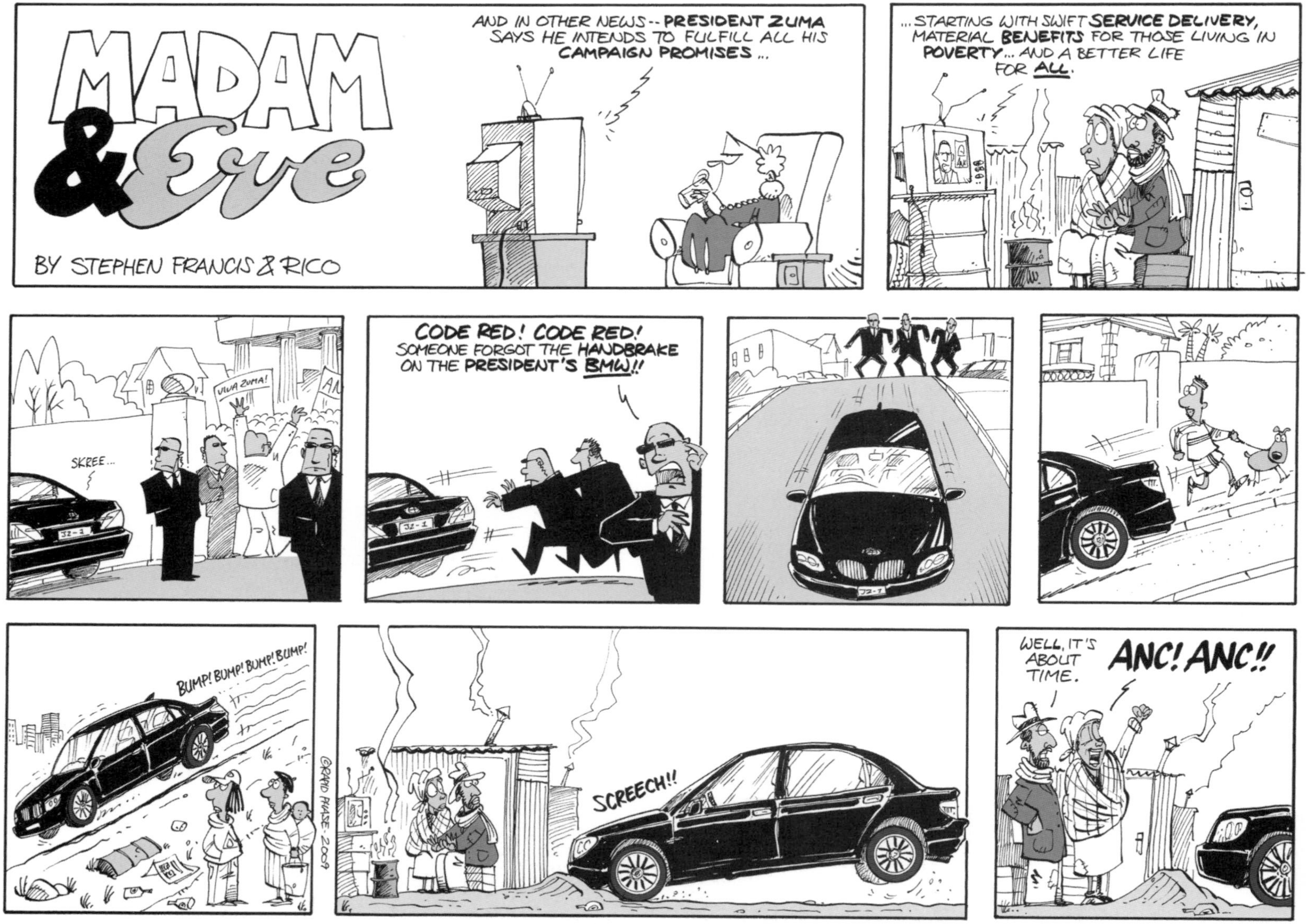
MADAM & Eve
BY STEPHEN FRANCIS & RICO
AND IN OTHER NEWS -- PRESIDENT ZUMA SAYS HE INTENDS TO FULFILL ALL HIS CAMPAIGN PROMISES ...
... STARTING WITH SWIFT SERVICE DELIVERY, MATERIAL BENEFITS FOR THOSE LIVING IN POVERTY ... AND A BETTER LIFE FOR ALL.
SKREE...
CODE RED! CODE RED! SOMEONE FORGOT THE HANDBRAKE ON THE PRESIDENT'S BMW!!
BUMP! BUMP! BUMP! BUMP!
SCREECH!!
WELL, IT'S ABOUT TIME.
ANC! ANC!!

COMING UP... "HOW LONG WILL ZUMA'S NEW HONEYMOON PERIOD LAST?
HE GOT MARRIED AGAIN?!
IN THIS INSTANCE "HONEYMOON PERIOD" REFERS TO THE LENGTH OF TIME PEOPLE OVERLOOK A PRESIDENT'S NON-DELIVERY.
HOW LONG WAS PRESIDENT MBEKI'S "HONEYMOON PERIOD?"
©RAPID PHASE - 2009
EIGHT YEARS.
MOM!!

AND IN OTHER NEWS, PRESIDENT ZUMA SAID THAT FROM NOW ON, THIS IS THE ERA OF COMPETENCE AND HARD WORK.
...LAZINESS AND NON-PERFORMANCE WILL NOT BE TOLERATED.
©RAPID PHASE - 2009
WILL YOU STOP DOING THAT?!

...AS PRESIDENT ZUMA RECENTLY SAID... "NOW THE REAL WORK BEGINS!"
©RAPID PHASE - 2009 www.madamandeve.co.za
ME TOO!! FROM NOW ON... THE REAL WORK BEGINS!
WHAT THE HELL HAS SHE BEEN DOING ALL THESE YEARS?

IF ZUMA APPOINTED EVE TO HIS CABINET... WHAT DO YOU THINK SHE'D BE?
©RAPID PHASE - 2009
...DEFINITELY NOT MINISTER OF ENERGY.

OKAY CLASS! YOU HAVE 45 MINUTES TO COMPLETE YOUR BIOLOGY EXAM. READY? BEGIN.
"QUESTION ONE: THROUGH CELLULAR DIVISION, IT CAN LITERALLY MULTIPLY OVERNIGHT RESULTING IN GREATLY INCREASED NUMBERS."
©RAPID PHASE - 2009
www.madamandeve.co.za
"PRESIDENT ZUMA'S CABINET."

GOOD NEWS, EVE. THE HOUSEHOLD ELECTION RESULTS ARE IN. I'M PRESIDENT.
...AND I'VE DECIDED TO APPOINT MOM AS MY DEPUTY PRESIDENT.
CONGRATULATIONS. ...WHAT ABOUT ME?
www.madamandeve.co.za
YOU? I'M COUNTING ON YOU TO RESTRUCTURE THE CABINET.
©RAPID PHASE 2009

GOOD NEWS, EVE! AS **PRESIDENT** OF THIS HOUSEHOLD, I'VE FINALLY DECIDED ON MY NEW **CABINET**!
www.madamandeve.co.za
CONGRATULATIONS! YOU'RE MY NEW "MINISTER OF DOMESTIC MAINTENANCE!"
WOW.
©RAPID PHASE · 2009
...DOES IT COME WITH A BIG **WAGE INCREASE**?
POSSIBLY.
...BUT YOU'LL HAVE TO TAKE IT UP WITH MY NEW "MINISTER OF YOU MUST BE JOKING."

CONGRATULATIONS, EVE, ON YOUR APPOINTMENT AS "MINISTER OF DOMESTIC MAINTENANCE."
THANK YOU.
VROO
OOM!
©RAPID PHASE · 2009
www.madamandeve.co.za
VROOOM!
WHO'S THAT?
OH. THAT'S MY NEW **DEPUTY** MINISTER.

WHO'S THAT?
WELL, SINCE YOU APPOINTED ME "**MINISTER OF DOMESTIC MAINTENANCE**" I FIGURED I'D NEED A NEW **DEPUTY** MINISTER.
THAT'S RIDICULOUS.
IS IT?! GO ASK HELEN ZILLE AND HER **ALL-MALE CABINET**!!
©RAPID PHASE · 2009
www.madamandeve.co.za
...AND WHO WAS **THAT**?
MY NEW **SPOKES-PERSON**.

I WAS THINKING YOU COULD MAKE ME A **PRESENT** OF FIVE BUCKS.
BECAUSE...
I JUST READ THAT THE **MINISTER OF TRANSPORT** ACCEPTED A R 1.1 MILLION **MERCEDES BENZ** FROM A BUNCH OF GRATEFUL CONTRACTORS.
...SO I FIGURE GIVING **ME** A LOUSY **FIVE BUCKS** SHOULDN'T BE A PROBLEM.
©RAPID PHASE · 2009 www.madamandeve.co.za
MAYBE SHE FAILED TO SEE THE CORRELATION.

WHAT REALLY HAPPENED...
HAVE YOU DECIDED WHAT TO DO YET, MINISTER?
NOT YET. IT'S A DIFFICULT CHOICE.
KEEP THE MERCEDES... OR GIVE **BACK** THE MERCEDES...
©RAPID PHASE · 2008
KEEP THE MERCEDES...
VROOOOM!!

Guaranteed style.
Guaranteed class.
©RAPID PHASE · 2009 www.madamandeve.co.za
Guaranteed future lucrative contracts.
Mercedes Benz S500
The next best thing to having a relative in government.

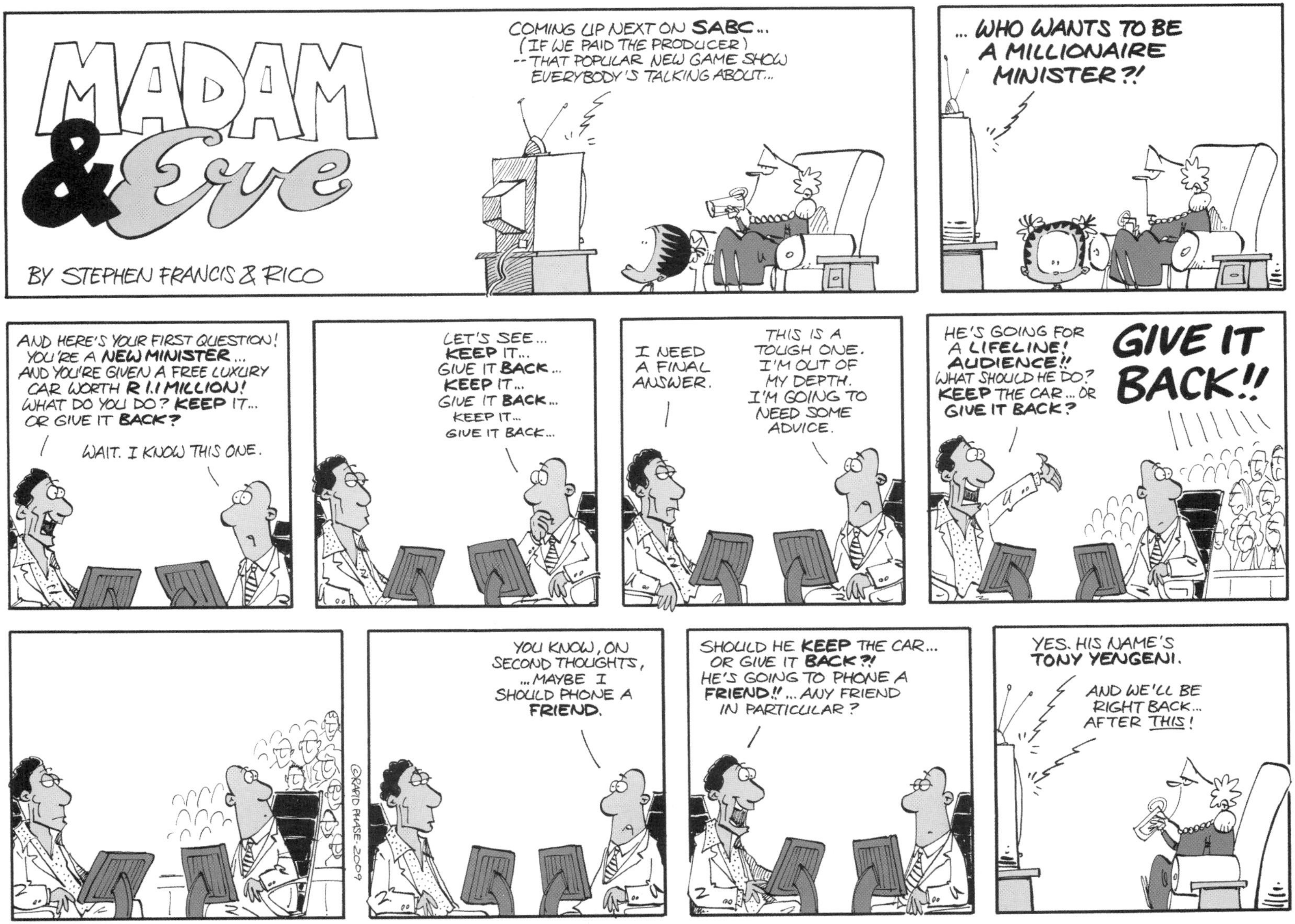
MADAM & Eve
BY STEPHEN FRANCIS & RICO
COMING UP NEXT ON SABC... (IF WE PAID THE PRODUCER) --THAT POPULAR NEW GAME SHOW EVERYBODY'S TALKING ABOUT...
... WHO WANTS TO BE A MILLIONAIRE MINISTER?!
AND HERE'S YOUR FIRST QUESTION! YOU'RE A NEW MINISTER... AND YOU'RE GIVEN A FREE LUXURY CAR WORTH R1.1 MILLION! WHAT DO YOU DO? KEEP IT... OR GIVE IT BACK?
WAIT. I KNOW THIS ONE.
LET'S SEE... KEEP IT... GIVE IT BACK... KEEP IT... GIVE IT BACK... KEEP IT... GIVE IT BACK...
I NEED A FINAL ANSWER.
THIS IS A TOUGH ONE. I'M OUT OF MY DEPTH. I'M GOING TO NEED SOME ADVICE.
HE'S GOING FOR A LIFELINE! AUDIENCE!! WHAT SHOULD HE DO? KEEP THE CAR... OR GIVE IT BACK?
GIVE IT BACK!!
©RAPID PHASE 2009
YOU KNOW, ON SECOND THOUGHTS, ...MAYBE I SHOULD PHONE A FRIEND.
SHOULD HE KEEP THE CAR... OR GIVE IT BACK?! HE'S GOING TO PHONE A FRIEND!! ... ANY FRIEND IN PARTICULAR?
YES. HIS NAME'S TONY YENGENI.
AND WE'LL BE RIGHT BACK... AFTER THIS!

... AND COMING UP NEXT... A NEW SERIES NOBODY'S EVER **HEARD** OF, BUT WE BOUGHT IT ANYWAY...
... FOLLOWED BY A LOCAL **SITCOM**... UNLESS THE PRODUCERS PULLED IT BECAUSE THEY HAVEN'T BEEN **PAID** YET...
www.madamandeve.co.za
... WHICH WOULD USUALLY BE FOLLOWED BY **NEWS**... BUT I JUST HEARD THE DIRECTOR QUIT...
©RAPID PHASE · 2009
... WHICH **REMINDS** ME. IF ANYONE KNOWS OF ANOTHER "PRESENTER" JOB... HERE'S MY C.V.
BOY, MORALE AT THE **SABC** IS GETTING REALLY LOW.

COMING UP NEXT... THAT POPULAR SITCOM, "**ONE AND A HALF MEN.**"
AHEM
©RAPID PHASE · 2009 www.madamandeve.co.za
... FORMERLY "**TWO** AND A HALF MEN" ... BUT WE HAD TO LET ONE OF THEM **GO**, DUE TO CASH FLOW PROBLEMS.
COULD SOMEBODY PLEASE **BAIL OUT** THE **SABC**?!!

HUH? SHE'S **SINGLE?** WHY, SHE GOT MARRIED **SIX MONTHS** AGO!
©RAPID PHASE · 2009
WAIT A MINUTE -- **THAT** GUY FELL DOWN A MINE SHAFT! HE'S BEEN DEAD FOR OVER **THREE YEARS!**
www.madamandeve.co.za
-- AND WE'LL BE BACK -- WITH MORE **ISIDINGO RE-RUNS** SHOWN IN NO PARTICULAR ORDER.
WILL SOMEONE PLEASE BAIL OUT THE **SABC**?!!

...AND DON'T MISS THE NEXT EPISODE OF "THE BOLD AND THE BEAUTIFUL."
UH... SORRY. I MEANT "THE BOLD." DUE TO BUDGET CONSTRAINTS WE COULDN'T AFFORD "THE BEAUTIFUL."
...THEN THAT POPULAR SOAP "SOME OF MY CHILDREN" ...FOLLOWED BY "STRICTLY COME SKIPPING."
AND NOW, UP NEXT... "NOT SO SPECIAL ASSIGNMENT."
WILL SOMEONE PLEASE BAIL OUT THE SABC?!
www.madamandeve.co.za
©RAPID PHASE · 2009

THIS JUST IN -- A MOB OF ANGRY PRODUCERS HAVE JUST STORMED THE GATES OF THE SABC BECAUSE THE BROADCASTER OWES THEM MONEY.
ACCORDING TO REPORTS, THE PRODUCERS HAVE BROKEN THROUGH THE MAIN DOORS AND ARE BEGINNING TO OVERRUN THE --
PAY NOW!
NO!! I'M ON YOUR SIDE! THEY HAVEN'T PAID ME EITHER!!
GET GO OF MY TIE! IT'S SPONSORED!!
FINALLY! NOW THIS IS GOOD TELEVISION!!
www.madamandeve.co.za
©RAPID PHASE · 2009

LOOK AT ALL THOSE BODYGUARDS!
THAT GOVERNMENT OFFICIAL MUST REALLY NEED PROTECTION.
ROUTE TO CAR--CLEAR!
CHECK THE ROOFTOPS!
www.madamandeve.co.za
©RAPID PHASE · 2009
WHO IS IT? A MINISTER? AN AMBASSADOR?
...SABC BOARD MEMBER.
INCOMING!!

AND IN OTHER NEWS, A BUSINESSMAN INTENDS OFFERING PRESIDENT ZUMA **ONE BILLION RANDS** IN ORDER TO FIGHT **CRIME**.
www.madamandeve.co.za ©RAPID PHASE · 2009
FORMER PRESIDENT **MBEKI** TURNED THE DEAL DOWN, SAYING "WE DON'T HAVE A PROBLEM WITH **CRIME** IN THIS COUNTRY... WE HAVE A PROBLEM WITH **PERCEPTION** OF CRIME."
IS THAT TRUE? WE HAVE A PROBLEM WITH **PERCEPTION** OF CRIME?
WELL...
...ALL I KNOW IS THAT A COUPLE OF **PERCEPTIONS** STOLE OUR TV LAST MONTH.
MOM!!

WHAT ARE YOU WATCHING?
IT'S A NEW AFTERNOON PROGRAMME ON **SABC**.
...DAILY LESSONS TO HELP STUDENTS PREPARE FOR THEIR MATRIC EXAMS.
THE "**SABC EDUCATIONAL CHANNEL**", HUH? WHAT SUBJECT IS ON NOW?
©RAPID PHASE · 2009 www.madamandeve.co.za
"**ACCOUNTING AND BUSINESS ETHICS**."
QUICK! GIVE ME THE REMOTE!

SIR, THE **PRODUCERS** AND ACTORS ARE STILL AT THE GATES!!
THROW OUT ANOTHER ACCOUNTANT.
SABC
WE ALREADY GAVE THEM **THREE**, SIR.
RIGHT! THEN IT'S TIME FOR "OPERATION FISHING POLE!"
www.madamandeve.co.za
IS THAT A **REAL** COMPANY **CHEQUE** ON THE LINE?
YEP.
©RAPID PHASE · 2009
THAT'S **COLD**, SIR.
...YOU WANT TO KEEP YOUR **JOB** OR **NOT?!**

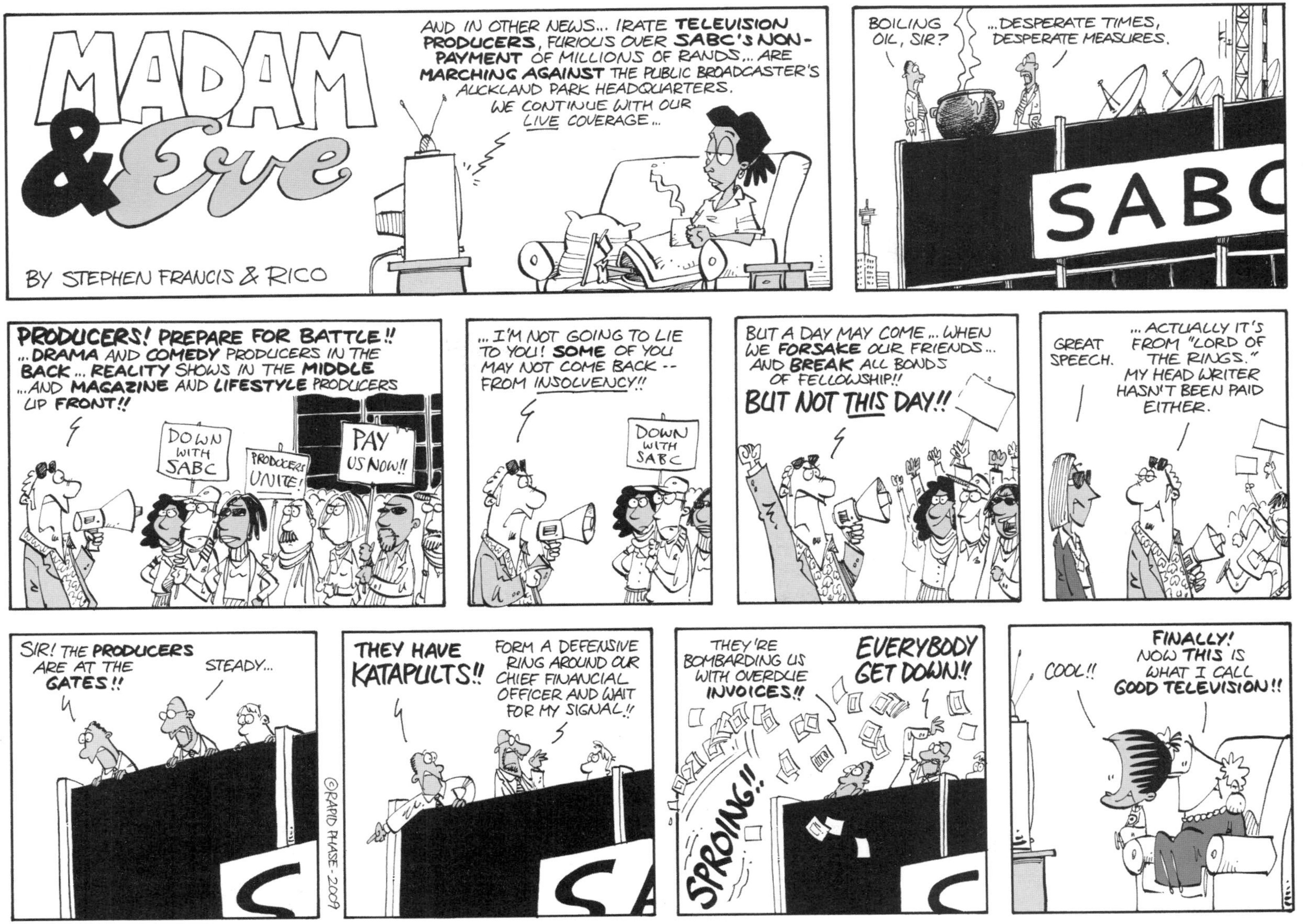
MADAM & Eve
BY STEPHEN FRANCIS & RICO
AND IN OTHER NEWS... IRATE TELEVISION PRODUCERS, FURIOUS OVER SABC'S NON-PAYMENT OF MILLIONS OF RANDS... ARE MARCHING AGAINST THE PUBLIC BROADCASTER'S AUCKLAND PARK HEADQUARTERS. WE CONTINUE WITH OUR LIVE COVERAGE...
BOILING OIL, SIR?
...DESPERATE TIMES, DESPERATE MEASURES.
SABC
PRODUCERS! PREPARE FOR BATTLE!! ...DRAMA AND COMEDY PRODUCERS IN THE BACK... REALITY SHOWS IN THE MIDDLE ...AND MAGAZINE AND LIFESTYLE PRODUCERS UP FRONT!!
DOWN WITH SABC
PRODUCERS UNITE!
PAY US NOW!!
...I'M NOT GOING TO LIE TO YOU! SOME OF YOU MAY NOT COME BACK -- FROM INSOLVENCY!!
DOWN WITH SABC
BUT A DAY MAY COME... WHEN WE FORSAKE OUR FRIENDS... AND BREAK ALL BONDS OF FELLOWSHIP!!
BUT NOT THIS DAY!!
GREAT SPEECH.
...ACTUALLY IT'S FROM "LORD OF THE RINGS." MY HEAD WRITER HASN'T BEEN PAID EITHER.
SIR! THE PRODUCERS ARE AT THE GATES!!
STEADY...
©RAPID PHASE-2009
THEY HAVE KATAPULTS!!
FORM A DEFENSIVE RING AROUND OUR CHIEF FINANCIAL OFFICER AND WAIT FOR MY SIGNAL!!
THEY'RE BOMBARDING US WITH OVERDUE INVOICES!!
EVERYBODY GET DOWN!!
SPROING!!
COOL!!
FINALLY! NOW THIS IS WHAT I CALL GOOD TELEVISION!!

LOOK AT THIS! THEY JUST **REDEPLOYED** A GOVERNMENT OFFICIAL.
WHAT'S "REDEPLOYED?"
WELL, YOU KNOW HOW YOUR COUSIN VUSI WAS REALLY **BAD** AT HIS JOB OF **STEALING CARS?**
YEAH?
©RAPID PHASE · 2009
NOW, HE ONLY **BLOWS UP ATM'S.**
YEAH?
www.madamandeve.co.za
... **THAT'S** REDEPLOYMENT.
GOTCHA.

SINCE THE ELECTION, **MINISTERS** HAVE BEEN RUSHING OUT TO BUY THE MOST **EXPENSIVE** LUXURY CARS THE **MINISTERIAL HANDBOOK** WILL ALLOW.
©RAPID PHASE · 2009
"... **MINISTERIAL HANDBOOK?!**" -- I'D LOVE TO GET A LOOK AT THAT.
Congratulations!
YOU'RE A MINISTER!
CHAPTER ONE: "WELCOME TO THE BLUE LIGHT CLUB!"
MOM!! ARE YOU DAY-DREAMING AGAIN?!

MR PREMIER -- IS IT **TRUE** THAT **R 500.000.000** IN **GOVERNMENT TENDERS** WERE ILLEGALLY AWARDED TO **SPOUSES** OR **RELATIVES?**
www.madamandeve.co.za
ABSOLUTELY NOT!!
BANG!!
©RAPID PHASE · 2009
CRASH!!
CALL MY COUSIN'S FURNITURE COMPANY. TELL HIM HE'S IN **BIG** TROUBLE.
YES, SIR.

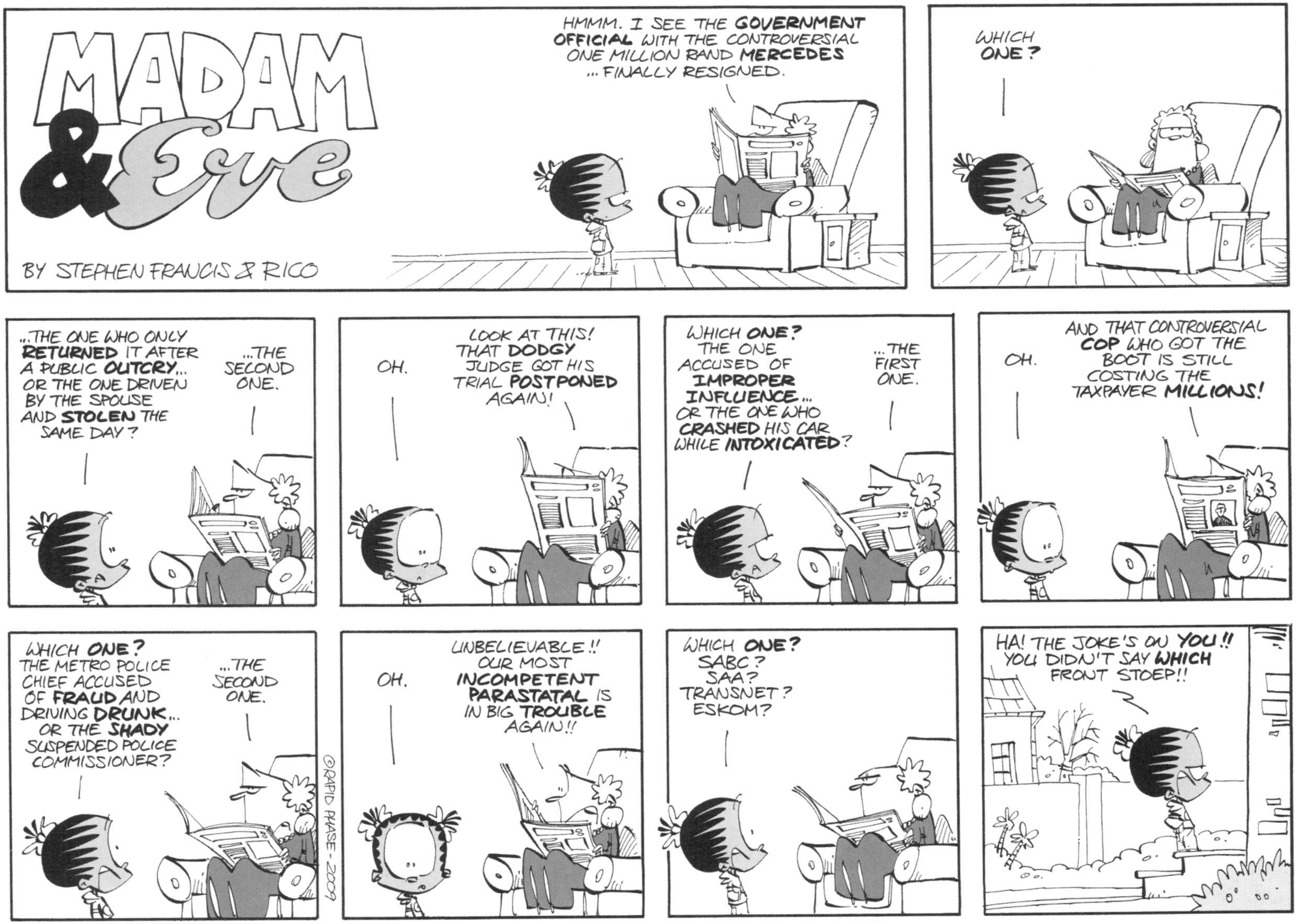
MADAM & Eve
BY STEPHEN FRANCIS & RICO
HMMM. I SEE THE GOVERNMENT OFFICIAL WITH THE CONTROVERSIAL ONE MILLION RAND MERCEDES ... FINALLY RESIGNED.
WHICH ONE?
...THE ONE WHO ONLY RETURNED IT AFTER A PUBLIC OUTCRY... OR THE ONE DRIVEN BY THE SPOUSE AND STOLEN THE SAME DAY?
...THE SECOND ONE.
LOOK AT THIS! THAT DODGY JUDGE GOT HIS TRIAL POSTPONED AGAIN!
OH.
WHICH ONE? THE ONE ACCUSED OF IMPROPER INFLUENCE... OR THE ONE WHO CRASHED HIS CAR WHILE INTOXICATED?
...THE FIRST ONE.
AND THAT CONTROVERSIAL COP WHO GOT THE BOOT IS STILL COSTING THE TAXPAYER MILLIONS!
OH.
WHICH ONE? THE METRO POLICE CHIEF ACCUSED OF FRAUD AND DRIVING DRUNK... OR THE SHADY SUSPENDED POLICE COMMISSIONER?
...THE SECOND ONE.
©RAPID PHASE - 2009
UNBELIEVABLE!! OUR MOST INCOMPETENT PARASTATAL IS IN BIG TROUBLE AGAIN!!
OH.
WHICH ONE? SABC? SAA? TRANSNET? ESKOM?
HA! THE JOKE'S ON YOU!! YOU DIDN'T SAY WHICH FRONT STOEP!!

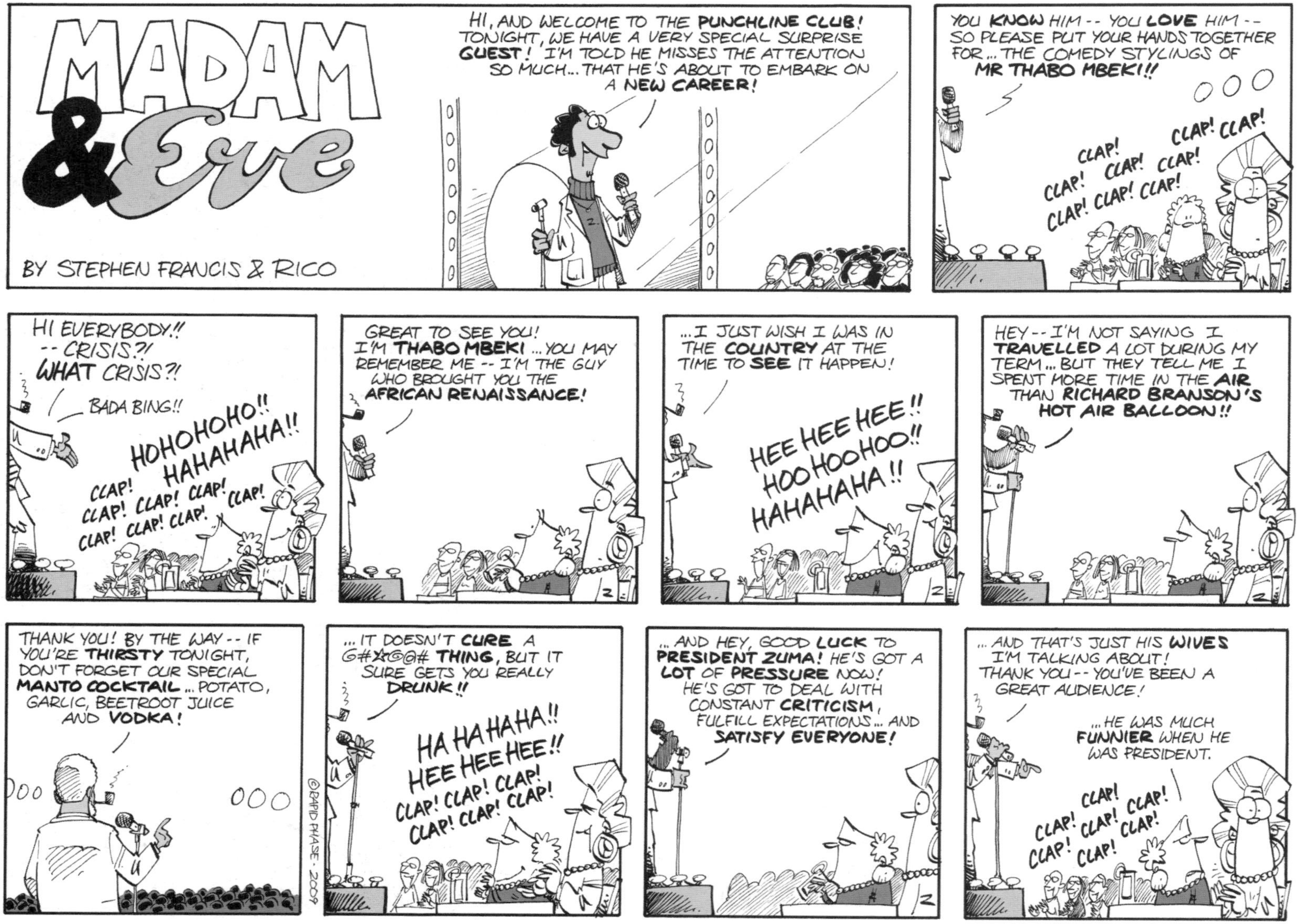
MADAM & Eve
BY STEPHEN FRANCIS & RICO
HI, AND WELCOME TO THE PUNCHLINE CLUB! TONIGHT, WE HAVE A VERY SPECIAL SURPRISE GUEST! I'M TOLD HE MISSES THE ATTENTION SO MUCH... THAT HE'S ABOUT TO EMBARK ON A NEW CAREER!
YOU KNOW HIM -- YOU LOVE HIM -- SO PLEASE PUT YOUR HANDS TOGETHER FOR... THE COMEDY STYLINGS OF MR THABO MBEKI!!
CLAP! CLAP! CLAP! CLAP! CLAP! CLAP! CLAP! CLAP! CLAP! CLAP!
HI EVERYBODY!! -- CRISIS?! WHAT CRISIS?!
BADA BING!!
HOHOHOHO!! HAHAHAHA!!
CLAP! CLAP! CLAP! CLAP! CLAP! CLAP! CLAP! CLAP!
GREAT TO SEE YOU! I'M THABO MBEKI ... YOU MAY REMEMBER ME -- I'M THE GUY WHO BROUGHT YOU THE AFRICAN RENAISSANCE!
... I JUST WISH I WAS IN THE COUNTRY AT THE TIME TO SEE IT HAPPEN!
HEE HEE HEE!! HOO HOO HOO!! HAHAHAHA!!
HEY -- I'M NOT SAYING I TRAVELLED A LOT DURING MY TERM... BUT THEY TELL ME I SPENT MORE TIME IN THE AIR THAN RICHARD BRANSON'S HOT AIR BALLOON!!
THANK YOU! BY THE WAY -- IF YOU'RE THIRSTY TONIGHT, DON'T FORGET OUR SPECIAL MANTO COCKTAIL... POTATO, GARLIC, BEETROOT JUICE AND VODKA!
©RAPID PHASE · 2009
... IT DOESN'T CURE A G#☆@@# THING, BUT IT SURE GETS YOU REALLY DRUNK!!
HA HA HA HA!! HEE HEE HEE!!
CLAP! CLAP! CLAP! CLAP! CLAP! CLAP!
... AND HEY, GOOD LUCK TO PRESIDENT ZUMA! HE'S GOT A LOT OF PRESSURE NOW! HE'S GOT TO DEAL WITH CONSTANT CRITICISM, FULFILL EXPECTATIONS... AND SATISFY EVERYONE!
... AND THAT'S JUST HIS WIVES I'M TALKING ABOUT! THANK YOU -- YOU'VE BEEN A GREAT AUDIENCE!
... HE WAS MUCH FUNNIER WHEN HE WAS PRESIDENT.
CLAP! CLAP! CLAP! CLAP! CLAP! CLAP! CLAP!

Panel 1: GUESS WHAT?... I JUST BOOKED SEXWALE AND MANUEL TO SPEAK AT MY BOOK CLUB.

Panel 2: **TOKYO** SEXWALE AND **TREVOR** MANUEL?! | ACTUALLY, IT'S **BOB** SEXWALE AND **VUSI** MANUEL. THEY LIVE DOWN THE ROAD. TREVOR AND TOKYO ARE FAR TOO **BUSY.**

Panel 3: BUT NEXT MONTH WE'VE BOOKED **MBEKI** AS OUR GUEST SPEAKER. **THABO** MBEKI?!

www.madamandeve.co.za

Panel 4: YEP.

©RAPID PHASE - 2009

Panel 5: LET ME RUN SOMETHING BY YOU: FIRST OFF, YOU GIVE ME **FIVE RANDS.**

www.madamandeve.co.za

Panel 6: THEN, **TOMORROW** I GIVE YOU BACK **SEVEN RANDS!** ...THAT'S A TWO RAND PROFIT ON A FIVE BUCK INVESTMENT.

©RAPID PHASE - 2009

Panel 7: OKAY, IT'S A **PONZI SCHEME.** BUT BEING AN EARLY INVESTOR, YOU'RE AT THE BOTTOM OF THE **PYRAMID** SO YOU'RE GOLDEN.

Panel 8: **SLAM!!** ...TOLD YOU THIS NEEDED **POWERPOINT!!**

Panel 9: DO YOU KNOW WHO **ELVIS PRESLEY** WAS? OF COURSE.

Panel 10: ...WASN'T HE THAT SOUTH AFRICAN SINGER WHO WORKED IN THE CIVIL SERVICE? **CIVIL SERVICE?!**

©RAPID PHASE - 2009

Panel 11: SURE! HE HAD THAT BIG HIT-- **"LOVE MY TENDER."**

Panel 12: WELL, I BET **YOU** DON'T KNOW WHO THE BLACK-EYED PEAS ARE, EITHER!!

FREEZE!!
GASP
BEFORE I TAKE YOUR MONEY-- FIRST: ARE YOU TWO FROM OVERSEAS?
NO. WE'RE PROUDLY SOUTH AFRICAN! WHY?
WE'RE DOING OUR PART TO PROMOTE SOUTH AFRICA'S REPUTATION AS A CRIME-FREE ENVIRONMENT, ESPECIALLY DURING INTERNATIONAL SPORTING EVENTS.
IT'S OKAY TO ROB THEM! THEY'RE JUST LOCALS!
I USED TO LIVE IN ENGLAND. DOES THAT COUNT?
©RAPID PHASE - 2009

09:20am
Have found the perfect car to hijack.
09:40am
We are on route to the chop shop with our white mercedes, license VST1106GP.
WHOOOOO!!
09:45am
We hear loud sirens behind us on the M1.
©RAPID PHASE - 2009
www.madamandeve.co.za
09:46am
For some unknown reason, the police have found us.
ARE YOU ON TWITTER AGAIN?!

TIC TIC TIC
SCREECH!!
©RAPID PHASE - 2009
www.madamandeve.co.za
MADAM!! TEXTING WHILE DRIVING IS DANGEROUS!!
I KNOW! WHEW THAT WAS A CLOSE ONE.
...WAIT TILL I TELL MOM!!

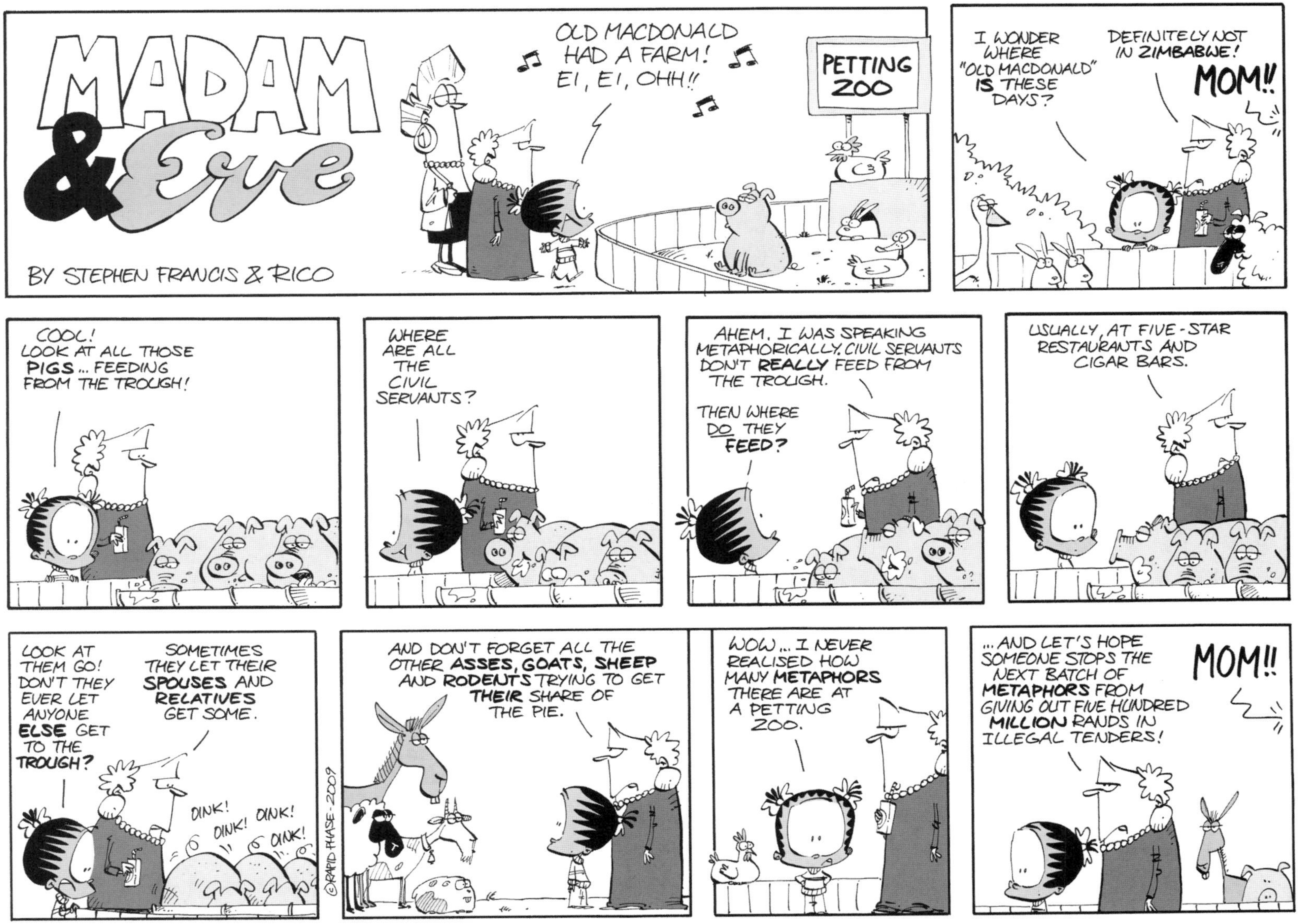
MADAM & Eve
BY STEPHEN FRANCIS & RICO
OLD MACDONALD HAD A FARM! EI, EI, OHH!!
PETTING ZOO
I WONDER WHERE "OLD MACDONALD" IS THESE DAYS?
DEFINITELY NOT IN ZIMBABWE!
MOM!!
COOL! LOOK AT ALL THOSE PIGS... FEEDING FROM THE TROUGH!
WHERE ARE ALL THE CIVIL SERVANTS?
AHEM. I WAS SPEAKING METAPHORICALLY. CIVIL SERVANTS DON'T REALLY FEED FROM THE TROUGH.
THEN WHERE DO THEY FEED?
USUALLY, AT FIVE-STAR RESTAURANTS AND CIGAR BARS.
LOOK AT THEM GO! DON'T THEY EVER LET ANYONE ELSE GET TO THE TROUGH?
SOMETIMES THEY LET THEIR SPOUSES AND RELATIVES GET SOME.
OINK! OINK! OINK! OINK!
©RAPID PHASE · 2009
AND DON'T FORGET ALL THE OTHER ASSES, GOATS, SHEEP AND RODENTS TRYING TO GET THEIR SHARE OF THE PIE.
WOW... I NEVER REALISED HOW MANY METAPHORS THERE ARE AT A PETTING ZOO.
...AND LET'S HOPE SOMEONE STOPS THE NEXT BATCH OF METAPHORS FROM GIVING OUT FIVE HUNDRED MILLION RANDS IN ILLEGAL TENDERS!
MOM!!

HMM... YOU'RE **LUCKY** THIS TIME. NO CAVITIES.
www.madamandeve.co.za
©RAPID PHASE · 2009
BUT STAY AWAY FROM **SWEETS** AND EAT LOTS OF FRUIT AND VEGETABLES.
THANKS, DOC.
DOCTORS ON STRIKE
UNFAIR WAGES!
BY THE WAY-- IS THERE A **DERMATOLOGIST** HERE? I'VE BEEN GETTING A **RASH** ON MY LOWER **BUTTOCK**.
MORE PAY!!
DON'T PUSH YOUR LUCK.
STRIK

SCALPEL...
CLAMP... STAPLER... BLACK MARKER...
©RAPID PHASE · 2009
WELL?
GOOD JOB, DOCTOR. GET SOME REST. I'LL TAKE IT FROM HERE.
ON STRIKE! MORE PAY!

I'M AFRAID I HAVE GOOD NEWS AND BAD NEWS. WHICH DO YOU WANT TO HEAR FIRST?
G-GIVE ME THE **BAD** NEWS.
YOU HAVE A VERY, VERY SERIOUS ILLNESS.
GASP! THEN... WHAT COULD POSSIBLY BE THE **GOOD** NEWS?
www.madamandeve.co.za
I THINK THEY'RE FINALLY AGREEING TO OUR 50% WAGE INCREASE!
©RAPID PHASE · 2009
DOCTOR STRIKE, MD.
A NEW MINISERIES FOR TELEVISION. COMING SOON TO SABC. ...MAYBE.

WHAT ARE YOU LEARNING AT SCHOOL THESE DAYS?
LET'S SEE...
www.madamandeve.co.za
HOPSCOTCH, JUMP ROPE, AND BARBIE IN THE MORNING... AND THEN TELEVISION AND VIDEO GAMES IN THE AFTERNOON.
WHAT KIND OF SYLLABUS DO THEY CALL THAT?!
©RAPID PHASE - 2009
THEY DON'T. OUR TEACHER'S ON STRIKE AGAIN.

BLAM!! POW!! BANG!!
BE SURE NOT TO MISS TOMORROW'S EPISODE: "BATMAN STRIKES BACK!"
©RAPID PHASE - 2009
ON STRIKE!
MORE PAY!
JOKER UNFAIR
THIS CULTURE OF STRIKING IS REALLY GETTING OUT OF HAND.

GASP
NO... IT CAN'T BE!!
©RAPID PHASE - 2009
THERE MUST BE SOME MISTAKE! IT'S ALL SO UNFAIR!!
www.madamandeve.co.za
WHY ME?? WHY ME?!!
AAAAH!!
...TEACHER'S STRIKE JUST ENDED.

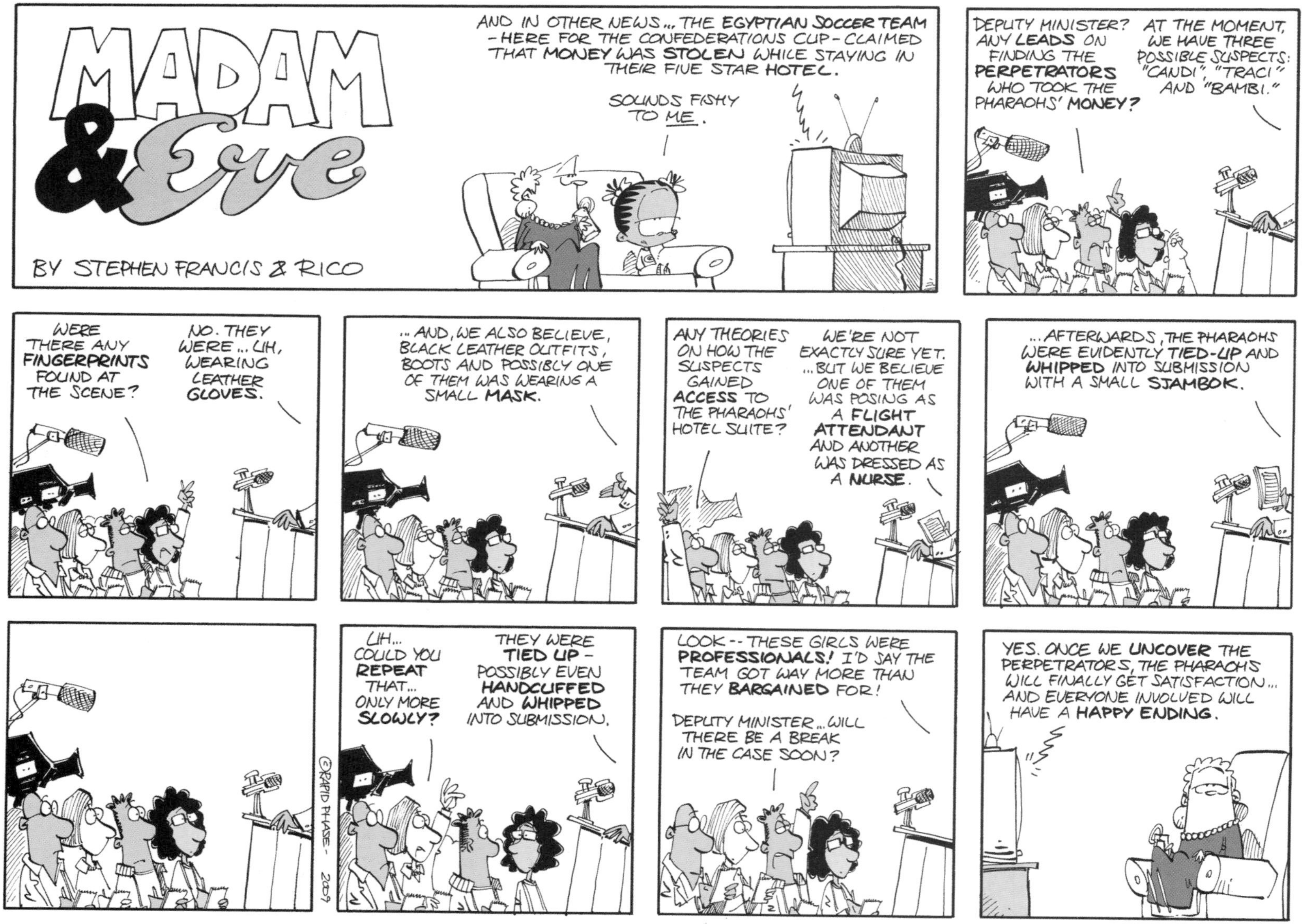
MADAM & Eve
BY STEPHEN FRANCIS & RICO
AND IN OTHER NEWS... THE EGYPTIAN SOCCER TEAM - HERE FOR THE CONFEDERATIONS CUP - CLAIMED THAT MONEY WAS STOLEN WHILE STAYING IN THEIR FIVE STAR HOTEL.
SOUNDS FISHY TO ME.
DEPUTY MINISTER? ANY LEADS ON FINDING THE PERPETRATORS WHO TOOK THE PHARAOHS' MONEY?
AT THE MOMENT, WE HAVE THREE POSSIBLE SUSPECTS: "CANDI", "TRACI" AND "BAMBI."
WERE THERE ANY FINGERPRINTS FOUND AT THE SCENE?
NO. THEY WERE... UH, WEARING LEATHER GLOVES.
... AND, WE ALSO BELIEVE, BLACK LEATHER OUTFITS, BOOTS AND POSSIBLY ONE OF THEM WAS WEARING A SMALL MASK.
ANY THEORIES ON HOW THE SUSPECTS GAINED ACCESS TO THE PHARAOHS' HOTEL SUITE?
WE'RE NOT EXACTLY SURE YET. ...BUT WE BELIEVE ONE OF THEM WAS POSING AS A FLIGHT ATTENDANT AND ANOTHER WAS DRESSED AS A NURSE.
...AFTERWARDS, THE PHARAOHS WERE EVIDENTLY TIED-UP AND WHIPPED INTO SUBMISSION WITH A SMALL SJAMBOK.
©RAPID PHASE - 2009
UH... COULD YOU REPEAT THAT... ONLY MORE SLOWLY?
THEY WERE TIED UP - POSSIBLY EVEN HANDCUFFED AND WHIPPED INTO SUBMISSION.
LOOK -- THESE GIRLS WERE PROFESSIONALS! I'D SAY THE TEAM GOT WAY MORE THAN THEY BARGAINED FOR!
DEPUTY MINISTER... WILL THERE BE A BREAK IN THE CASE SOON?
YES. ONCE WE UNCOVER THE PERPETRATORS, THE PHARAOHS WILL FINALLY GET SATISFACTION... AND EVERYONE INVOLVED WILL HAVE A HAPPY ENDING.

CHECK OUT THESE RECENT EVENTS! FIRST, PRESIDENT OBAMA GOES TO CAIRO...
THEN... A BIG PYRAMID SCHEME COLLAPSED.
AND AFTER THAT, A BUNCH OF PHARAOHS GET THEIR MONEY STOLEN FROM A FIVE STAR HOTEL.
©RAPID PHASE · 2009
THERE'S GOT TO BE A CONNECTION!
GO HOME TO MUMMY!!

www.madamandeve.co.za
©RAPID PHASE · 2009
WHERE'S EVE?
SHE TOOK THE DAY OFF.
THEN WHO ARE YOU?
I'M YOUR INTERIM MAID.
WHERE'S SHE GOING?
INTERIM TEA BREAK.

COME BACK. COME... COME... COME... COME... COME...
COME... COME...
CRASH!
©RAPID PHASE · 2009
Eskom
NO ELECTRICITY TARIFF INCREASE!

MOM - ARE YOU SURE THOSE ARE COMFORTABLE WALKING SHOES?
YEP! ...GOT YOUR WATER BOTTLE?
www.madamandeve.co.za
YEP.
WHERE ARE YOU TWO GOING?
MEGAWATT PARK! WE HEARD THERE'S A BIG ESKOM HIKE -- AND WE DON'T WANT TO MISS IT!
©RAPID PHASE · 2009
YOU TELL THEM. ...I'M STILL ON MY TEA BREAK.
FORWARD HO! HUP! HUP! HUP! HUP!

PRESIDENT ZUMA... SIR, WHAT HAPPENS IF WE DON'T REACH THE 500 000 NEW JOBS BY DECEMBER YOU PROMISED?
SIMPLE.
©RAPID PHASE · 2009
...WE DOUBLE DOWN! AND I PROMISE ONE MILLION NEW JOBS BY APRIL!!
www.madamandeve.co.za
UH, AND IF WE DON'T REACH THAT TARGET, SIR.
WE ADMIT WE CAUGHT A BAD FLOP, WE KEEP RAISING AND BLUFF UNTIL WE GET TO SEVENTH STREET.
...SIR?
...ONLINE POKER. MY WIVES LOVE IT.

©RAPID PHASE · 2009
SHAME. MOM'S DOING A FINAL **MOONWALK** IN MICHAEL JACKSON'S MEMORY.
NOT REALLY. I JUST WASHED THE KITCHEN FLOOR.

AND IN OTHER NEWS, A LIFELIKE **HOLOGRAM** OF MICHAEL JACKSON WILL PERFORM FOR FANS ON A LONDON STAGE NEXT MONTH.
A HOLOGRAM?
©RAPID PHASE · 2009
CAN YOU BELIEVE THAT, EVE? WHAT IDIOT WOULD WANT TO WATCH A **PERFORMING HOLOGRAM?!**
... EVE?
YOU HAVE TO ADMIT IT LOOKS REAL.
NO WONDER THE RUG NEVER LOOKED PROPERLY VACUUMED.

Panel 1: EVE -- THERE'S NO TELLING WHEN THIS **RECESSION** WILL END. WE NEED TO TIGHTEN OUR BELTS.

Panel 2: (©RAPID PHASE - 2009)

Panel 3: I ALREADY **TIGHTENED** MINE. SEE?

Panel 4: -- AND STOP **WEARING MY BELTS**!!

Panel 5: AND THEY'RE OFF!! IT'S **MASSIVE UNEMPLOYMENT** COMING OUT OF THE GATE! MASSIVE UNEMPLOYMENT... FOLLOWED BY LONGTERM RECESSION AND BELT TIGHTENING! (©RAPID PHASE - 2009)

Panel 6: AND COMING INTO THE HOME STRETCH... THEY'RE NECK AND NECK! IT'S MASSIVE UNEMPLOYMENT... BELT TIGHTENING... AND WAIT -- HERE COMES **PRICE HIKE**!! (www.madamandeve.co.za)

Panel 7: ...AND IT'S A **PHOTO-FINISH!** MASSIVE UNEMPLOYMENT AND BELT TIGHTENING... FOLLOWED BY PRICE HIKE, LONGTERM RECESSION... REPOSSESSION... AND FINALLY BANKRUPTCY AND LIQUIDATION BRINGING UP THE REAR!

Panel 8: WHAT ARE YOU WATCHING?

DURBAN JULY.

Panel 9: I JUST INVENTED A NEW **CHOCOLATE BAR**. I CALL IT A "CREDIT CRUNCH."

Panel 10: A "**CREDIT CRUNCH**?"

IT'S THIN, BITTERSWEET AND DEFINITELY NOT SUGAR-COATED. (©RAPID PHASE - 2009)

Panel 11: ...AND WHEN YOU GET TO THE END, YOU'RE MOSTLY LEFT WITH **PEANUTS**.

Panel 12: SOUNDS FATTENING.

NOT AT ALL. IN FACT, AFTERWARDS YOU HAVE TO TIGHTEN YOUR BELT.

WISHING WELL
I WISH...
SPLISH!
I WISH THIS RECESSION WAS OVER ALREADY!
©RAPID PHASE - 2009

AND IN OTHER NEWS... PRESIDENT ZUMA ARRIVED IN LYBIA THIS WEEK TO ATTEND A MAJOR SUMMIT.
WHAT'S A "SUMMIT?"
IT'S WHEN A BUNCH OF PEOPLE GET TOGETHER AND SPEND THE ENTIRE DAY TALKING WITHOUT ACTUALLY DOING ANYTHING.
I WISH I COULD BE PART OF A "SUMMIT."
YOU CAN.
EVE HOLDS ONE EVERY DAY IN THE KITCHEN DURING TEA BREAK.
www.madamandeve.co.za
©RAPID PHASE - 2009

LOOK AT THIS PAMPHLET... "RUNNING WATER." "RUNNING WATER (PURIFIED)."
"ELECTRICITY (SQ)"
"HOUSING: LARGE, MEDIUM AND ECONOMY SIZE."
...WHAT KIND OF A TAKE-AWAY MENU IS THIS?!
"MISTER SERVICE DELIVERY."
www.madamandeve.co.za
©RAPID PHASE - 2009

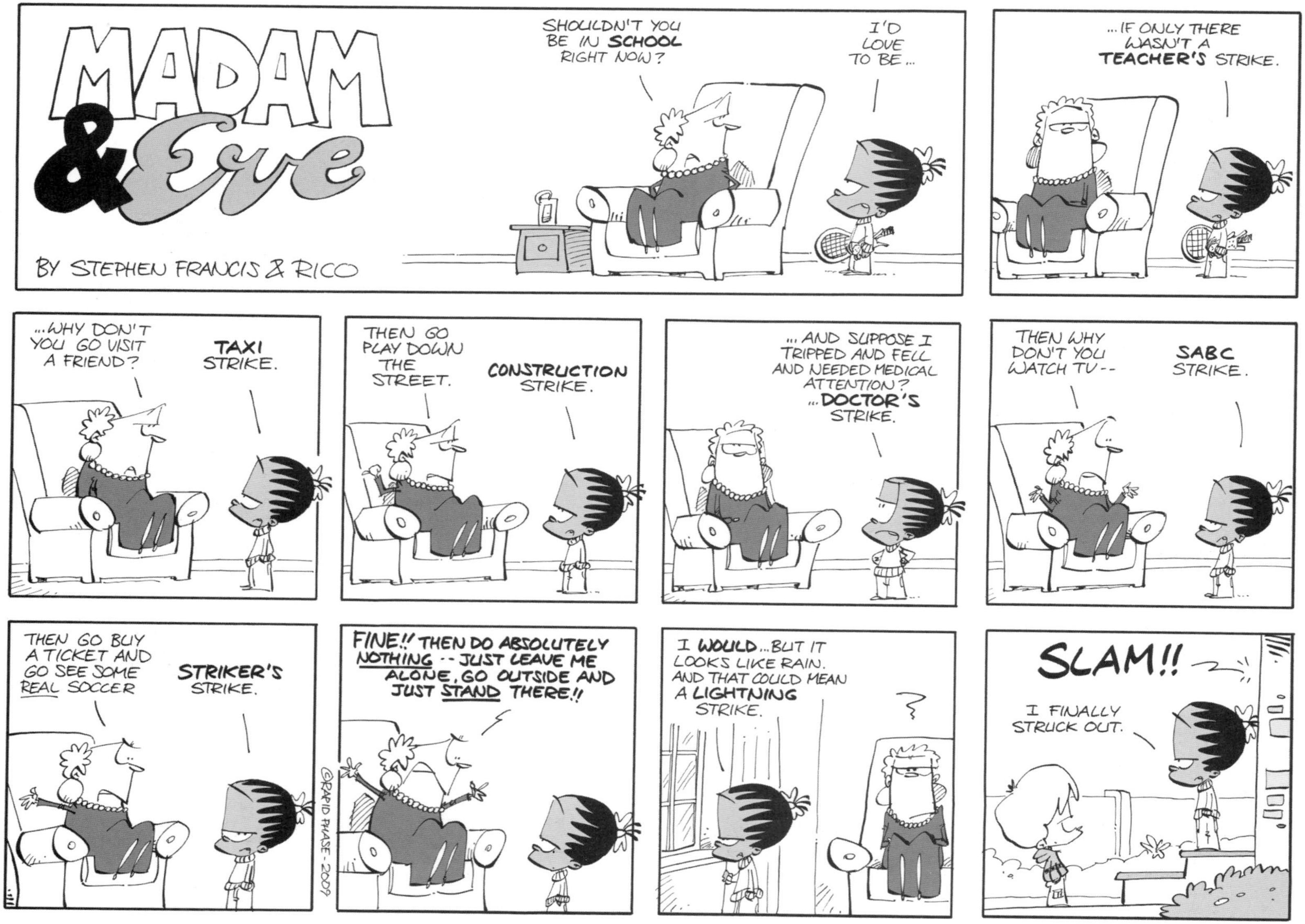
MADAM & Eve
BY STEPHEN FRANCIS & RICO
SHOULDN'T YOU BE IN SCHOOL RIGHT NOW?
I'D LOVE TO BE...
...IF ONLY THERE WASN'T A TEACHER'S STRIKE.
...WHY DON'T YOU GO VISIT A FRIEND?
TAXI STRIKE.
THEN GO PLAY DOWN THE STREET.
CONSTRUCTION STRIKE.
...AND SUPPOSE I TRIPPED AND FELL AND NEEDED MEDICAL ATTENTION? ...DOCTOR'S STRIKE.
THEN WHY DON'T YOU WATCH TV--
SABC STRIKE.
THEN GO BUY A TICKET AND GO SEE SOME REAL SOCCER
STRIKER'S STRIKE.
©RAPID PHASE · 2007
FINE!! THEN DO ABSOLUTELY NOTHING -- JUST LEAVE ME ALONE, GO OUTSIDE AND JUST STAND THERE!!
I WOULD...BUT IT LOOKS LIKE RAIN. AND THAT COULD MEAN A LIGHTNING STRIKE.
?
SLAM!!
I FINALLY STRUCK OUT.

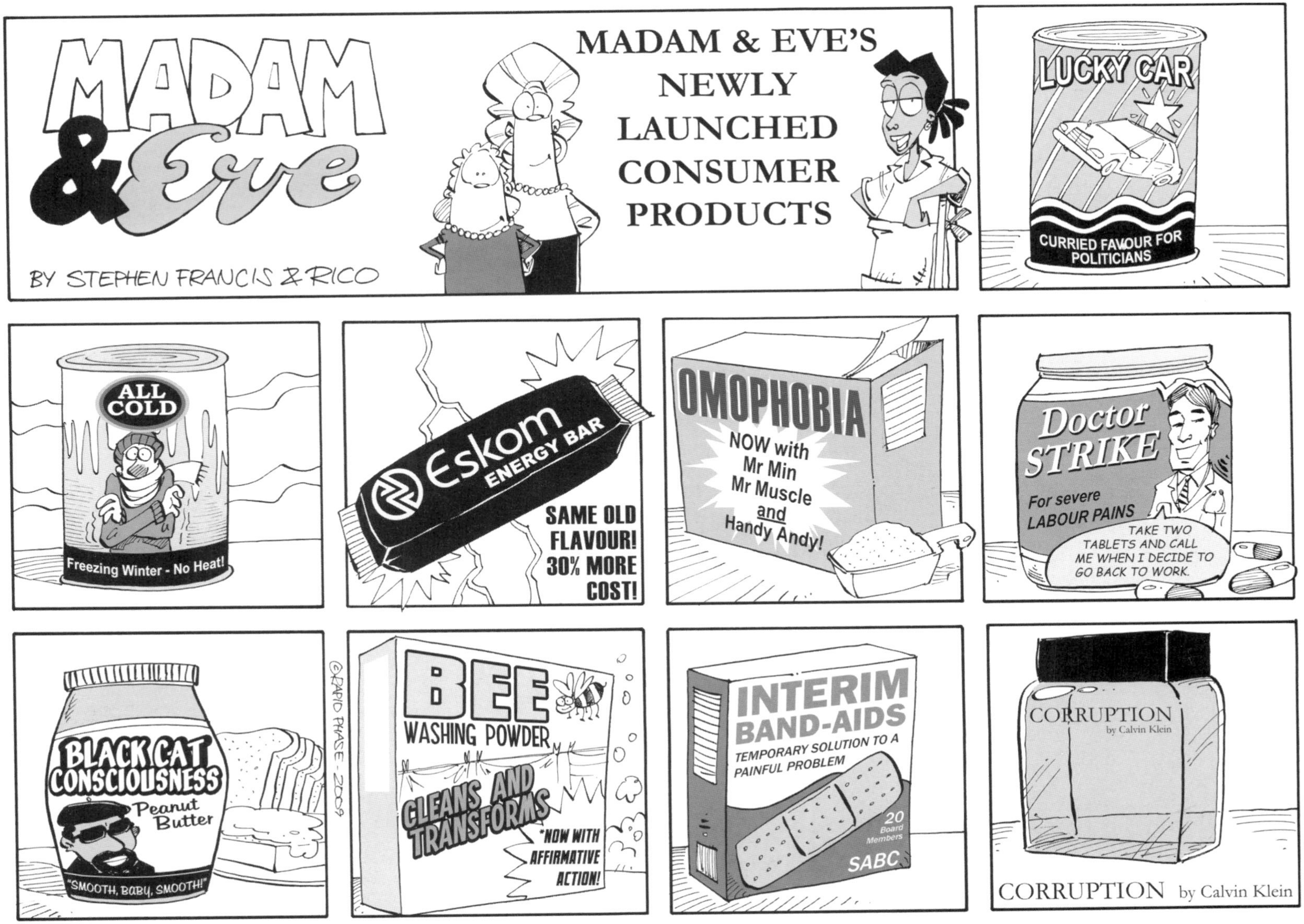
MADAM & EVE
BY STEPHEN FRANCIS & RICO
MADAM & EVE'S NEWLY LAUNCHED CONSUMER PRODUCTS
LUCKY CAR
CURRIED FAVOUR FOR POLITICIANS
ALL COLD
Freezing Winter - No Heat!
Eskom ENERGY BAR
SAME OLD FLAVOUR! 30% MORE COST!
OMOPHOBIA
NOW with Mr Min Mr Muscle and Handy Andy!
Doctor STRIKE
For severe LABOUR PAINS
TAKE TWO TABLETS AND CALL ME WHEN I DECIDE TO GO BACK TO WORK.
BLACK CAT CONSCIOUSNESS
Peanut Butter
"SMOOTH, BABY, SMOOTH!"
©RAPID PHASE - 2009
BEE
WASHING POWDER
CLEANS AND TRANSFORMS
*NOW WITH AFFIRMATIVE ACTION!
INTERIM BAND-AIDS
TEMPORARY SOLUTION TO A PAINFUL PROBLEM
20 Board Members
SABC
CORRUPTION by Calvin Klein
CORRUPTION by Calvin Klein

MADAM!!
EVE IS GOOD!! EVE IS FUNNY!!
EVE WORKS HARD! SHE DESERVES MORE MONEY!!
www.madamandeve.co.za ©RAPID PHASE - 2008
SHE HIRED A PRAISE SINGER?
RAISE SINGER.

HEEHEE! HOOHOO! HAHAHA!!
WHAT'S SO FUNNY?
GWEN JUST GOT THIS SMS.
"PLEASE DON'T FORGET TO PAY YOUR TV LICENSE."
BWAHAHAHA! HEEHEEHEE!! HAHAHAHAHA!! HOHOHO!!

AND IN OTHER NEWS, MEMBERS OF SABC MANAGEMENT WILL BE ATTENDING A SPECIAL TWO-WEEK BOSBERAAD...
...IN AN ATTEMPT TO DISCOVER WHY THE PARASTATAL LOSES SO MUCH MONEY.
www.madamandeve.co.za
THE SABC BOSBERAAD WILL BEGIN IN PARIS, FRANCE.
©RAPID PHASE · 2009
...WITH FURTHER MEETINGS IN MAURITIUS, RIO DE JANEIRO ...AND FINALLY NEW YORK CITY.

MIELLLIES!!
©RAPID PHASE · 2009
www.madamandeve.co.za
Mielies.com
Supplying all your Mielie needs online!
WE DELIVER!

EVE!! WHAT ARE YOU DOING IN THE KITCHEN?!
TEA BREAK!
CRASH!!
AND WHAT WAS THAT?!
©RAPID PHASE · 2009
...CUP BREAK.

THIS G#☆G☆ CHAIR!!
MOM!! WATCH YOUR MOUTH!!
AND WHY SHOULD I?!
©RAPID PHASE · 2009
...BECAUSE SOMEBODY MIGHT HEAR YOU!
WHO? I'M OUT HERE ALONE!
HARDEE G#☆G☆ DAW!!
HARDEE G#☆G☆ DAW!!

NO WORK NO MONEY
NO PURSE NO CHANGE
©RAPID PHASE · 2009 www.madamandeve.co.za
NO RANDS? NO COINS?
NO WAY, NO HOW!
SOMETIMES YOU HAVE TO KNOW HOW TO **TALK** TO PEOPLE.

DOOR CLOSED ON ACCOUNT OF WEATHER
BAM! BAM! BAM!
WHAT'S THIS SIGN MEAN: "CLOSED ON ACCOUNT OF WEATHER?"
©RAPID PHASE · 2009 www.madamandeve.co.za
CLOSED ON ACCOUNT OF **WEATHER** EVE FEELS LIKE GETTING UP TO **ANSWER** IT OR NOT.

LOOK MOM! OUR NEW GARDENER'S ALREADY PLANTED A **VEGETABLE GARDEN**!
"PEAS." "CARROTS." "ONIONS." "POTATOES."
©RAPID PHASE · 2009
"MADAM, YOU FORGOT TO PAY ME AGAIN THIS MONTH."
MUST BE A NEW VEGETABLE.

MADAM & Eve

BY STEPHEN FRANCIS & RICO

Hello. I am the new A-1000 and I'll be your ATM tonight. Would you like a little **pepper** with your transaction?

Just joking.

Please stand motionless for **palm** and **retina** scan.

WHIRRRRR

Beginning voice verification. Please repeat after me: I would like to open up a new expensive banking account.

I WOULD LIKE TO OPEN UP A NEW EXPENSIVE BANKING ACCOUNT.

© RAPID PHASE 2009

State your PIN number for our records.

EXCUSE ME ??!!

Trick question. Please stand in front of screen for **facial recognition**.

You look a little thin. have you been **eating** properly?

GIVE ME MY MONEY!! **NOW**!!

Your tone is unacceptable. Initiating mild **pepper spray**.

SPRITZ!!

YOU'RE IN BIG TROUBLE, BUSTER! ...I'LL BE BACK.

Hasta la vista, baby.

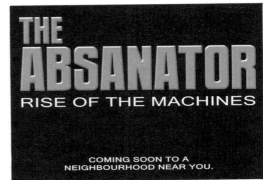

THE ABSANATOR
RISE OF THE MACHINES

COMING SOON TO A NEIGHBOURHOOD NEAR YOU.

TODAY, IN AN OUTSIDE PRESS CONFERENCE, SAPS OFFICIALLY LAUNCHED THEIR NEW ELITE UNIT "THE HAWKS", INTRODUCING THEIR NEW MASCOT.
GO! SPREAD YOUR WINGS FOR JUSTICE AND FLY!!
ZAP!!
©RAPID PHASE 2009
I TOLD YOU TO TURN OFF THE ELECTRIC FENCE.

WE RETURN WITH MORE LIVE COVERAGE ...AS THE SAPS LAUNCHES THEIR NEW ELITE CRIMEFIGHTING UNIT, "THE HAWKS."
LADIES AND GENTLEMEN... MEET OUR NEW MASCOT... SOON TO STRIKE FEAR INTO THE HEARTS OF CRIMINALS EVERYWHERE!!
GO! SPREAD YOUR WINGS FOR JUSTICE AND FLY!!
FLAP! FLAP! FLAP!
HEY!! COME BACK WITH MY PURSE!

NEXT QUESTION!
WHY DID THE SAPS DECIDE TO CALL THEIR NEW ELITE UNIT "THE HAWKS?"
...BECAUSE, LIKE HAWKS... JUST WHEN YOU LEAST EXPECT IT... THEY STRIKE!!
©RAPID PHASE - 2009
...MAYBE YOU SHOULD HAVE CALLED THEM "THE DOCTORS."
HEE-HEE.
HEH-HEH.
I HATE THE MEDIA.

AND... IN AN EFFORT TO KEEP HIS PROMISE TO "STAY IN TOUCH WITH THE PEOPLE"... PRESIDENT ZUMA WILL BE POSTING DAILY COMMENTS ON TWITTER.
TWEET!
©RAPID PHASE - 2009
Hi there! It's President Zuma. How'd you like to follow me around and see what I do all day?
First, in the interest of transparency... time for a shower! :-)
GWEN!!

YOU'RE NOT GOING TO BELIEVE THIS! PRESIDENT ZUMA STARTED TWEETING!
"TWEETING."
©RAPID PHASE - 2009
THE PRESIDENT STARTED "TWEETING..."
TWEETING: WRITING SHORT MESSAGES PEOPLE CAN SEE ON THEIR COMPUTERS AND CELLPHONES.
WHY DIDN'T SOMEBODY JUST SAY THAT?!

Hi. President Zuma here.
©RAPID PHASE - 2009
I'll be posting comments on Twitter today in the interest of transparency.
But please don't tell my wives. They think I should be out doing something about the service delivery riots.
JACOB!! ARE YOU TWEETING AGAIN?!!
UH-OH. GOTTA GO.

WE'RE LEARNING ABOUT COLLECTIVE NOUNS IN SCHOOL. ...KNOW ANY?
www.madamandeve.co.za
"A SCHOOL OF FISH."
"A PRIDE OF LIONS."
©RAPID PHASE · 2009
"A MURDER OF CROWS."
"A GAGGLE OF GEESE."
"A MERCEDES OF MINISTERS."
MOM!!

HOW MUCH IS THAT BEEMER IN THE WINDOW?
THE ONE WITH THE EXTRAS AND CHROME?
HOW MUCH IS THAT BEEMER IN THE WINDOW?
A MINISTER'S TAKING YOU HOME!

THE LONG WAIT FOR DELIVERY
WELL. IT'S ABOUT TIME.

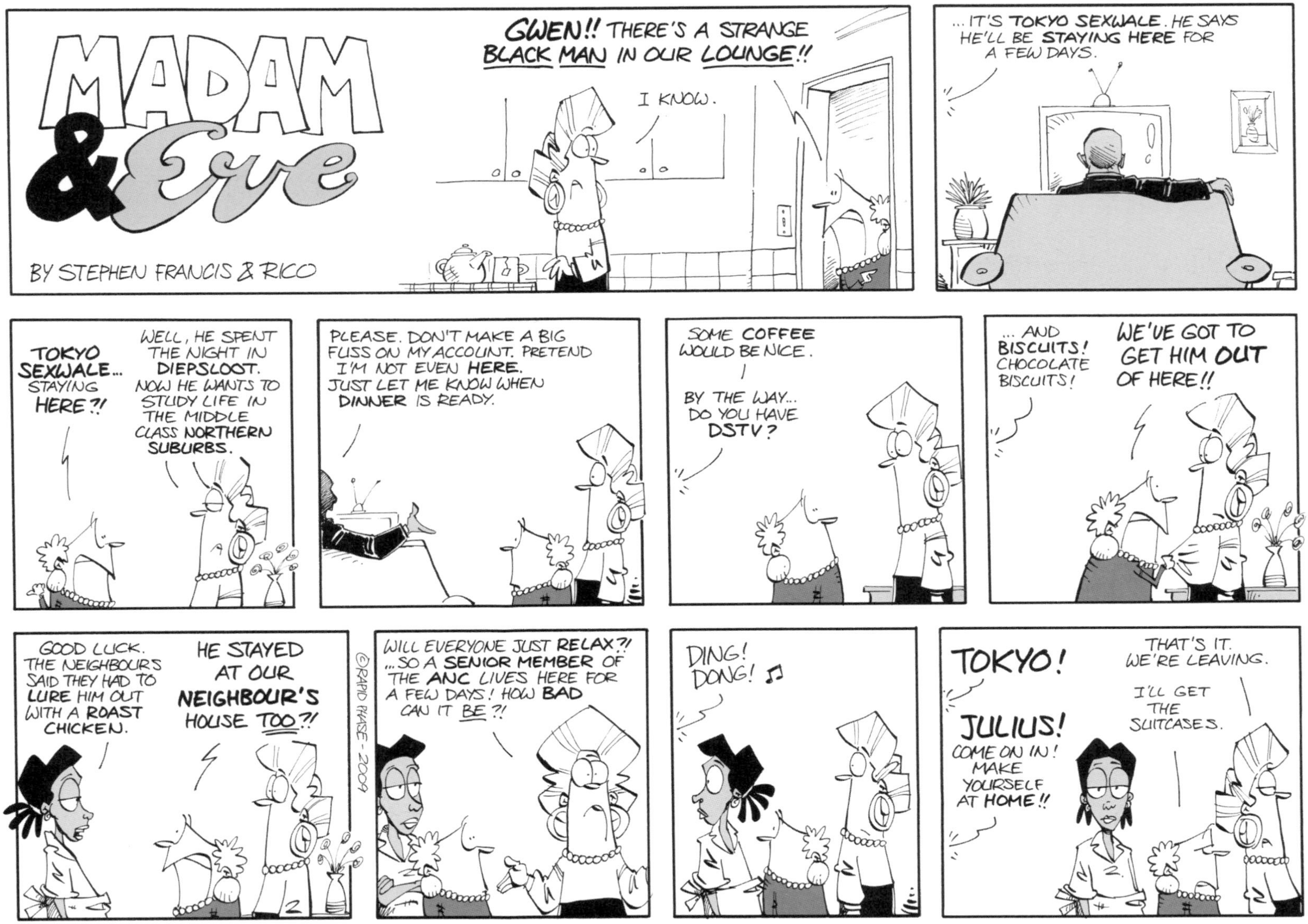
MADAM & Eve
BY STEPHEN FRANCIS & RICO
GWEN!! THERE'S A STRANGE BLACK MAN IN OUR LOUNGE!!
I KNOW.
...IT'S TOKYO SEXWALE. HE SAYS HE'LL BE STAYING HERE FOR A FEW DAYS.
TOKYO SEXWALE... STAYING HERE?!
WELL, HE SPENT THE NIGHT IN DIEPSLOOT. NOW HE WANTS TO STUDY LIFE IN THE MIDDLE CLASS NORTHERN SUBURBS.
PLEASE. DON'T MAKE A BIG FUSS ON MY ACCOUNT. PRETEND I'M NOT EVEN HERE. JUST LET ME KNOW WHEN DINNER IS READY.
SOME COFFEE WOULD BE NICE.
BY THE WAY... DO YOU HAVE DSTV?
... AND BISCUITS! CHOCOLATE BISCUITS!
WE'VE GOT TO GET HIM OUT OF HERE!!
GOOD LUCK. THE NEIGHBOURS SAID THEY HAD TO LURE HIM OUT WITH A ROAST CHICKEN.
HE STAYED AT OUR NEIGHBOUR'S HOUSE TOO?!
©RAPID PHASE - 2009
WILL EVERYONE JUST RELAX?! ...SO A SENIOR MEMBER OF THE ANC LIVES HERE FOR A FEW DAYS! HOW BAD CAN IT BE?!
DING! DONG! ♫
TOKYO!
JULIUS! COME ON IN! MAKE YOURSELF AT HOME!!
THAT'S IT. WE'RE LEAVING.
I'LL GET THE SUITCASES.

AND IN OTHER NEWS...
HUMAN SETTLEMENT
MINISTER **TOKYO SEXWALE**
ENJOYED HIS STAY IN
DIEPSLOOT SO MUCH...

...THAT HE PLANS TO
TRAVEL ACROSS SOUTH
AFRICA SPRINGING
"SURPRISE SLEEPOVERS"
ON PEOPLE
EVERYWHERE.

©RAPID PHASE · 2009

www.rapidphase.co.za

DING!
DONG! ♪

HI.
I'M
TOKYO
SEXWALE.

GOT
ANY I.D.?

HELLO. I'M **TOKYO
SEXWALE.** I'LL BE
SLEEPING OVER AT
YOUR HOUSE FOR
A FEW NIGHTS.

...I STAYED IN
DIEPSLOOT LAST WEEK...
NOW I WANT TO
EXPERIENCE LIFE IN
THE MIDDLE CLASS
SUBURBS.

©RAPID PHASE · 2009

THEN FROM **HERE**...
IT'S DURBAN, HOUT BAY,
MAURITIUS AND THEN I
PLAN TO STUDY LIFE AT
ALL OF **SOL KERZNER'S**
FIVE-STAR
RESORTS.

...YOU WON'T
EVEN KNOW
I'M HERE!
...ANYTHING
GOOD ON TV?

EVE!!

www.rapidphase.co.za

MORNING,
MISTER
SEXWALE.

⸱YAWN!⸱
WE'RE LIVING
UNDER THE
SAME ROOF.
CALL ME
TOKYO.

©RAPID PHASE · 2009

LET'S SEE. YOU SPENT THE
NIGHT IN **DIEPSLOOT**...
THEN **HERE** IN THE
NORTHERN SUBURBS... SO
I GUESS YOU'LL BE MOVING
ON FOR YOUR NEXT
"SURPRISE SLEEPOVER."

WELL, TO TELL YOU THE
TRUTH... I'VE ENJOYED
SLEEPING HERE SO MUCH...
I'VE DECIDED TO STAY
UNTIL **FRIDAY.**

⸱YAWN!⸱ YOU GOT
ANY COCO POPS?

ISN'T
THAT YOUR
ROBE
HE'S
WEARING?

...**AND**
MY
**BUNNY
SLIPPERS!**

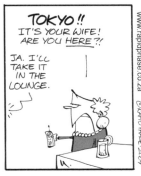

TOKYO!! IT'S YOUR WIFE! ARE YOU HERE?!
JA. I'LL TAKE IT IN THE LOUNGE.
HI HONEY!... NO, I'M NOT STILL IN DIEPSLOOT. I'M CURRENTLY SLEEPING OVER IN THE MIDDLE CLASS NORTHERN SUBURBS.
...WELL, I CAN'T REALLY TALK,... BUT OUR TV IS BIGGER AND THERE'S AN IRRITATING 80 YEAR OLD WOMAN WHO DRINKS A LOT OF GIN!
THAT DOES IT! EITHER HE GOES... OR I GO!
YES!
www.rapidphase.co.za
©RAPID PHASE 2009

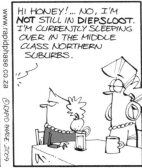

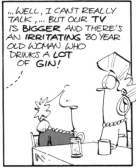

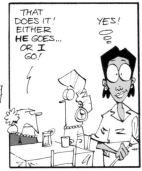

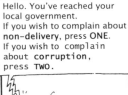

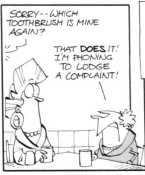

SORRY--WHICH TOOTHBRUSH IS MINE AGAIN?
THAT DOES IT! I'M PHONING TO LODGE A COMPLAINT!
Hello. You've reached your local government. If you wish to complain about non-delivery, press ONE. If you wish to complain about corruption, press TWO.
...if you wish to complain about Minister Sexwale showing up at your house unannounced and sleeping over, press THREE.
...WELL?
APPARENTLY, THEY'RE ALREADY AWARE OF THE PROBLEM.
©RAPID PHASE 2009
www.rapidphase.co.za

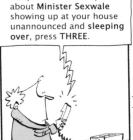

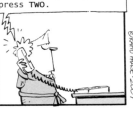

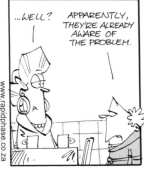

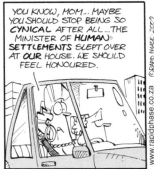

YOU KNOW, MOM... MAYBE YOU SHOULD STOP BEING SO CYNICAL AFTER ALL... THE MINISTER OF HUMAN SETTLEMENTS SLEPT OVER AT OUR HOUSE. WE SHOULD FEEL HONOURED.
TOKYO SLEPT HERE
TOKYO SEXWALE WAS HERE
TOKYO SLEPT HERE
TOKYO SLEPT HERE!
TOKYO'S ROOM!
Tokyo slept here!
Tokyo WAS HERE
TOKYO SLEPT HERE!
©RAPID PHASE 2009
www.rapidphase.co.za

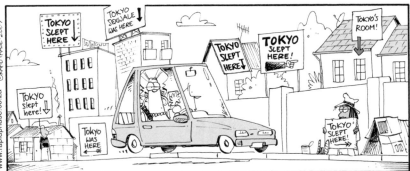

AND IN OTHER NEWS, PRESIDENT ZUMA IS SPENDING **MILLIONS** ON HIGH TECH SECURITY SYSTEMS FOR HIS DURBAN HOUSE.
©RAPID PHASE - 2009
Beepbeepbeepbeep
IF YOU ASK ME, WE NEED AN **UPGRADE** ON OUR **MOTION DETECTOR** SYSTEM.

WHAT'S THAT?
IT'S A **TIME CAPSULE!**
www.rapidphase.co.za
ONE DAY WE'LL OPEN IT UP AND SEE WHAT LIFE WAS LIKE IN **2009!**
NOW ALL WE NEED, IS A PLACE WHERE NO ONE WILL **DISTURB** IT FOR **YEARS** TO COME.
©RAPID PHASE - 2009
TRY UNDER THE RUG, BEHIND THE FRIDGE, OR AT THE BOTTOM OF OUR LAUNDRY BASKET.

©RAPID PHASE - 2009
SNIKT!
SNIKT!
AAAAAAAAAH!!!
WolverEVE
COMING SOON TO A THEATRE NEAR YOU

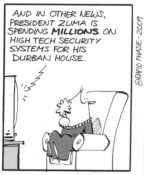

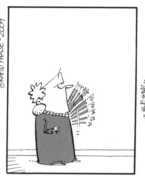

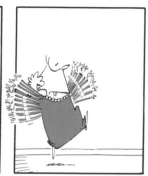

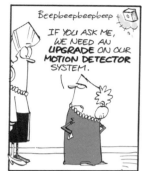

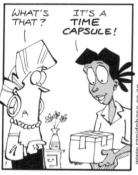

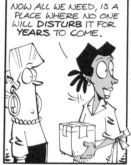

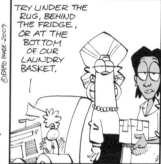

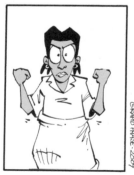

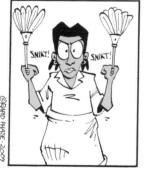

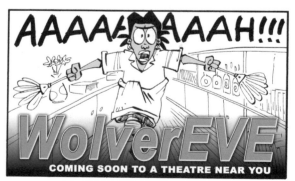

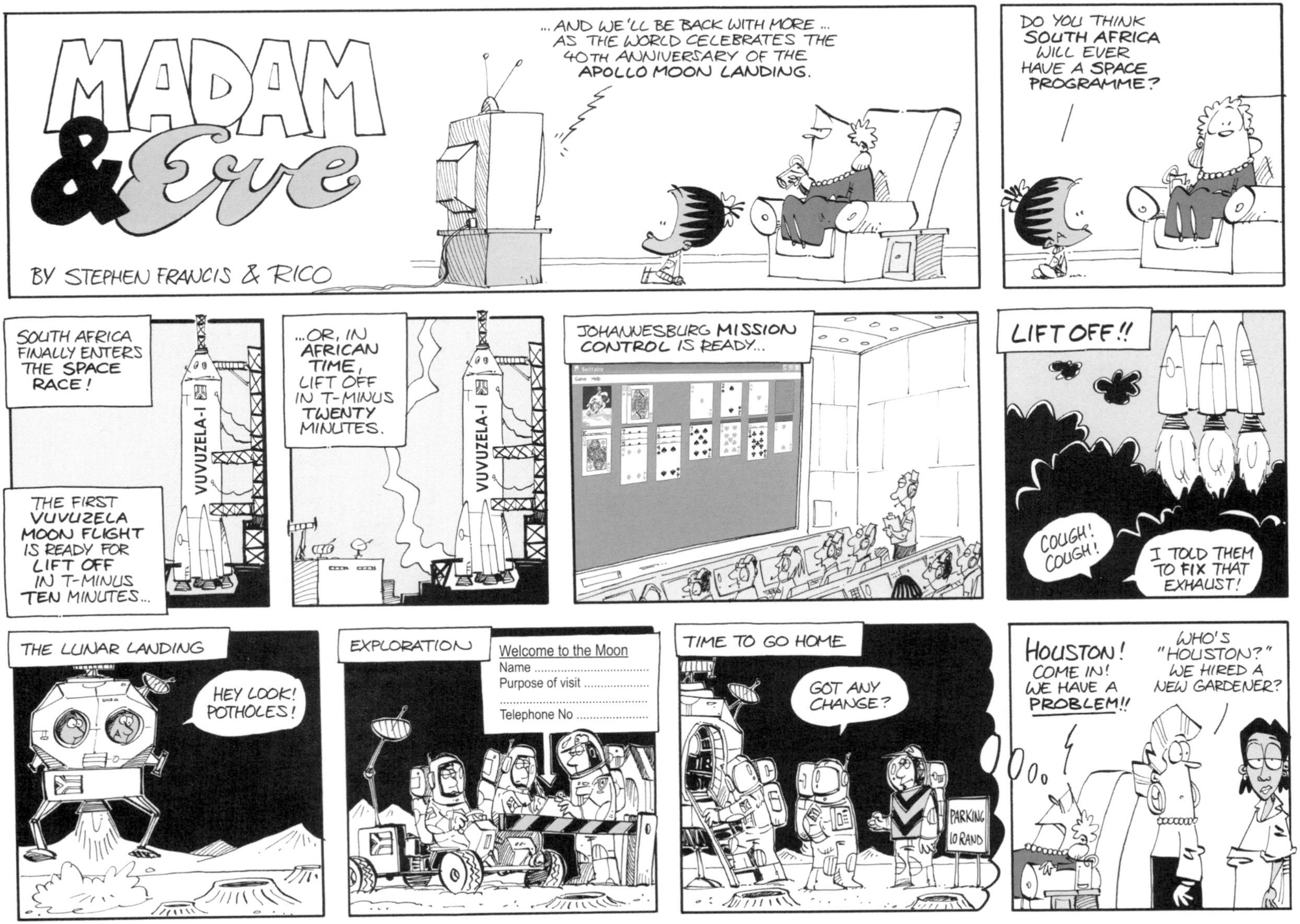
MADAM & Eve
BY STEPHEN FRANCIS & RICO
...AND WE'LL BE BACK WITH MORE ... AS THE WORLD CELEBRATES THE 40TH ANNIVERSARY OF THE APOLLO MOON LANDING.
DO YOU THINK SOUTH AFRICA WILL EVER HAVE A SPACE PROGRAMME?
SOUTH AFRICA FINALLY ENTERS THE SPACE RACE!
VUVUZELA-I
THE FIRST VUVUZELA MOON FLIGHT IS READY FOR LIFT OFF IN T-MINUS TEN MINUTES...
...OR, IN AFRICAN TIME, LIFT OFF IN T-MINUS TWENTY MINUTES.
VUVUZELA-I
JOHANNESBURG MISSION CONTROL IS READY...
Solitaire
LIFT OFF!!
COUGH! COUGH!
I TOLD THEM TO FIX THAT EXHAUST!
THE LUNAR LANDING
HEY LOOK! POTHOLES!
EXPLORATION
Welcome to the Moon
Name ....
Purpose of visit ....
....
Telephone No ....
TIME TO GO HOME
GOT ANY CHANGE?
PARKING 10 RAND
HOUSTON! COME IN! WE HAVE A PROBLEM!!
WHO'S "HOUSTON?" WE HIRED A NEW GARDENER?

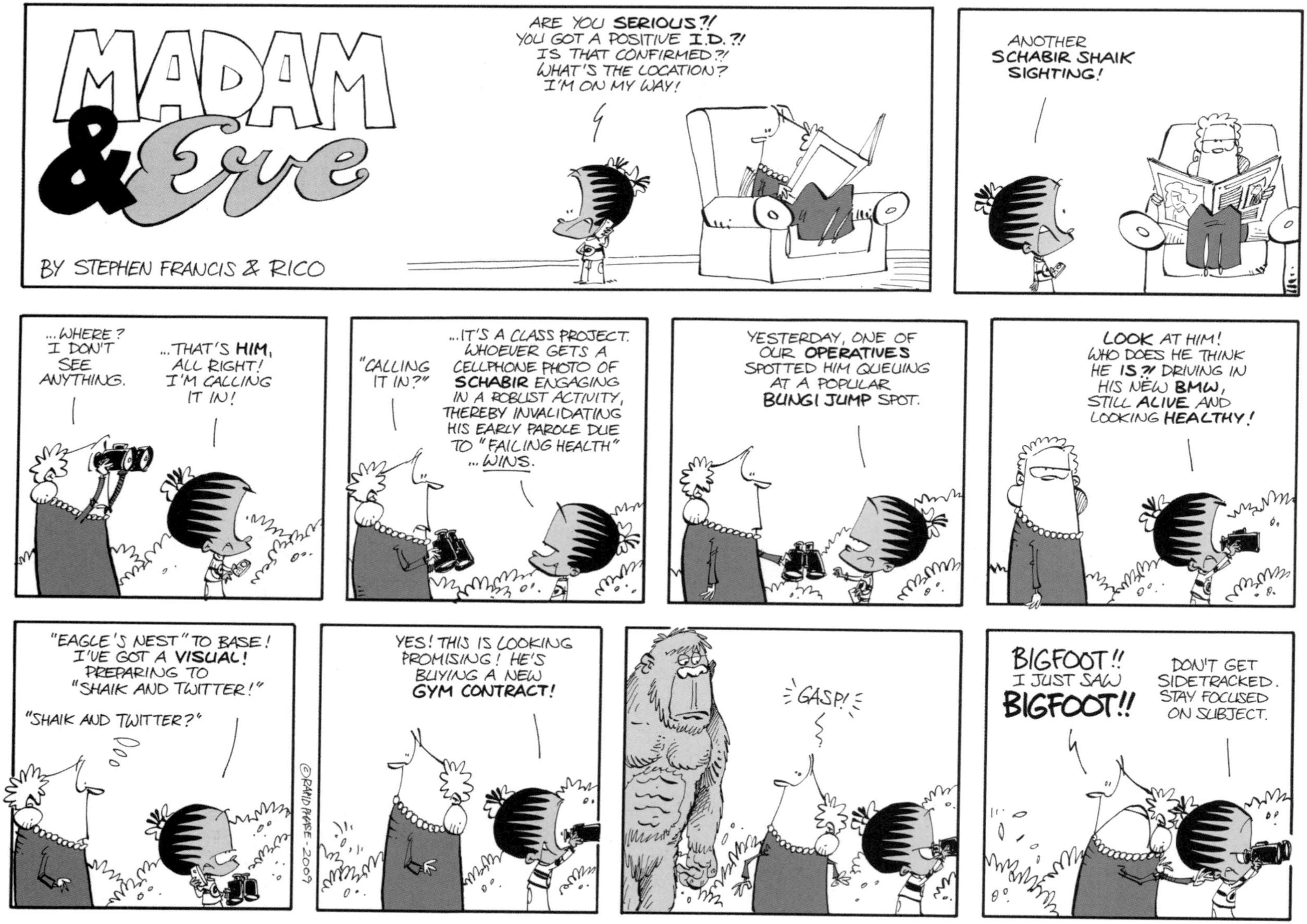
MADAM & Eve
BY STEPHEN FRANCIS & RICO
ARE YOU SERIOUS?! YOU GOT A POSITIVE I.D.?! IS THAT CONFIRMED?! WHAT'S THE LOCATION? I'M ON MY WAY!
ANOTHER SCHABIR SHAIK SIGHTING!
...WHERE? I DON'T SEE ANYTHING.
...THAT'S HIM, ALL RIGHT! I'M CALLING IT IN!
"CALLING IT IN?"
...IT'S A CLASS PROJECT. WHOEVER GETS A CELLPHONE PHOTO OF SCHABIR ENGAGING IN A ROBUST ACTIVITY, THEREBY INVALIDATING HIS EARLY PAROLE DUE TO "FAILING HEALTH" ...WINS.
YESTERDAY, ONE OF OUR OPERATIVES SPOTTED HIM QUEUING AT A POPULAR BUNGI JUMP SPOT.
LOOK AT HIM! WHO DOES HE THINK HE IS?! DRIVING IN HIS NEW BMW, STILL ALIVE AND LOOKING HEALTHY!
"EAGLE'S NEST" TO BASE! I'VE GOT A VISUAL! PREPARING TO "SHAIK AND TWITTER!"
"SHAIK AND TWITTER?"
©RAPID PHASE - 2009
YES! THIS IS LOOKING PROMISING! HE'S BUYING A NEW GYM CONTRACT!
GASP!
BIGFOOT!! I JUST SAW BIGFOOT!!
DON'T GET SIDETRACKED. STAY FOCUSED ON SUBJECT.

BY THE WAY... **EVE** SAID SHE CAN'T DO ANY WORK TODAY BECAUSE OF THE STRIKE.
STRIKE? **WHAT** STRIKE?!
STRIKE!!
GIN
1

MOM - WHERE ARE YOU GOING?
TO THE KERB. TO MAKE SURE OUR **DUSTBIN** GETS **EMPTIED**.
BUT YOU KNOW THE MUNICIPAL WORKERS ARE TOYI-TOYING ON **STRIKE**!
YEBO.
©RAPID PHASE · 2009
www.rapidphase.co.za
TWEET!
HAI!
HAI!
HAI!!
TWEET!
SEE? ALL GONE.

HERE A STRIKE. **THERE** A STRIKE. EVERYWHERE A STRIKE, STRIKE!
STRIKE
©RAPID PHASE · 2009
IS THERE ANY GROUP OF WORKERS WHO **HAVEN'T** GONE ON **STRIKE** YET?!
www.rapidphase.co.za
ON STRIKE!
LESS SECURITY
BAN ELECTRIC FENCES!
POLICE BRIBES TOO HIGH!
NO MORE GUARD DOGS!
LOWER WALLS!

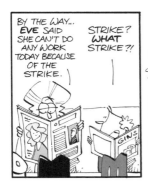

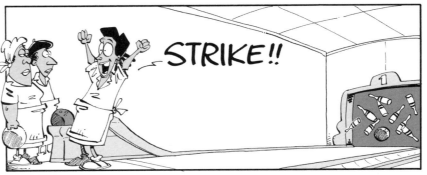

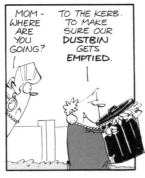

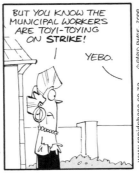

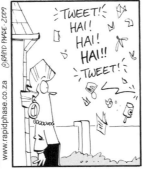

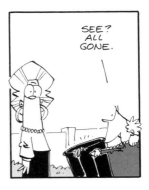

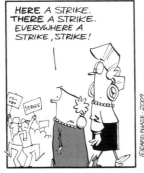

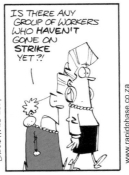

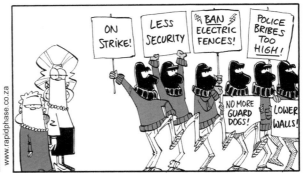

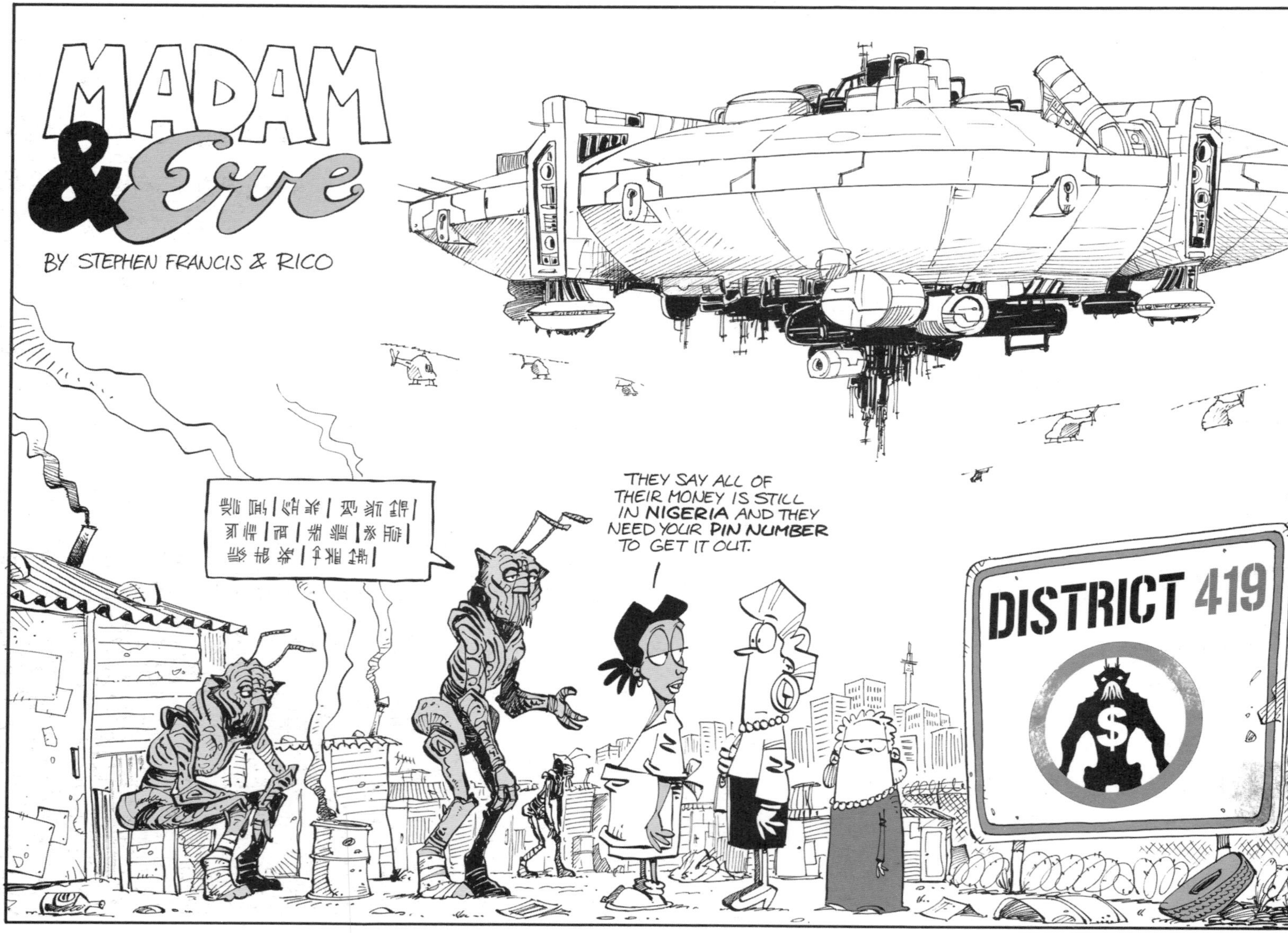
MADAM & Eve
BY STEPHEN FRANCIS & RICO
©RAPID PHASE - 2009
THEY SAY ALL OF THEIR MONEY IS STILL IN **NIGERIA** AND THEY NEED YOUR **PIN NUMBER** TO GET IT OUT.
DISTRICT 419
$